THE IMMIGRANT

THE IMMIGRANT

THE LIFE OF
MATTHIAS TOEBBEN

IN HIS WORDS

Praus Press
306 Greenup St., Covington, KY, 41011

Statue of German immigrant, John
A. Roebling. Donated to the city of
Covington by the Toebben family

FOR LAVERNE

MY WONDERFUL WIFE, DEVOTED MOTHER OF OUR FIVE CHILDREN, MY BUSINESS PARTNER, MY LOVE, AND BEST FRIEND. WITHOUT YOUR PATIENT SUPPORT AND UNDERSTANDING, IT WOULD HAVE NEVER HAPPENED.

No difficulty can discourage, no obstacle dismay, no trouble dishearten the man who has acquired the art of being alive. Difficulties are but dares of fate, obstacles but hurdles to try his skill, troubles but bitter tonics to give him strength; and he rises higher and looms greater after each encounter with adversity.

-ELLA WHEELER WILCOX

FOREWORD

There is only one predictable characteristic of life. That is, it's completely unpredictable. Life seems to delight in throwing hardships in our path, especially when we least expect them. They are inevitable and touch every one of us to varying degrees. Usually they present in the form of minor annoyances, but occasionally they may appear to be insurmountable obstacles. When beset by tribulations, some simply complain about their outrageous misfortune. Others see them as an opportunity. It's how we respond to setbacks that ultimately defines who we are. Those who confront and learn from them are those who succeed. It's just a matter of perspective.

Matth Toebben came to this country over sixty years ago with only ten dollars in his pocket, and a trainload of determination in his soul. Whether it was growing up under the oppression of Adolph Hitler or dealing with countless personal tragedies as an adult, Matth is one of those individuals who have repeatedly faced adversity and prevailed. When I moved to Northern Kentucky in 1978, I began the process of searching for a new home. I inquired about various local builders and received numerous suggestions from friends. One name was mentioned repeatedly: Matth Toebben, a man who had developed a reputation as a highly respected home builder. At social events individuals discussed the many stories about him and his successful activities. They became almost legendary, leaving in my mind the image of an extraordinary man. It took over forty years before I had the opportunity to meet him in person, and he more than lived up to my expectations.

Matth impressed me with his commanding presence, but it wasn't out of design or calculated. He simply exuded a confidence that was balanced by an equal level of humility. A firm handshake and engaging smile still make those around him feel like an important friend, a quality that has helped to make him so successful. A level of energy and passion for everything he does seemed to defy his actual age. It was readily apparent that he was a man of kindness and compassion. At the same time, I saw in the set of his jaw a determined look that might arise when confronted by a problem.

When considering a man having attained such a level of success, there might be a tendency by some to assume that he must have enjoyed some advantage or inherent privilege that helped pave the road to that success. For Matth, nothing came easy. Any achievements were solely the result of painstaking hard work, sheer perseverance, and a dedication to excellence. As a child, he grew up in a poor farming village under the scourge of Hitler's Nazi Germany. He came to appreciate the dangers of a powerful central government that promised everything and delivered only anguish. As a boy he learned to distrust the seductive power of a media that could twist the facts until they fit any agenda the government wanted to promote. He learned to rely on his own instincts and inherent sense of decency, qualities he carried with him to America.

It was a challenge to be an immigrant, coming to a new land with an unfamiliar language and a different set of cultural rules. Yet even as a young man, he was undeterred by those disadvantages. Rather, he attacked them head on until he ultimately overcame them with the patient support of his loving family and his faith in God.

There was a group, including myself and several friends, who played a weekly game of hearts for many years. When Matth was invited to join us, he brought with him his enthusiasm and positive attitude. He would talk about his life in Germany and his many business ventures in Kentucky, not as someone who liked to brag, but rather a man who had a passion for everything he did. He enjoyed sharing that enthusiasm with others. Every week he would regale us with a different story of his experiences, each tale more compelling than the last. I soon came to realize that Matth's life was more interesting than many of the fictional characters I had read about in novels, so when he asked me to consider the possibility of writing his story, I was both honored and excited.

Initial attempts to gather background information about his life were challenging. He finds texting and such other modern forms of communication to be cold and impersonal. Lost are the nuances of reading another's eyes, body language, the tone and pitch of voice, all those subtle things that help convey messages from one person to another. Matth prefers personal meetings where he is able to engage in an exchange of ideas. In spite of a severe language barrier, that is where he has been most successful in his career.

If you ask him a question over the phone, he will more than likely respond with an invitation to breakfast or a meeting in his office in order to discuss matters face-to-face. That's what we did. What resulted was over forty hours of recorded interviews and dozens more in personal conversations. They only served to reinforce my original impression of the man. He has overcome seemingly insurmountable obstacles to become one of the most successful and influential men in the Northern Kentucky community. There is no doubting the fact that he is a tough businessman, as most successful people are, but he is also one who has been fair and honest in all he has done. As you read his story, you will discover that Matth has been a man who is remarkably generous, never hesitating to help someone or some organization in need. While he has shunned acclaim, it has found him anyway, not because he has sought it, but rather because of his actions, working behind the scenes, making important things happen. He often did what others thought impossible and did so through sheer determination. Matth has spent his entire adult life being a doer, a consummate "mover and shaker" in his attempt to benefit the community. His many accomplishments have helped to reshape the culture of our area. His influence has been widespread. Over the past four decades, Matth has been on a first-name basis with many presidents, every Kentucky governor, each United States senator, and all Northern Kentucky congressmen. The *Cincinnati Enquirer* praised him as one of the four most influential people in Northern Kentucky.

Inclusion of all Matth's challenges and accomplishments are beyond the scope of just one book, so I have described just those that I feel most significantly reflect the major aspects of his life. I hope you enjoy reading his story as much as I enjoyed writing it.

-*T. MILTON MAYER*

THE AWARD

On May 13, 2008, the auditorium at the Northern Kentucky Convention Center in Covington was filled with almost a thousand people. I stood at the podium and gazed out over the crowd seated before me, my eyes partially blinded by the lights. My family and close personal friends were seated near the front, looks of pride on their faces. I knew I was expected to say something, so I had memorized a short acceptance speech the night before. However, in the moment, faced by all those in the large audience, my prepared script left me. I had no notes and my mind raced, searching for something to say. I had nothing. My only option was to speak from the heart and that's what I did.

"Besides my marriage to Laverne, and the birth of my five children, receiving the Northern Kentuckian of the Year Award is one of the proudest moments of my life. I thank each of the members of the selection committee and everyone else associated with Covington Catholic for considering me as this year's recipient. I am proud to be standing where so many other contributors to our community have stood before and I am humbly honored to be included in their company. I would be remiss if I didn't recognize the support of my wife, Laverne, the understanding of my family, and the Toebben Company employees who have all contributed so much to our success. Each of you can rightfully lay claim to part of this award.

"I have been blessed; blessed to have had a wonderful life, blessed to have had the support of a loving family, and blessed to have enjoyed a level of success well beyond my wildest expectations. I was fortunate enough to come to the United States over fifty years ago. It was a country that openly accepted an immigrant who could speak no English and had only ten dollars in his pocket. The people of this great land gave me a chance, an opportunity to pursue the American dream. As a result, I was successful, and I have always felt that it has been incumbent upon me to give back to the same country that gave so much to me. I believe that an individual must use any gifts or opportunities given by God to leave one's community and family better than they had been previously. That has always been my goal in both my professional and personal life. We owe it to our forefathers who sacrificed all to establish this great country. We all have a responsibility to them to make a difference. As I look around this auditorium, I see so many other distinguished individuals who have made that difference. Each of you have contributed so much of your time and resources to our Northern Kentucky community and are equally deserving of this same recognition. Working together, I know we will continue to do great things together. At the same time, we must encourage the next generation to continue with these same efforts.

Northern Kentucky Man of the Year Award
From left to right: Judith Toebben (wife of my brother John); Georges Gerdes; Christina Gerdes; Bill Gerdes; Marie Kreutzjans (my sister), Matth Toebben, Helen Finken; Angela Pohlabeln; Rudy Pohlabeln; Christina Drees, Agnes Wessels (my sister); Ben Wessels

"Occasionally a younger individual will approach me and ask me about the secret to success. My one-word response is always the same: passion. It's not about the accumulation of wealth and material objects. Rather, it's about the pursuit of your passion to the best of your ability. That is what will make you successful and happy. While doing so you must always be guided by four primary factors: God, family, community, and friends. All else is secondary. The good will follow if you remain focused on those four things. I believe they also form the basis for this award. Thank you again."

As the crowd applauded, I reflected upon my life and how fortunate I have been. I asked myself, "How did I get here?"

LORUP, GERMANY

It began in a small farming community in Germany. We were poor, but almost everyone in our small village of Lorup was poor. Our family didn't know any better. We were better off than some and not as well as others. It wasn't always the case, but war has a way of sucking the lifeblood out of any community, especially if your country was on the losing side. Before World War I, the economy in Germany was relatively prosperous, even in the peripheral farming communities like ours. Supplies were readily available, so my father, Rudolph Toebben, and his brother, Herman, were able to build a new home on a two-acre plot of land next to the house where they were born. The lumber was harvested from local forests and they made their own bricks on site. It was grueling work but something they embraced because they were making preparations for the future.

———————— ◆◆●◆◆ ————————

Before having a chance to move into the new home, my father and Herman were conscripted into Kaiser Wilhelm's army to fight in what would become "The war to end all wars." After four years of battle, my father returned as a decorated hero with multiple bayonet wounds and a heart problem. Unfortunately, Herman never made it back. He died of gunshot wounds in a trench just outside of Verdun, France. One would think that a return to peace would have brought about another period of relative prosperity for Germany, but that was not to be the case. The situation for the citizens worsened.

The small farming village of Lorup

A dark cloud began to hang heavy over Germany. The loss of World War I had taken a painful toll, both economically and culturally. Over seven million German soldiers were either killed or wounded during the conflict. It was a national disgrace that left Germany a broken country. In addition, the terms of the Treaty of Versailles were harshly punitive. The German army and air force were to be dismantled. Germany was also forced to pay $33 billion in reparations to the Allied Powers. This, in combination with the Great Depression, resulted in an economic disaster that was ultimately shouldered by the everyday German citizen. Widespread poverty resulted. The country was lost and desperate for a leader who could provide economic growth and restore national honor. Adolph Hitler and his National Socialist Party provided what the German people thought they needed, but any positive achievements during his early years were far outweighed by the political atrocities that marked his reign as chancellor. In addition, austere measures were enacted in order to support his ambitious war efforts. Those living in the coun-tryside were especially impacted by his unreasonable demands and strict governmental regulations. As the German economy continued to falter, Hitler's new World War made the situation worse. Poverty became the way of life in Lorup, a simple village of only about twelve hundred people. It was so small that the town was rarely shown on most maps of Germany. It was of no tactical significance and contained no industry, so it was mostly forgotten by the Nazi movement.

The beauty of living in a small village was that it was a homogeneous community. The citizens were bound together by a common belief in their Catholic faith. Before Hitler, all life centered around the church, the family, and the community. Serious disputes were unusual and, when they occured, were handled personally. People treated their neighbors with respect, but everything changed after the rise of Hitler's National Socialist Party. Our community slowly became divided as some individuals fell to the seductive hatred of the Nazis. Since Lorup was so isolated from the industrial and political centers of Germany, the local citizenry was unaware of Hitler's hidden sinister agendas. We were unaware of his slaughter of the millions of Jews and political dissidents. We didn't know about Heinrich Himmler's final solution.

Lorup had several village leaders and a few influential citizens who were official members of the Nazi party. However, an uncomfortable number of the local citizens were Nazi sympathizers. They tended to keep their political affiliations a closely guarded secret, and we seldom knew who they were. Casual conversation between neighbors could be dangerous. You had to weigh your words carefully before speaking. Even a former friend could turn you in for treason.

It was 1920 when my father returned from WWI and married my mother, Anna Schmitz. They moved into the home my father and his brother had built. By local standards the home was reasonably large with four bedrooms. However, once my parents began their family, things became crowded with them and nine children under one roof. We didn't notice. It was a good home where our family was held together with strong bonds of love and mutual respect. Regardless of the circumstances, my parents always found a way to put food on the table and maintain a roof over our head. They worked hard and sacrificed all in order to care for us.

The home my father and uncle built. The barn is to the right. My mother and grandparents are standing in front

Day to day living was a challenge. Hitler's government confiscated all durable goods for the war effort so there were few raw materials available for tradesmen. Rubber and leather were almost impossible to come by so traditional shoes were a luxury we enjoyed only when attending church on Sundays. During the week we wore wooden shoes made by our neighbor, Franz Jansen. That's how he made a living. He would cut a twelve-inch section of a birch log and split it in two. A single shoe was crafted out of each half with a hatchet and hand tools. Using a small pocket knife, he would carve roses into the tops of the girl's shoes to make them look more feminine.

Franz Jansen carving shoes

Mr. Jansen was a kind man who would eventually lose four of his five sons in Hitler's war. He was no supporter of the Nazi regime. Almost every household in Lorup lost at least one son during the war so Hitler had few supporters in our community. It wasn't until much later when I also became a parent that I fully understood the absolute devastation they experienced when losing a child.

Fabric was as scarce as rubber and leather, so finding clothing was just as difficult as getting shoes.

We had to make do with whatever we had. Mother would constantly have to hem and re-hem pants and dresses so they could be passed down from child to child. When clothing was worn beyond repair and no cloth replacements were available, she would resort to sewing gunny sack material or anything else she could get her hands on to clothe us.

Indoor plumbing was a luxury enjoyed by only the very rich in the larger cities. In fact, I had never heard the words "toilet" or "flushing" until well after the war. Our bathroom consisted of an outhouse inside the barn. That was horrible to use in the winter time, especially with a foot of snow on the ground and the cold wind howling outside the walls. I always made sure I went before going to bed, while there was still a little daylight left. I didn't want to be wandering around outside in the night. I had heard the other kids tell horror stories about wolves stealing small children in the darkness and carrying them away. It wasn't until I was older that I found out the stories weren't true. The biggest threat of all wasn't wolves; it was the Nazis.

Our only source of fresh water was a well across the road in our aunt's side yard. At least three times a day my older sisters would place a yoke over their shoulders and hang a wooden water bucket from each side. They'd fill them and carry the water back to the house where mother would use it for cooking or washing. They also had to make multiple trips to fetch water for the animals.

Farm of my Aunt Elizabeth Schmits, across the road from our house. On the right is a man carrying water buckets with a yoke over his shoulders

We had a large water barrel about thirty inches high which the girls would have to fill. Then they would add brown liquid soap to the water and hang a washboard over the side of the barrel to clean the clothes. There was no wringer, so the clothes had to be squeezed by hand to remove as much water as possible. Then they were hung outdoors on a rope line to dry. In the winter, clothes would remain hanging outside, sometimes as long as a week, until they freeze-dried. Then they would be hung from a line in the kitchen ceiling where they would finally dry from the heat of the cooking stove.

There was no soap available for purchase in stores, so my mother would boil a large pot of beef fat and add lye. When the mixture cooled, she'd cut it up into squares and that's what we used for bathing.

———————————— ◆◦◆ ————————————

My father was an imposing figure who stood over six-foot-two, seemingly without an ounce of body fat. He had a strong chin, piercing blue eyes, and a full head of curly white hair, which he combed neatly for Sunday Mass. His physical strength was matched only by the quality of his character. He was soft-hearted but would never allow his emotions to show, a trait deeply in-grained among German men of the time, especially those living in rural communities. Like many small-town farmers, he was a man of very few words, preferring to allow his actions to speak for him. Dad was a proud man who asked for little but was always willing to give, to help others when needed. As a decorated war hero, he was highly respected by the men who served under him and by the citizens of Lorup. Serving in Kaiser Wilhelm II's army for four years in the First World War gave him the confidence of a leader and the ability to overcome adversity, no matter how severe it might be. It was a trait he tried to instill in his children.

My mother had spent her entire life in Lorup, rarely traveling more than five miles from home. She was of average height and build for women in those days. Her eyes were a tender blue and she carried herself with an air of stubborn determination. Mom's entire life revolved around caring for her husband and children. It was a selfless dedication frequently seen in the women around our tiny farming community. She helped with the farm, cooked three meals a day from scratch, cleaned, and did wash, all the while providing nurturing comfort for the family. She gave all of herself to us to the point of exhaustion, but never once did I ever hear her complain. She always wore a smile and made herself available to us no matter how tired she might be. Though father did most of the labor around the farm, our mother was the glue that held the family tightly together.

———————————— ◆◦◆ ————————————

In spite of Hitler's early promises, Germany descended into a state of chaos as the war machine ate up more and more re-sources. It was a time when nothing could be taken for granted, not clothing, not food, and least of all, life.

My parents' first two children were boys: John and Matth. They both died when they were very young. We had no doctors at that time because everything was rural and so primitive. I was never told exactly what had happened to them, but I suspect they both suffered from severe respiratory problems, maybe the croup or pneumonia. In any event, they died within a year of each other and were buried side-by-side in the St. Marian Catholic Cemetery where they remain to this day. The loss of their first two children was devastating for my parents. My mother spent the rest of her life worrying constantly about the health of her subsequent children.

My sister Marie was the next in line. As the oldest living child, she took on the responsibility for much of the hard work on the farm and helping Mom raise the younger children. I was very close to her and she took me under her wing until she married Nick Kreutzjans, a young German soldier. It wasn't as though he wanted to serve in Hitler's army. He had no choice. If he had refused, he would have been shot for treason and his family would have been severely punished. It was a miracle that he had actually survived his entire four years of combat. Most didn't.

The next two children were girls: Elizabeth and Anna. They both married farmers and lived out the rest of their lives in Germany.

Dad and my sister Anna in the kitchen, next to the stove. It served as the only source of heat in the house during the winter months. Dad is wearing his wooden shoes

My twin brother and I were born on May 16, 1931. We were our parent's seventh and eighth children. I was born first and weighed a mere three pounds. Rudy came thirty minutes later, weighing five-and-a-half pounds. My brother was named Rudolph, after my father. We called him Rudy. I was named Matthias, after my mother's father. We were twins only in that we were carried by Mom at the same time and were born on the same day. Regardless, we shared a special bond only twins could understand.

My twin brother Rudy (right) and me (left) dressed in our
good Sunday clothes

Our house's only source of heat came from the cooking stove
in the kitchen. The winters could be brutal and even dangerous
especially for young infants, so mom took extra care to protect
us from the cold. Because of my small size, I was sickly and
suffered from severe asthma so I was particularly vulnerable
to respiratory problems. There were no doctors or medicines
available. Whenever I became ill, my mother would sit me on her
lap and slowly rock me back and forth until my breathing difficulties passed. Sometimes it took a few hours, other times it could
take days. Occasionally it would be almost a week, but she would
never leave my side at those times. I think she was afraid she
might lose another child to breathing problems just like her first
two. The asthma plagued me throughout my childhood and ado-
lescence. There were times when I would awaken in the night to
find mom sitting on the edge of my bed, just watching me. When I
asked her what she was doing she would say, "I was worried about
the planes flying over us." Even as a young boy, I knew better.

Mom tried to breast feed Rudy and me, but after bearing so
many children, and such poor nutrition on her part, there just
wasn't enough breast milk for twins. We had a neighbor up the
road, Elizabeth Gerdes, who had delivered a son just three months
before Rudy and I were born. She had a great deal of breast milk
so one of my sisters would carry me to her house several times a
day to feed. My aunt lived directly across the road from us and
she had had a daughter nine months previously. She was still
producing milk, so they would take Rudy over there to be fed.
It was an excellent example of the close family and community
support we enjoyed.

After Rudy and I came Helena, who we called Lainie. She had beautiful white curly hair that glowed when she was outside in the sunlight. Her wide smile and bright blue eyes always brought a ray of sunshine to even the darkest of days. Unfortunately, she wasn't with us long enough. Lainie was eleven when she developed severe pain in her belly. I think it was probably just appendicitis, but no treatment was available. Her appendix ruptured, and she died shortly afterward. Lannie was buried next to her older brothers behind the Lorup Catholic Church. The loss was a hard blow for our entire family.

Our sister Tekla was born in 1940, two years after Lainie. In 1957 she married Henry Reiken, a supervisor in the local highway department. They still live in Germany. Agnes was born a year after Tekla. She was seventeen when she moved to America where she met and married Ben Wessels, who would become very instrumental in my eventual success in the United States. They did well in the construction business and owned many apartment buildings in Northern Kentucky. My youngest brother, John, was named after our older brother who died as a toddler. At age fourteen he left home to be trained by the Volkswagen Corporation in Wolfsburg. He also wound up emigrating to America and started his own automobile repair business there. He subsequently developed a large sports complex along I-275 and the AA Highway.

With all us children and our parents living under the same roof, it was a difficult life, but we were all happy nevertheless. We simply didn't know any other way. We just did what we had to do to survive. Except for Hitler's war, we all enjoyed a wonderful childhood united by our faith in God and surrounded by the love that only a close family can provide.

Our family posing in front of the ktichen windows. Standing from left to right: Agnes, Rudy, Ann, Marie, Elizabeth, Me, and Tekla. Seated: Father, John, and Mother

THE TAPPING

Life in the rural farming areas was primitive and harsh compared to the conditions in urban communities. As rough as things were, I discovered that our lives were better than others'. This was especially true as Hitler's war continued to drain the country. At least we had a roof over our heads. We didn't have the modern conveniences of the cities, but we did enjoy several benefits that the city dwellers didn't. First of all, we didn't live in a target-rich environment so the Allied forces had little interest in bombing us. The second was that living in a remote farming area allowed us to remain fairly self-sufficient from a food standpoint.

The Toebben family had begun accumulating farm land about a mile down the dirt road from our house. Over time, each generation added to the original property until it eventually stood at about fifty acres. Our family farmed the land and grew everything we needed. The sandy soil around Lorup was conducive to growing potatoes which became a mainstay of our diet. In good times some of the villagers would help with the harvest. These were not the best of times, however. We had to do everything on our own.

There was also an ample crop of kale, rutabaga, cabbage, sugar beets, and rye that we harvested for our own personal use. Father would place the potatoes in his wagon and bring them to the front of our home where the Nazis would confiscate half for the army. The rest would be sold to distributors who would stop by with a truck once a week. What we didn't sell, we kept for ourselves. Mother would cook the vegetables and seal them in gallon jars that kept everything fresh for several years if necessary. Once a year Father would butcher a two-year-old cow and Mom would jar the beef in the same way. A pig was butchered twice a year and Mom used the meat to make sausages and bacon which she hung from the kitchen beams for drying.

Harvesting potatoes in the fields for our own use.

During the winter, the livestock was kept in a barn attached to our house. In the summer, we would herd the cows back down the dirt road to the fields for grazing. Every morning Marie would milk the cows and carry the milk cans back home using a bicycle. It was hard work, but Marie never complained. It was her job. Father would pour the milk into five-gallon cans and transport it to the local dairy in Lorup. That was where the Nazis seized half of it for the troops.

Commercial tobacco was unavailable, so a small parcel of our land was set aside to grow tobacco for father. After harvesting, it was hung from the barn rafters to dry. Then dad would shred it into fine strips. There was no cigarette paper and dad's only pipe was strictly an ornamental gift, given to him by the men he commanded during the First World War.

It had a hand-carved ivory bowl with the names of all the men who served under him carved into the sides. Since the pipe wasn't an option, he would make his own cigarettes by rolling the tobacco in a piece of newspaper. What resulted was something that look much like a large cigar with newsprint on the wrapper. It smelled like burning socks, but we didn't complain. When you had cows, chickens and pigs living in an attached barn, the tobacco smell blended in with the others to the point that we didn't notice any of them. It was simply part of life in our home. Dad died of emphysema at age seventy-two, probably because of smoking those homemade cigarettes every day.

Pipe given to Dad by the men who served under him during WW1

Our meals were prepared by Mom and the older girls. A block or two of dried peat would be placed in the stove. Every spring peat blocks were harvested from surrounding bogs. Peat is formed by rotting vegetation and is a soft precursor to coal. Using special spades, four-by-four-by-ten-inch blocks would be cut and placed in the sun for several months to dry. It took about five days to harvest enough peat for an entire year.

Once the peat blocks were lit, mother and the older girls would boil pots of water on the stove for cooking. Breakfast usually consisted of eggs and fried potatoes with a little bit of bacon or sausage. Sometimes Mom would boil fresh milk and mix it with day-old bread and serve that for breakfast. Every once in a while, she was able to get a little sugar. She would butter some bread and sprinkle it with the sugar. That was a great treat for us!

Women loading peat blocks onto a wagon after they had been drying in the sun for several months

For lunch, we would usually have bean soup or left-overs from the day before. Dinnertime was different, especially on Sundays. That was a meal we looked forward to all week. We would get dressed for church and afterward return home where we all ate a great meal of a roast, vegetables, potatoes, and gravy. Sometimes mom would wrap sliced apples in bread, bake it and serve it as dessert. There was nothing I enjoyed better than our Sunday dinners together.

We all sat at a large kitchen table that was made from hand-hewn lumber. On each side of the table were wooden benches where we children would sit. Mom and Dad sat on either end on chairs. We would all share stories about what we had done the previous week. There was the inevitable teasing that family members usually do to each other.

With all those children, things generally got out of hand, but everyone immediately stopped, and became quiet when we heard the tapping. It was the sound of father's wooden shoe on the floor. He didn't have to say a word. The message was clear. We were getting too loud and needed to quiet down a little. I can still hear that tapping sound today.

I remember one particular dinner when there was talk of the war. Father never spoke of his experiences. I think they were too painful. I later found out that most combat veterans were also re-luctant to discuss what they had seen and done during war. Rudy suddenly said, "People in town say that you were a hero in the last war, Dad. Is that true? How many men did you kill?"

"Did you win any medals?" asked one of my sisters.

We all erupted in louder conversation about war and speculated about how Dad became a hero. We stopped when we heard the familiar sound. It was Dad, slowly tapping on the floor. That was it. All discussion immediately came to a halt.

Father was annoyed but didn't raise his voice. He quietly set his spoon and down next to his plate. He adjusted the spoon so it was lying perfectly perpendicular to the edge of the table. After a second, he looked each of us in the eye and said, "There's nothing heroic about taking another man's life. War is not some glorious game. It's brutal beyond imagination and nothing good comes from it. Young men die or lose arms and legs because the leader of one country decides that he must attack the leader of another. For what reason? Because of a dispute over land or ideas? Because of a perceived insult, a bruising of someone's pride? Government leaders sit in their palaces or castles while the common people like us are forced to shed our blood. Then the survivors are given the task of picking up the pieces when all is done. Hundreds of thousands of men on both sides died in the last war and nothing was resolved. Towns and families were devastated, and it drove Germany to the point of financial ruin. Even in Lorup, the burden has been heavy, and for what? Not pride and certainly not glory. No, war results in nothing but pain and suffering. Now we have Hitler's war to deal with and the consequences are going to be even more severe. We've already seen almost every family in Lorup suffer the loss of at least one son or father. People across the country are starving. When you hear stories about the nobility of war, you don't believe them, not for a minute. There is no glory in killing another man." I had never heard my father say so much at one time.

Several years into the war, life was becoming bleak for those in the larger cities. Allied bombing runs were destroying the German infrastructure. Homes and even entire cities were levelled. The degree of destruction was beyond comprehension. Fathers and sons were either dead or still fighting in Hitler's losing cause. Families were devastated, and it wasn't unusual to see a dozen or so refugees struggling down the dirt road in front of our house every day, searching for safety. They came starving and begging for food. Early in the morning my dad would gather up a sack of potatoes and leave it by the front door for those who wandered by. Sometimes Mom would add slices of bacon and bread. We didn't have a lot to give away, but she would always find something for them. She would never let a single person go past our home without offering them something to eat.

LIFE UNDER NAZI RULE

Initially, Hitler delivered on some of his promises. He authorized construction of major roads like the Autobahn and a multitude of buildings in the big cities. Almost everyone had a job. His plan was to have a Volkswagen in the garage of every German family. That didn't happen. Hitler abandoned the citizenry and headed in a direction dictated by his ego and insane quest for world dominance. He dreamt of establishing a glorious Third Reich but that's not what happened. Life in Germany became more and more oppressive as tyrannical rules and regulations plagued our community. Nazi informants ensured that everyone was in compliance with the Fuhrer's wishes. Violators were arrested and shipped to detention camps like Esterwegen, just six kilometers away. Supplies of rubber, leather, and fabric had already been depleted. Other goods were being rationed. Younger and younger men were being conscripted into the army, never to return home.

The war machine demanded increasingly more and more from the farmers. Half of all milk, grain, vegetables, and meat was confiscated and shipped away by train. This meant less food available for families and farm animals. I heard my father once say, "I openly accept our responsibility to feed the hungry and needy, but not Hitler's delusions." Father defied the regulations at great risk to himself. He hid bushels of vegetables and grain in the back of our barn. When an animal was to be butchered, father did it in the middle of the night lest any Nazis see him.

I remember one incident when my father needed to grind oats and rye for the farm animals. It was a noisy process, so he did it hidden inside the barn. Rudy and I were helping him but the dust from the grinding began affecting my asthma, so Dad asked me to stand guard outside. I was to let him know if any Nazis were approaching by tapping my wooden shoe against the barn's door.

I waited and kept checking the road in both directions. It wasn't long before I saw a cloud of dust in the distance, indicating that a vehicle was approaching. That could only mean one thing, a Nazi car was coming. I tapped on the side of the barn with my shoe, but my dad couldn't hear me. It was the noise from the grinder drowning out my signal. The closer the car came, the harder I kicked. I panicked and kicked the barn door so hard my wooden shoe split in two. It gave my father just enough time to turn off the grinder and hide what he was doing. Two men in in Nazi uniforms and swastika arm bands passed by with just a cursory glance in my direction.

Dad came out and looked down at my broken shoe. He laughed, "I guess you'll be walking around barefoot on one side for a while, Matth." He was teasing me. That afternoon we went to see Franz Jansen who had a new pair of wooden shoes ready for me the next day.

———————————— ◄•●•► ————————————

As bad as it was, life for others under the Nazis was unimaginably worse. I knew of only one Jewish family in our region. They were horse and livestock traders who lived in the town of Werlte, about ten kilometers away. They would come by on occasion to see if we had any pigs or calves to sell. It took several months before we realized that we hadn't seen them in quite a while. They just seemed to have disappeared. When father asked other farmers in Lorup, he found out that the entire family had been "relocated." We didn't know what that meant at the time, but we suspected it wasn't good. Eventually we heard that they were detained as political prisoners in a jail somewhere. We didn't find out about the Hitler's "Final Solution" until much later when the allied forces defeated the Nazis and uncovered the atrocities at the extermination camps in Auschwitz and Dachau. Over six million Jews were murdered in what was to be known as the Holocaust. Another five million including gays, those with physical or mental afflictions, communists, priests, resistance political leaders, and multiple others were executed. Eight million German citizens and soldiers lost their lives. The numbers don't even include the millions who died fighting the Nazis. It was a tragedy that would scar the conscience of Germany for a century.

HERR HILMER

It was mid-summer when Mom was planning to cook up a pot of bean and potato soup for dinner. Dad told Rudy and me that he wanted us to help him dig up some vegetables. I was happy that father asked me since I was usually too sick with my asthma to do much. We hooked the horses to the wagon, the same one that had been used by his great grandfather, and headed down the road for a mile. The early morning ride was peaceful, the only sounds being from the birds singing and the breeze blowing through the trees. I was looking forward to dinner that night. Mom made the greatest soups and fresh bread.

There had been a fair amount of rain that summer and the fields were still a lush sea of green. We unhitched the horses from the wagon and hooked them up to the plow. Dad unearthed the potatoes while Rudy and I cleaned them and placed them in baskets along with some of the beans we had already picked. I tried to keep up with my brother, but he was healthier and stronger than me. The dust and pollen started affecting my lungs to the point that I couldn't breathe. The harder I tried, the more difficult it became. I had desperately wanted to do well and not disappoint Dad, but the dust got to be too much. I finally had to sit down to catch my breath. Tears welled up in my eyes and I was so embarrassed I held them tightly shut.

When I sensed my dad standing over me, I looked up at him. "What's wrong, Matth?" he asked.

"I can't breathe. I can't do anything. I can't even load potatoes."

He sat down next to me, put his arm around my shoulder, and reassured, "Don't rush. The harder you try, the worse it will be. Just relax and try to take slow, deep breaths." He breathed with me and his strong voice calmed me down as I tried to match each of my own breaths with his. After a few minutes, I slowly improved. He waited with me for a little bit and said, "When you feel better, get back up and help Rudy. This asthma problem is a little test God has given you to see how you handle it. It's the way life is sometimes. It throws problems at you, but it's how you respond to them that makes you who you are. Always remember, when things seem the darkest, never give up. Keep pushing forward, no matter the size of the obstacles, and you'll never fail." I remembered those words for the rest of my life. Whenever it looked like failure was imminent, I kept pushing on. There was always a light at the end of the tunnel. It was the only time I can remember Dad speaking to me from the heart like that.

After several more minutes I got up and rejoined my brother. I didn't make the mistake of trying to keep up with him, but I pushed myself as hard as I could.

◆◦◆◦◆

"Hello, Rudolph," a deep voice rang out from across the back fence. A neighbor approached the property line. It was Gunter Hilmer. The actual Nazi party in Lorup consisted mostly of a few town and police officials. However, there were a number of silent Nazi sympathizers in the region. We seldom knew for sure who they were, but Hilmer was suspected of being one. He and my father had grown up together and had been friends since childhood, but they differed in their political philosophies.

"Hello Gunter," my father replied and reached across the back fence to shake the man's hand.

"I see you brought the twins out to help you today."

"Trying to teach them a little farming," replied my father.

"They should be old enough to join Hitler's Youth Corps in a few years."

A frown creased my father's face. He didn't want his sons joining any of Hitler's paramilitary groups. "That's still many years away and my boys aren't interested in politics anyway."

"They should be. They're going to want to share in the glory." Then Gunter Hilmer proceeded to boast about Hitler's annexation of Austria, "The Austrians welcomed Hitler with open arms and cheered as he entered. Then it was Poland. They dropped their guns and ran like dogs as soon as we crossed the border. He has reclaimed most of the lands stolen from us in that damned Treaty of Versailles. There will be no stopping our return as the new Reich, a grand and powerful empire."

My father paused for a few seconds before replying. "There will be no glorious empire. The Americans have entered the war, Gunter. You watch. This will soon be over. Hitler will lose and we will have to pay the price."

"Nonsense!" shouted the neighbor. His face turned red. "The Americans are weak and lack resolve. They can't wage two separate wars on opposite sides of the world. They will be too busy with the Japanese to mount an effective campaign against us. We will bring them to their knees just as we did the French. The Blitzkrieg is already destroying London and Britain will fall within the year. Then we'll take Russia."

Father slowly shook his head from side to side and replied, "You're wrong, Gunter. I fought the Americans in the last world war, and they are anything but weak. They have consistently shown themselves to be courageous foes. We were up against a Colonel George Patton and his tank corps at the Battle of Saint-Mihiel. He and his men were ferocious warriors. You will find that the American soldier is relentless and should not be dismissed. Germany has again overestimated its abilities and will not be able to defeat them. Hitler will fail and when he does, the people of Germany will suffer for his folly. This time the punishment will be even harsher than that dished out in Versailles."

I watched as my father and our neighbor argued for the next ten minutes, Hilmer's arms flailing about as his voice grew louder. At one point he made the mistake of pointing his finger at my father's chest. Most men would have received a broken arm or worse in return for such actions, but father remained calm. Finally, Gunter said between clenched teeth, "You'd better be mindful of what you're saying, Rudolph. Some would interpret your criticisms of the Fuhrer as treason." He turned and walked away toward his house.

———————————◆◦◆◦◆———————————

At dinner that night my father told the story of the argument. My brothers and sisters were proud that he took such a strong stand and held his ground against Herr Hilmer. Almost no one in Lorup liked the man.

My mother remained quiet for a while. She was a strong-willed woman but seldom spoke up at dinner when political issues were discussed, preferring to defer to my father on such matters. Tonight, however, she felt compelled to say something. I always believed she was afraid that her family might be in danger. Her words were intended to be more of a lesson for my siblings and me rather than a challenge to our father.

"Rudolph, you must be very careful when criticizing Hitler, especially in public. You can't trust anyone."

"I'm not worried. It was a simple disagreement between neighbors. Gunter has been a close friend of mine for most of my life and would never turn me in for speaking my mind."

"He's also a good friend of the mayor who is an official member of the Nazi Party. Gunter is a strong supporter of Hitler and the war effort. Everyone in the village knows that."

"This won't be a problem, Anna. You'll see. It will have been completely forgotten by tomorrow," replied my father, but he sounded less convincing.

My oldest sister, Marie, said, "That's what the Federle family thought before Mr. Federle became an outspoken critic of the Fuhrer. One night a car pulled up to their house and he simply disappeared. He hasn't been heard from since. Rumor is that he was arrested and placed in a prison for political dissidents in Esterwegen. Everyone knows that anyone who speaks out against Hitler winds up there. The Federle family is now fatherless and destitute."

People seldom discussed Germany's camps in public because they were afraid that if the wrong person overheard them, they might get an official visit from the police and wind up in the same prison. Everyone was afraid. We later found out that the fear was well founded. Many of the political prisoners at Esterwegen were executed and buried in mass graves.

Marie added, "A cousin of my friend Gretel Weber told her that several Catholic priests in their village had been arrested for treason. It seems they criticized the oppression of the Nazi government in their Sunday sermons. They were reported by some of their own parishioners. Can you imagine? Priests turned in by their own parishioners." She looked at everyone around the table. We were all worried.

My mother said, "Germany is not what it once was, Rudolph. Civility is gone and insanity has taken over. You can trust no one, not even those who had once been close friends." Mother had made her point and there would be no further discussion. We all ate the rest of our meal in silence. Afterward, my father walked out the door and headed across the road to my uncle's barn. Guns had already been confiscated and private ownership was illegal, but Dad had hidden a double-barreled shotgun in the barn's thatched roof. He returned with it, loaded the gun with shells, and placed it next to our front door. It was a dangerous maneuver. Punishment for gun possession could be death.

My father was a brave man who had fought valiantly in the First Great War. He was afraid of no one, but as he looked at the gun over the next several weeks, I could see the concern in his eyes. The presence of a gun in the house would jeopardize the safety of his entire family. He could never protect them from the Gestapo if they decided to raid our home. Late one night, when it appeared as though Hilmer had not reported him, I saw father return the shotgun to its hiding place in the thatched roof. He used a nail to mark the location with a small scratch in the wall. He never retrieved it again until after the war.

THE PARACHUTES

Initially, the village of Lorup was of no military interest. We were spared the ravages of conflict until the war neared its climax. Unfortunately, our location was directly in the flight path of allied bombers whose mission it was to destroy Germany's infrastructure. We had just finished breakfast when we heard the loud explosions. The entire house shook, and small bits of plaster fell from the ceiling.

"Bombs!" exclaimed my father. "Not near, but close enough."

Mother tried to huddle us into the cellar, but we were determined to see what was happening. We had all heard about bombs falling and destroying entire cities, but we had never actually seen or heard one explode before. Looking up into the bright blue sky I could make out what looked like a silvery speckled cloud extending as far as I could see. The planes were high in the air but even at that distance the noise from their engines was unmistakable.

"Allies. Look like B-17 Flying Fortresses," said my father. "They've crossed the English Channel and flew through Holland to get here."

"Are they going to bomb us?" I asked my father.

"No, son. They're probably headed farther northeast to the industrial centers in the Ruhr Valley area. They're trying to cripple Hitler's ability to wage war."

Then we heard the sounds of what seemed like a giant hornet's nest. It was dozens of smaller planes chasing the bombers and firing at them.

Allied B-17 Flying Fortress armed with multiple defensive machine gun turrets. However, they were no match for the speedier Messerschmitt fighter planes

"Messerschmitt fighters," said Dad. "They're attacking the B-17s."

"Why don't the bombers fight back?" I asked.

"They are. They have a number of guns on board but there are too many of the German planes and they're very fast. The bombers' gunners have trouble hitting them."

"Why don't the Americans have their own fast planes like the Messerschmitts?"

"They do but it's a long way across the Channel to here and the smaller planes can't carry enough fuel to make the trip. They have to turn back leaving the bombers unprotected. They're sitting ducks like this. It'll be a miracle if any of them make it back in one piece."

Just then the rear of one of the bombers exploded, blowing the entire tail section off. Then another plane was hit, and then another. The pilots immediately released their bombs and a half-minute later the ground again shook like nothing I've ever felt before. My insides rattled, and the sound of the explosions was deafening. Smoke billowed up all along the horizon.

"That was less than a kilometer away," said my father. "We should take cover because a lot more of those planes are sure to drop their loads if they're hit."

I looked at my dad and said, "I thought you said they weren't going to bomb us."

"They aren't, Matth. They're trying to drop their bombs in unpopulated areas before their damaged planes crash somewhere and kill civilians. They just don't always know for sure where those bombs will land."

I looked back up at the battle in time to see the sky fill with giant white balloons. They were the parachutes of Allied airmen escaping their crippled planes. It looked like for them the war might be over, but most of them never made it to the ground. They were defenseless and no longer able to fight but they were killed anyway. The German fighter planes shot the pilots to pieces while they were hanging from their chutes. Dad told me it was prohibited by the terms of the Geneva Convention. Even some German Luftwaffe generals forbade the practice, but many pilots refused to adhere to those rules. I was surprised to hear that they actually even had rules for killing people in war. That made no sense to me, but I was just a kid. What did I know? It was a brutal massacre that I vividly remember to this day. Only a few of the men made it safely to the ground. Dad was right when he said there was no nobility in war.

More planes and bombs began to fall from the sky, so we retreated back into the safety of the house. Father disappeared in the direction of the fallen airmen. When we saw the bombers return several hours later, there were a lot fewer of them remaining. So many lives were lost on both sides that day. The air battle repeated itself almost every day, more and more men being killed each time. It was wrong. Even as a child I realized it was such a tragic waste of life. Eventually the American escort fighters began using accessory fuel tanks, so they were able to extend their flight distance and protect the bombers through their entire mission. As the tide of the war changed, more and more American planes made their way safely back to their bases across the channel

I found out years later that my father and several other villagers tried to help the downed airmen, but they were too late. Most of them had become hung up in the trees where they died of their wounds before they could be cut down. Others disappeared into the peat bogs and couldn't be found. Those few that made it to the safety of solid ground tried to hide but were usually captured or shot before they could reach cover.

WALDO AND HUNTER

The walk from our home to the center of the village and school was a little over a mile. After classes, many of my friends would stop at a field or even on the road and start playing soccer. The balls we used were nothing like the ones seen today. We would make them from dried pig bladders that we would stuff with hay. When one would wear out, we'd just make another.

When I was healthy, I could run as fast as anyone. Unfortunately, those good days were few and far between. I wasn't very good at sports because my asthma usually kept me from playing well and on the bad days I couldn't keep up with the others. Trying to push through like my father suggested seldom worked, so when it came time to choose up sides, I was always selected last. Friends tried to use me as a goalie thinking that if I didn't have to run so much, I could play. Even that position was more than I could handle. The others would groan when they had the last choice and wound up with me on their side. Rudy tried to cover for me but there was just so much he could do. No one wanted me on their team.

It became too embarrassing, so whenever my friends would decide to start up a game, I would instead walk home to get my cane pole and hike over to the Fleischlot River to fish. When our German Shepherd, Waldo, saw me leaving with my gear, he would take off after me, wagging his tail and barking repeatedly until he caught up. Actually, he was part German Shepherd and part something else. We didn't know exactly what that something else was, but the family loved him anyway. I liked to fish so I was alone with the dog a great deal of the time. Sometimes, that's the way I wanted it.

The river was more like a stream in that it was mostly narrow and shallow, but in some areas, where the river would bend around a curve, it would carve a deep pool. That's where I'd throw in my line. There weren't a lot of fish, but the afternoons were enjoyable anyway. I mostly caught bluegills and an occasional eel. Sometimes there were enough to fillet and pickle with a mix of vinegar, sugar, and onions. That was pretty good eating. Usually there weren't enough to take home to help feed the family, so I'd threw them back to catch another day.

On one lazy afternoon, the fish weren't biting at all. I looked up at the trees and saw that the wind was blowing out of the north. I understood. Several months earlier I was having similar bad luck when an old man stopped and asked me, "How are they biting?"

"I've had a few nibbles but no real bites," I replied.

The old man looked up to the trees just like I had just done and said to me, "Watch the leaves, son. The winds blowing out of the north today. The fish never bite when the wind is coming from that direction."

I remembered his words and decided I wasn't going to catch anything that day, so I pulled in my line. It was too nice a day to head back home so I began skipping stones across the water. Waldo would occasionally lift his head to see what was going on if there was a loud splash, but then after a few seconds, he'd get bored and rest his head back down on his front paws. Suddenly he stood up. I could tell something was bothering him by the way his ears popped forward as he stared across the water. He was agitated. When I looked down stream, I saw what had caught Waldo's attention. It was another dog running along the opposite bank and barking. It was a mixed breed like Waldo and it was an extremely ugly-looking thing, scrawny with patches of fur missing. He was guarding a herd of sheep feeding along the other side of the water. A minute later I saw the herdsman coaxing the animals along as they grazed. If one of the sheep wandered off from the rest, he'd whistle out a signal. The dog would jerk his head up and look around until he found the wayward animal. Then he would take off and chase the renegade back to the main group. I studied the dog for some time as he methodically ran back and forth, keeping the flock together. He was thin and mal-nourished looking, certainly not as strong as Waldo, but he was fast and seemed very smart.

After several minutes, the dog suddenly bolted off at a full speed away from the herd. I couldn't see any sheep he might have been after and I wasn't sure what he was up to until I saw a large jackrabbit flush out of the brush. The dog gave chase as it was zigging and zagging across a field. *No dog can outrun a jackrabbit,* I thought. *No dog can do that.* Within ten seconds, the dog proved me wrong and brought his prize back to the herder. He laid the rabbit at the man's feet and was wagging his tail in excitement. He ran around in small circles, barking until the owner rewarded him with a pat on the head and a treat.

I was so impressed I waded across a shallow part of the stream to talk to the herder. Waldo followed. "I like your dog," I said.

The herder said nothing, simply nodded.

"What's his name?" I asked.

"Never gave him one. Never found a need to. When I want his attention I just whistle and he knows what to do."

"Smart dog," I said.

"Yes, but he's a little too skinny. Good enough for herding sheep but that's about it. He certainly can't protect my herd from predators." He looked at Waldo and asked, "What's your dog's name?"

"Waldo," I replied. "He's smart and big enough to scare off wolves."

"We don't have any wolves in this part of Germany, but I still like the dog. He's a fine-looking animal." He scratched Waldo behind the ear.

I thought for a second before replying, trying to decide if I was going to get into trouble for what I was about to do. *How bad could it be,* I wondered before saying, "Would you like to trade?"

The man looked at Waldo for a second and replied, "Can he herd sheep?"

"No but he's a good learner."

"I imagine I can teach him what he needs to do. It's a deal, son." We shook hands on it. The man took a piece of rope and tied it around Waldo's neck like a collar and offered him some dried beef, a rare delicacy for a dog. That was it. The deal was done, and Waldo now belonged to the sheep herder. My dog and best friend left me without hesitation.

Before he could walk away, I asked the herder, "Can I have one of those treats?"

"Sure, but don't give him too many. You'll spoil him."

I gave my new dog the treat and he seemed to understand. He followed me back across the stream, gazing back at his former owner just once before walking beside me as we went home.

———————◆◆◆◆◆———————

The following week my father noticed the strange new dog hanging around our house. "Anna, where'd he come from?" he asked my mother.

She looked at me and said, "Matth brought him home from fishing a few days ago."

He turned to me. "Matthias, where'd you get that dog? He's just about the ugliest thing I've ever seen." When he called me Matthias instead of Matth it usually meant I was in trouble and would have some serious explaining to do. I had been expecting this reaction, so I had my story prepared. I still wasn't sure just how much trouble I might be in. "I traded him for Waldo."

"What? You traded our fine German Shepherd guard dog for this sickly-looking mutt? He looks like he's starving. The next good breeze will probably knock him over."

I didn't bother reminding father that Waldo wasn't a full blood German Shepherd. There wasn't any purpose in it. "I agree, he doesn't look like much, but looks can be deceiving. He's a special dog. He's smart and runs faster than any other dog you've ever seen. He can even chase down a jackrabbit in no time."

"A jackrabbit!" laughed my father. "Did you hear him, Anna? Your son actually thinks this mangy dog could catch a jackrabbit. I think you must be dreaming, Matth."

"I've seen him do it with my own eyes. You take us to a field and I'll prove it to you."

"I have to head down to the farm this morning to repair a section of fence. You and your new dog can come with me and we'll see what he can do." I helped father hitch up the horses to the wagon, one a chestnut mare and the other a spotted draft gelding. Without having to be told, the dog jumped into the back and we headed out on the thirty-minute trip to the land. It was a peaceful morning. The quiet was disturbed only by the rhythmic sounds of the horses' hooves on the road, and birds singing in search of a mate. The trees on either side of the road were reaching out, almost as if to touch their counterparts on the other side. The dog was busy searching the surroundings and sniffing the air. He must have caught the scent of something because as soon as we pulled up to our land, he jumped down and began searching through the brush. A large rabbit flushed out and headed across the field. Without a single command, the dog took off after the rabbit, which zigged and zagged for about fifty meters. The dog was fast but not as fast as the rabbit. He didn't bother trying to chase directly behind it. He had learned he'd never catch it that way. Rather he anticipated the rabbit's next move and headed for the spot where the animal would zag next. It took two tries but within fifteen seconds the dog had it. He proudly brought the rabbit back to us and laid his prize at my feet. I named my new dog "Hunter."

"I wouldn't have ever believed it if I hadn't seen it with my own eyes. Looks like you made a good trade after all, Matth," said my father as he tousled my hair.

While father repaired the fence, the dog flushed a second rabbit and added him to his catch. That night mother and Marie prepared a stew of rabbit, sauerkraut, potatoes, and onions. Rabbit was considered a delicacy that we seldom got to enjoy, so when father said grace that night, he thanked God for the meal and our health. He also thanked me and Hunter for providing the rabbits. For one of the few times in my young life, I was as proud as I could be.

ST. MARIANS CHURCH

Hitler was raised by his mother as a Roman Catholic. By the time he became a teenager, he rejected all forms of religion as being contrary to what he believed to be the facts of science. His goal was to make Germany a secular state, but he was acutely aware of the political ramifications of persecuting a Catholicism that dominated so much of German culture at the time. As a compromise, Hitler drafted and signed a non-interference agreement with the church. It was called the Reichskonkordat and it allowed the Catholic churches to function openly as long as priests and nuns avoided all discussion or participation in political matters. It was an agreement that many priests and Hitler himself almost immediately violated.

Some historians believe that Hitler was somewhat intimidated by the size and influence of the church, but I sometimes wondered if he was simply afraid of the wrath of the nuns who used to teach him as a boy. Obviously, a joke, but those of you who might have been taught by nuns would understand the humor. My entire family and almost everyone else living in Lorup was Catholic. In fact, I had never met a Protestant until I moved to Borger for my apprenticeship in cabinetry construction. We believed in one merciful, almighty God. We believed in the Ten Commandments and the existence of heaven and hell, but also in the forgiveness of sins. We all had our human failings, but we strove to live by the teachings of Jesus Christ.

St. Marian Church, located about a kilometer from our home, was a central part of our lives. It was a beautiful brick building that was constructed at least several centuries previous. Both side walls were adorned with stained glass windows depicting different stories from the Bible. There was a magnificent steeple where the bells would ring every Sunday to signal the beginning of Mass. During the war, the bells fell silent. Hitler had ordered them removed so they could be melted down to create casings for artillery shells. Near the end of the war, the steeple was damaged by bombs when the Allied armies invaded Germany. It has since been rebuilt and enlarged.

St. Marian Church. Damage to the steeple occured as a result of artillery fire during the Allied invasion. At the time of this photograph, it had been repaired, but the scars can still be seen.

Our previous priest had been arrested midway through the war for speaking out against Hitler's regime. His replacement, a priest by the name of Father Herman Otten, was a young man who stood about six-foot-four. He towered over everyone in the parish and had a loud resonating voice that he wasn't reluctant to use it when he wanted to make a point. The children were all afraid of him to say the least.

Rudy and I were altar boys. We had studied the Latin responses to all the prayers in the mass and knew them by heart. We had practiced the ceremony repeatedly and knew exactly what we were expected to do at different points during the service. We thought we were well prepared, but for me there was a problem serving my first Sunday mass, a problem that I considered to be a catastrophe at the time. As the priest instructed, I had prepared the water and wine before the service, but I had failed to pour enough wine into one of the cruets. It was almost empty. When I brought the silver tray holding the cruets of water and wine up to the alter for the consecration, the large priest scowled at me and said in his deep voice, "There almost no wine here! Go back and get some more."

I was terrified as I walked back into the sacristy. The bottle of wine was still sitting where I had left it, on a glass tray. It had a small lip around its perimeter to prevent bottles from sliding off. I picked up the wine bottle, removed the cork, and tried to pour more wine through the tiny cruet opening. It was a difficult maneuver even in the best of circumstances, and this definitely wasn't one of those. I was nervous and shaking so badly I bumped the bottle against the tray's rim. It slipped out of my hand and wine ran all over the tray. I tried to pick the bottle up as soon as it happened, but it was too late. It was already almost empty. Now I was in real trouble, with an empty cruet and an empty wine bottle. I just stood there trying to figure out what I could do so I filled the cruet with water, hoping the priest wouldn't notice. Then I had to figure out what to do with the tray full of wine. I panicked and lifted the corner of it to my mouth. I drank it all, licked up what was left, and tried to clean up the remaining evidence with a rag.

After Mass, the priest was in the sacristy, removing his outer vestments when he noticed the wine-stained rag sitting on the counter. He looked over at the empty wine bottle and asked in a loud voice, "What happened here?"

This was a man of God Almighty and I had messed up. Now, I was destined for hell. I was so scared I started crying. I told him the story of what had happened. I told him how I was nervous and how the wine just slipped out of my hand. "I didn't know what to do with it, so I drank it!" I cried. I thought I was going to get a thrashing, but instead the priest looked down at me and smiled. He said, "Well Mathias, did you enjoy all that wine?"

I shook my head. "No, father. It was terrible." I was feeling nauseated.

He chuckled and said, "Don't worry. Everything's going to be fine. We all make mistakes, even priests." He reassured me by patting my shoulder. A minute later I rushed outside and vomited. While walking home, I thought about what had happened that morning. I had learned an important lesson. I realized that though he was a priest, he was not someone to fear. He was a man anointed by God, but still just a man like most men...and a kind one at that.

Our school sat just to the left of the church, about a hundred meters back from the road. It merged two age groups together in each class. Every day began with morning Mass. School was in session eleven months out of the year with a couple of weeks off at Christmas and Easter. We were given a one-month break in the summer. Throughout the year, children had to help with the farm so the nuns were lenient in accepting excuses for absences.

The nuns were tough but fair. They didn't tolerate a great deal of nonsense and discipline was meted out with regularity. Usually it was in the form of a ruler slap across the knuckles or a smack in the back of the head. Sometimes it was more severe. I don't remember exactly what I had done wrong on one particular day, but it must have been something pretty bad. Sister Droste was a small woman and I could never quite tell how old she was. With the large habits around their heads you could only see a small part of their face and their hands were always hidden up their sleeves; hidden until they pulled out a ruler to smack you. Anyway, I did something very wrong one day and Sister Droste handed me a paring knife. It was also hidden up her sleeve. She told me to cut a switch from a crepe myrtle bush outside. I was in big trouble and didn't know how I could get out of it. Selecting a switch was a delicate matter. I didn't want to bring back one that was too big because it would hurt more. If I returned with one too small, she would go out to cut her own and that would be the worst situation of all. Sister Droste was an expert on switches. I knew I was going to get flogged one way or the other, so I selected a medium-sized shoot that I hoped would appease the good Sister. On the way back inside, I saw a stack of newspapers sitting in one of the rooms adjacent to ours. They gave me an idea. I grabbed a handful of them and stuffed the paper down the back of my pants.

I returned with the whip and bent over the bench to receive my punishment. When she hit me, I faked a howl but didn't feel anything. I grinned at my success but the noise of the switch hitting my bottom didn't make a slapping sound. Rather it was more of a crunching. My grin soon melted away when she said, "Matthias, why don't you head over to the corner for a minute and remove whatever you have in your pants." I did and when I again bent over the bench, she really let me have it.

By the time I got home that afternoon my mom had already found out about what I had done. We had no telephones or internet at the time, but mothers always seemed to know such things as soon as they happened. It was kind of the same way they could see around corners and through walls. Mom secretly gave me a pillow to sit on at dinner that night. Nothing was said to my father, and that was good.

The first time I returned to Germany was in 1959. One of the people I looked up when I got to Lorup was little Sister Droste. I thanked her for being such a great teacher and told her how much I respected her. She smiled and pretended to remember me, but I doubt she did. It had been too many years and too many switches ago.

COLLATERAL DAMAGE

War is not a surgically precise endeavor. Death and destruction are meted out arbitrarily and they are widespread in spite of all efforts to contain them. When a gun is fired, the bullet exits the muzzle in excess of two thousand feet per second. If the bullet misses its target it continues forward until it is stopped by something or someone else.

During bomb runs, the bombardier zeroes in on a target miles below him. Flying in a plane at two hundred miles per hour means that a target can be missed by several miles if the ordnance package is released a few seconds late or if the plane must take evasive measures to avoid anti-aircraft fire. Once target acquisition is confirmed, the process becomes a sterile matter of simply pressing a button. Once released, no decisions are made. Just like a bullet, a bomb's singular purpose is to destroy anything it hits. The projectile makes no moral decision regarding the potential loss of innocent civilian lives. Those victims are referred to by the euphemistic phrase, "Collateral damage."

I thought the day when the Messerschmitt fighter planes fired on the defenseless parachuting bomber crews would be the worst image of the war I would ever see. I was wrong. As the Allied fighters were able to extend their range farther into the industrialized areas of Germany, the air battles over Lorup intensified. German and American planes were shot out of the sky on a regular basis and the ejected bomb loads were landing closer to our village, some landing within fifty meters of our school. The building shook and the windows rattled to the point of breaking. It was terrifying, and we all took cover under our desks. As a result, the village constructed a series of bunkers placed along the roadways. They were simple trenches covered by boards and camouflaged with sod.

I witnessed just one civilian casualty during those months, but it wasn't from an errant bomb. I was walking home from school one afternoon with several of my friends. A group of smaller children followed a few meters behind. One of them was little Peter Abeln, the youngest brother of one of my best friends. We heard the fighter planes above us. The sounds of machine gun fire erupted as several planes engaged in the life and death battle of a dogfight. The air battle was in the clouds and a little to the north, so we paid little attention to them. We had gotten used to the noise and explosions and no civilians had ever been killed before. The air war was just a way of life for us. We continued walking home as we laughed and talked about the kind of things children usually discuss: tough teachers, chores, soccer, and plans for the afternoon.

The first thing I noticed was several puffs of dirt rising directly at my feet. A split-second later I heard what sounded like bees buzzing past my head. Realizing what was happening, I immediately told the others to take cover in one of the nearby makeshift bunkers. We ran as fast as we could. I heard a "thud," like the sound of a melon hitting the ground. I turned to see what had happened and saw young Peter lying on the ground just outside the bunker. He wasn't crying but something was definitely wrong. The other children were splattered with droplets of blood. It took a half second for me to process what I was seeing. The top two inches of the little boy's head were gone. He had been hit by one of the stray bullets. We all stood still, frozen in disbelief. The boy was laughing and talking one minute and the next he was dead, just like that. We ran for help but there was nothing anyone could do.

The randomness of the death shook me. The same could have happened to any of us that day. It was the arbitrary way in which we were walking together that made the only difference between life and death. The image of young Peter's headless body burned its way into my soul. I cried myself to sleep that night. It was the first time I had ever seen someone near me die so violently. It wouldn't be the last. Unfortunately, I would see many more before the war came to an end.

The funeral was held several days later. Almost everyone in Lorup attended. I remember the priest talking about the senselessness of the boy's death. After the service, I overheard some of the village leaders talking. "Stray bullet from one of the fighter planes. Bad luck," said one.

Then I heard Gunter Hilmer claim, "Had to be from one of those damned American planes. If they would stop meddling in German affairs, this would have never happened. They're the ones to blame."

None of the regular town folk commented. They were afraid to. Thoughts about how some churchgoing Christians could support the Nazi movement left me perplexed for the rest of my life.

◆•◆

As the air battles over Germany became more frequent, we noticed an increased German military presence near Lorup. They patrolled our village on a regular basis, and the local police were on high alert to look out for enemy airmen who might have safely parachuted from their disabled planes.

I was about twelve years old when I was watching some of my friends playing soccer near the school. It was a bad day for me and, as usual, my asthma prevented me from joining in the game. We all looked up when we heard a loud explosion a few thousand meters above us. An American plane had flames pouring out of both sides of its fuselage. It veered to its left and collided with the wing of another bomber. Both planes fell and soon the sky was filled with over a dozen parachutes. We watched in horror as half the men were badly wounded by machine gun fire from the Messerschmitts. Several of the airmen landed in the pine tree woods a hundred meters away. Five of us ran over to the area and we found one man hanging down from the trees, but he was obviously dead from multiple bullet wounds in his chest. A second one was still alive and hanging from his parachute along one of the lower branches. One of my friends climbed the tree and cut the chute free. When we got him down, we saw that blood covered his entire left leg and he could barely stand up. One of us stood on either side of the man and helped him walk toward town for help. A woman whose husband had died on the Russian front rushed out of her house and offered the man some warm coffee. He smiled and replied in German, "Danke."

We hadn't noticed Gunter Hilmer, my father's childhood friend, neighbor, and Nazi sympathizer standing nearby. He rushed over and slapped the coffee out of the pilot's hand, splashing it over the man's face and the woman who had offered it to him. Hilmer turned to her and yelled, "You don't help the enemy. I should have the SS arrest you for treason!" He turned to us and added, "You'd best not be here when I return, or they'll arrest you also."

After Mr. Hilmer disappeared around the corner calling out for the police, my friends and I helped the pilot toward a barn several hundred yards away. It was too difficult for just one of us, so we all took turns holding him up until we made it to safety. The barn door was ajar, and when we entered we found two other airmen already hiding inside. Our pilot was in better shape than either of them. One appeared to be dying from his wounds and the other looked like he wouldn't last very long. There was nothing we could do but try to make the men comfortable. We climbed up to the loft and threw down hay in order to make a bed for them, but with their severe injuries I knew their fate was inevitable.

About five minutes later I heard a noise. I walked outside and snuck a peek around the corner of the barn. "A car is coming!" I yelled to those inside. I knew it would be the police or SS because there were no other automobiles in Lorup.

The pilot said just one word to us. We didn't understand English but had a pretty good idea about what he meant. "Go!"

He was a good man and I didn't want to leave him, but I knew there was no other choice but to go. We ran across a field as fast as we could, toward the cover of some pine woods. Halfway there I started wheezing so badly I thought my lungs might explode. I pushed on just like my father had always told me. By the time I reached the trees, breathing was so difficult I almost passed out. I rested and looked back in time to see the black sedan coming to a sudden halt in front of the barn, kicking up gravel and dust in all directions. Four men in black uniforms jumped out and drew their pistols. Several minutes later, only the black uniforms exited the barn. They had no prisoners with them.

STRAFING

In time, we saw no more German aircraft attacking the Allied planes, so they were able to bomb Germany's industrial centers at will. Father said that it was because the Allies had destroyed the German Luftwaffe and stymied Hitler's ability to manufacture replacement planes. "This war will soon be over," he told me. "Whoever rules the sky wins the war." He seemed happy and sad at the same time.

"What's wrong?" I asked. "I thought defeating Hitler was a good thing."

"I've been through war," he replied. "Sometimes the final stages bring the worst killing and destruction." I would soon find out what my father meant.

———————————— ◆•●•◆ ————————————

It was a beautiful early spring morning in 1945. The weather had been unseasonably warm, and a few wild flowers were already beginning to bloom. The skies were a clear blue interrupted by only an occasional white billowy cloud. I hadn't had an asthma attack in several months, so I was pleased when father asked me to help him in the fields. In spite of the war, work still had to be done to prepare for spring planting. As we rode out to the farm, I could see that the land on both sides of the road had been scarred by the occasional errant bomb and jettisoned long-range fuel tanks. The American pilots tried their best to avoid populated areas, and it was a miracle there weren't more civilian casualties. When the British fighters took over more of the aerial responsibilities in our region, things changed. They were more aggressive when it came to attacks on civilian targets. My father told me it was because Hitler had bombed London and the rest of England so ruthlessly. In spite of prior international agreements to avoid aerial attacks on non-military sites, Hitler soon authorized the targeting of those very same facilities. Thousands of innocent men, women, and children were slaughtered as a result, leaving many of the British furious and seeking revenge. Unfortunately, many of them saw all German citizens as Nazis, deserving of reprisals. Everyone and every place became a potential target as far as some Brits were concerned.

My job that morning was to hitch up the horses to the tooth harrow, a piece of equipment used to loosen the soil. I walked behind, guiding the harrow in neat parallel rows, just like my father showed me. I had grown but still had trouble seeing over the top of the harrow. It was hard work and I struggled a bit, but I was happy to be able to do my part in helping Dad. I paused for a minute to wipe the sweat from my brow and gaze over our land. There was a gentle breeze blowing out of the north and the birds joined together in their daily chorus of songs. It couldn't have been a more perfect or peaceful day. It felt good to be working side by side with dad. Though I was only twelve, I felt like I had just joined that exclusive fraternity reserved only for adult men.

The next time I paused to rest I noticed that things were different. The birds' singing had stopped. It had been replaced by a loud buzzing, like a nest of angry hornets. I had heard that same sound too many times before. Then came the staccato bursts of machine gun fire. Father and I looked up to see two British fighter planes strafing something in the distant valley. It turned out to be a civilian train that was on its way to the town of Werlte, just five kilometers away. One after another, the planes took turns making their passes. They fired their guns until the train's engine finally exploded and the locomotive came to a halt. They made several more passes, firing heavily on the passenger compartments.

"Why do they keep firing on the train? The engine is already destroyed," I asked.

"They must think it's carrying military personnel," said my dad. Once they were finished, he added, "We'd better get off this hill. If they see us, they might decide to come after us next."

"But we're not soldiers!" I yelled.

"They might not know that, and they might not care. We need to release the horses!"

Dad helped me unhitch the horses from the harrow and I chased them over to an adjoining field where they would be safe. As soon as I finished, we heard the planes coming.

———————— ◆◦◆ ————————

British Spitfire fighter plane. Dad and I were defenseless

"Hurry, into the ditch!" yelled dad. It was a two-foot trench along the side of the road, created by centuries of rain and erosion. It was shallow, but it was the only cover available. We hoped it would be enough to protect us if the planes decided to attack. Seconds later they did, with their guns firing. I could see the flames shooting out from the barrels. They were rapidly approaching us in a line perpendicular to the ditch. I was terrified, but because of the direction of their attack, they couldn't get a clean shot at us. My relief was soon replaced by panic when we saw the planes banking so they could attack from a direction parallel to the road. We were sitting ducks and I knew we didn't stand a chance. Father huddled me close and tried to shield me with his body. I buried my head against the ground and said a silent prayer asking God to somehow protect us from this certain death.

God must have heard me. We could still hear the machine guns, but they weren't directed at us. We looked up to see the planes veering north toward a more attractive target. It was a black car speeding down a road just a quarter-kilometer away. The only people who could drive a car like that were Nazi officials. I guessed the Brits decided it was a better target than a farmer and his son. The planes destroyed the car and it crashed into a tree along the side of the road. Three men in military uniforms jumped out and ran to take cover in a house nearby. The planes fired on the home repeatedly until it started burning. One of the three men must have been killed inside because only two escaped the fire and headed to another home nearby. That one was also strafed until it caught fire. Within minutes it was totally engulfed in flames. We didn't see anyone trying to escape so we figured the two men inside had been killed.

We had been spared, but for only a few minutes. The planes began to again head back in our direction. Suddenly, they veered to the west, back toward Holland. "Thank God," said father. "I think they must have run low on fuel."

The entire incident reinforced to me just how random and unfair war could be. It wasn't always just about men in one uniform killing men in other uniforms. Just like my young friend Peter Abeln who had lost the top of his head from a stray bullet, everyone, even innocent citizens, were potential casualties. Usually it was from what they referred to as "collateral damage." Other times, it was intentional. Even the good guys could be as bad as the bad guys. Sometimes it was hard to tell the difference. I never could understand how God could allow this to happen, why innocent people had to die such a violent death. Even as an adult, I realized there were no easy answers to my questions.

ALLIED INVASION

It was in the late afternoon about six months later when we noticed a farmer and his family herding a flock of sheep down the dirt road in front of our house. We didn't recognize any of them, so we knew they weren't from Lorup. They had to have travelled a long distance. They all looked tired and sickly.

"Hello," said my father.

"Hello," replied the man in a weak voice. I noticed some of the children had been crying. The mother carried a listless baby in her arms. I was afraid it might be dead.

"Where are you from?" asked father as he looked at the infant.

"We had a small farm about fifteen kilometers northeast of here. We've been traveling all night."

"Had?"

"The Allies have invaded Germany and the German army set up a defensive line just to the west of our village. We were caught in the middle of artillery crossfire. I don't know which side did it, but our home and farm were completely destroyed. We lost our youngest son and I barely had enough time to bury him before we had to run. My wife and the children are in shock. I'm trying to take them someplace safe, but I don't even know if such a place even exists anymore."

Father nodded in understanding. Then he said, "Your family doesn't look like they can travel much farther and there's nothing up the road for another ten kilometers. The children need to rest and eat. You should stay with us for the night. You'll be safe here. My wife Anna has been cooking some bean soup with bacon and we have a little bread. We don't have a lot of room, but we will make space for you."

"But our sheep. They're all we have left."

"You can put them in our barn. They'll be safe there."

The man looked reluctant to accept what he probably saw as an offer of charity. It ran contrary to his deep-seated German sense of pride. He tried to remain strong, but I thought I could see a tear in his left eye. He looked back at his family and after a few seconds he relented. "Thank you," he said. Mom helped the woman and her children inside where they ate for the first time in several days.

Father didn't seem all that surprised at the information regarding the Allied invasion. I knew he had a radio, though possession of one was forbidden by the Nazis. They were nervous, and everyone was suspected of possible treason. If someone found out that Father had a radio and was listening to enemy broadcasts, the punishment would be death. At night I had seen him in the corner of the kitchen, with the radio close to his hear so he could keep the volume down. He knew the Allied army was coming.

The rest of us had seen trucks of fresh German troops passing through Lorup for the past month, so we all knew something was up. Even as a child I could tell how desperate the situation was for Nazi Germany. Father said the country had exhausted most of its reserves in the failed "Battle of the Bulge." The new soldiers were boys, just a few years older than me. Their eyes were open wide with fear. Defeat was imminent and Hitler's dreams of a Third Reich were rapidly collapsing around him.

The following morning, we could hear the sounds of what seemed to be a loud thunder storm in the distance, but the skies were clear and there was no rain.

"Allied Howitzers," said my father. "No more than ten kilometers away." Our visitors looked terrified.

"At least they aren't the Russians," added my father. We had all heard the rumors of widespread murder and rape by Stalin's troops. Father had advised the girls to hide and remain hidden if they saw any soldiers coming, lest they also become victims. The explosions frightened our overnight visitors and they insisted on leaving. Father tried to convince them that it would be safer to remain with us, but they continued their journey anyway, to where I never found out. I don't think they even knew. We never saw them again and I suspect they didn't survive.

The battle intensified. In the afternoon, we saw a small convoy of trucks retreating down the road. They were carrying wounded German soldiers and armaments away from the front. A few hours later, the sounds of artillery were getting closer. Father said, "We'd better leave. The fight is getting too close." Hitler had ordered all German civilians to stand their ground and defend the "Fatherland" with their lives. The Fuhrer had failed to consider two significant problems. First of all, his Nazi regime had already confiscated all guns years ago and the civilians had nothing left with which to fight. The second was that most of the civilians outside the large industrial cities didn't care about Hitler or his grand ideas for Germany's future. The common people despised the Nazis and all they stood for.

"We must prepare to leave now!" Father insisted. He hitched up the horses to our two wagons as Mom and the rest of us loaded ourselves and as much food as we could gather. Dad picked up the reins and turned around to be sure everyone was on board. When I looked up at him I was shocked by what I saw. My father, the unflappable hero who had already witnessed years of the unspeakable ravages of war, had tears in his eyes. That was the only time I had ever seen my father crying. I checked on my mother and saw a frightened look on her face. I realized that dad must have told her about some of the things he had seen in war. *What does this mean?* I thought. *What does dad think is going to happen to us?* I was terrified.

We continued down the dirt road, past our farmland and away from the village. We ran into some others who were also fleeing. They told us that the German army was sustaining heavy losses as the Allied forces pushed forward. The town of Borger had already fallen and Lorup was next in line. There were reports of deserters scattered across the countryside. They were being shot on sight by German officers. Sometimes civilians were also killed.

We eventually took shelter four kilometers away in a barn that belonged to one of my uncles, Matthias Schmits. Dad, Rudy, and I dug trenches behind the barn so we had a place to take cover if the Allies started firing at us. Meanwhile my sisters threw a lot of straw down from the loft in order to make beds for everyone. Through the night we could hear the sounds of Allied artillery getting closer. The noise was frightening. We never knew whether or not the barn might take a direct hit.

The next day my father told Rudy and me to take a white sheet and hang it from the barn's thatched roof to show the Americans that we weren't German army. He hoped they wouldn't target us. Just as we were finishing, a car containing two German officers came speeding down the road toward us. Their vehicle screeched to a halt in front of the barn, throwing a cloud of dust in all directions. A captain jumped out, drew his Luger pistol from its holster and pointed it directly at my father's head. I can still remember the inlaid red swastika on the handle. "Is that a white flag? The Fuhrer commanded all citizens to fight to the death. You know the penalty for surrender!"

Without blinking an eye, my father acted confused as he looked up at the sheet. "Oh, no, no, no. That's not a white flag. Some of our children were frightened and wet on that sheet last night. We had to hang it up there to dry out. We're in the barn ready to make our stand." I thought my father was dead right there, but he sold the story and the captain lowered his weapon.

The German officer raised his right hand and said, "Sieg heil." He jumped back into his car and sped away looking for more deserters. I noticed he was running away from the battle lines while expecting us to fight with nothing more than shovels and pitchforks.

———————————◆◆◦◆◦◆———————————

By the next day, the sounds of gunfire became less frequent. Rudy, father, and I hiked through a pine forest to see if it was safe to return to our house. We stood on a small rise and looked out through the trees. We could see a line of American tanks coming down a road just a few hundred meters away. There was a muddy peat bog area along the same river bank where I used to fish. There was a bridge across it, but it was narrow and the tanks had to traverse it single file. On the other side sat a small barn. We saw a young German soldier run inside through a rear door. He was carrying a bazooka and he cut a hole through the barn wall to aim his weapon. As soon as the line of tanks began crossing the bridge, he picked them off one by one, destroying two of them. The tanks behind couldn't pass the damaged ones because they'd get stuck in the peat bog, so they had to push the crippled ones aside and into the bog. The German soldier must have run out of shells because he started firing with his rifle. One of the tanks fired back and the barn exploded in a ball of fire. The soldier ran to escape but he was engulfed in flames. We could hear his screams for help. He only made it a few meters before he was killed by the tank's machine gun.

———————————◆◆◦◆◦◆———————————

We spent our second night in the barn with sporadic rifle and artillery fire all around us. The next morning, Rudy remained with the family while Dad and I followed the pine forest back to our house. We let all the cows and pigs into the back yard so they wouldn't burn to death if the house and attached barn caught fire. Father decided we should try to retrieve some of our goods, so I stood outside and reached in a window as he handed me pewter plates and other things that I stacked outside under a tree. As I reached in for a load of clothes, an artillery shell exploded against the wall, just above me. Reaching so far inside the window is what saved me from getting killed. I guess God was watching over me just like He had done when Dad and I were pinned down together in the trench. Father yelled, "We'd better get out of here. We can get our stuff later when the battle's over."

As we were trying to run back into the trees, another artillery shell exploded just a short distance away. We both dropped to the ground but neither of us was injured. I realized that from a distance, the Allies couldn't tell if we were German soldiers or not, so we decided to run back to the barn to rejoin the family. We would remain there until we could be sure the battle for Lorup was completely over.

It was almost a week before it was safe to return home. We were happy to discover that our house and those of our neighbors' had not burned. We were unhappy to find that the Americans had set up their camp just a half-kilometer down the road. We weren't sure how they would treat us. We hoped it would be better than the Russians. As least we were again able to sleep in our own beds.

The following morning mom prepared our first hot meal since we had left. It was fried potatoes, eggs, a little bacon, and hot milk that we poured over stale bread. I remember it as the best meal I had ever eaten. Suddenly the front door burst open and there stood two American MPs holding machine guns. My sisters jumped up to hide like my father had told them to do. I'll never forget the voice of the one MP as he raised his hand and yelled, "Whoa! Sit down!" We didn't know English, but the meaning was obvious. The girls stopped in their tracks and returned to their seats, frightened to death. The men kept their guns trained on us but didn't appear to be threatening. They tried to talk to us, but they didn't speak German and none of us could speak English. One of them knew a little French and my dad had spent some time in France during the First World War, so they were able to communicate a little. He reassured the Americans that there were no German soldiers hiding anywhere, but encouraged them to search the house if they'd like. One did while his partner kept an eye on us. When finished they were satisfied and lowered their weapons. Father finally figured out that the soldiers mostly wanted food. Because of the fighting, there was no market for eggs and ours would spoil before we could use all of them, so mom handed over as many as the two MPs could carry. They left happy and we were all relieved.

The next morning the same two MPs returned and this time their rifles were slung over their shoulders. They wanted more eggs and a few chickens. Mother again gave them as many eggs as she could spare, and father took them out to the coop where they selected a dozen chickens. In exchange, they gave my mother a can of coffee and a tin of tea. Mom hadn't had either of those items available in years and she was thrilled to get them. The soldiers also gave her $10. She placed the money in a tin and hid it on the top of a kitchen shelf. That money was to come in handy years later.

———————————— ◆◦◆ ————————————

On April 30, 1945, Adolf Hitler committed suicide inside his bunker in Berlin. Germany surrendered shortly afterward. By the time the fighting stopped, over seven million Germans had been killed and countless more severely injured. It amounted to almost ten percent of the population. In addition, over six million Jews had been massacred. Many American soldiers remained in Lorup to maintain order and help reestablish a local government. They were admittedly an occupational force but always treated us with respect and dignity. We were happy to have them. Many of them helped to repair some of the damage incurred during the battle for Lorup.

KARL KLUHNE

The German economy gradually improved after the war. Within several years, life slowly returned to normal. Supplies became more readily available and construction jobs in Lorup returned. My parents again had an open market for their crops and livestock.

At age fourteen, I finished my official school training and it was time for me to pursue a career. I was named after my mother's father who was a tailor so it was assumed that I would follow in my grandfather's footsteps. He began teaching me the necessary skills and, in time, I actually became good enough that I would help Mom hem old clothes.

Arrangements had been made for me to do an apprenticeship with a local master tailor. By then I was looking forward to pursuing a career that demanded precise workmanship and a certain level of creativity. The day before I was about to start my official training, my mentor died of a heart attack in the bog while harvesting peat blocks for his stove. My career as a tailor was derailed before it had gotten started. I was devastated and didn't know what to do. My asthma prevented me from becoming a farmer like my father and there weren't many other career options available in Lorup at the time. My chances for a successful future were looking grim. I approached my father hoping for the same words of reassurance he had given to me years ago during a severe asthma attack in the fields. He said nothing more than, "I'm sure everything will work out." That was it, no pat on the shoulder, no encouragement, just those few words.

He resumed the process of hitching the horses to the wagon and heading out to the farm as though our short conversation had never taken place. I later learned it didn't mean that Dad didn't care about me. He thought about the future happiness of all his children. He was simply unable to express his feelings with words. He relied more on his actions to show how much he loved his family: protecting us from harm, providing a roof over our head, and putting food on the table.

Two months later, I still had no career prospects. Dad approached me and without any preliminary discussion said, "I've arranged for you to begin a three-year apprenticeship as a cabinet maker." Nothing more was said, but I was thrilled. There wasn't much demand for cabinet makers at the time, but the post-war German economy was recovering, and it wouldn't be long before home construction returned. That meant a greater demand for carpenters and cabinet makers. I would soon find out that my new journey would be both a blessing and a curse.

The apprenticeship was to be with a master cabinet maker in the town of Borger, about six kilometers away. The only travel options we had were walking, riding a horse, or driving the wooden wagon. Dad needed the last two to work the farm and the distance was too far to walk, so Dad searched around for other possibilities. Eventually he found an old bicycle. The chain was frozen with rust and it had flat tires, but he was able to fix the chain and patch the holes in the inner tubes. The tires were a problem since there was still little rubber available in post-Hitler Germany, so my dad searched until he was able to gather scraps of rubber tire from other discarded bikes. He then glued them together until he had made two complete tires from the pieces. The wheels were uneven but that's what I rode down the dirt roads to Borger. I looked like one of those cartoon characters trying to ride a bike with square tires. I started on my journey to Borger at 5:00 AM on my first day and could hear the ka-plup, ka-plup of the wheels for the entire six kilometers. I was sure the bike was going to fall apart before I got there but get there it did by 7:00 AM. With regular tire repairs the bike served me well for three years.

The Master carpenter in charge of my apprenticeship was Karl Kluhne, a man who had come to Germany as a refugee from Hungary years earlier to ply his trade. I was the only student in his apprentice program and I soon discovered why. Kluhne was a tyrant who treated his apprentices like dogs. He was one of the most spiteful individuals I had ever met. I was given a simple room in the attic of his house. It contained a hard bed, no furniture, and no heat.

There was no machinery, so all work had to be done by hand. Raw lumber was sawed to the necessary size and smoothed with planes. Kluhne frowned upon the use of nails. Everything was held together with hidden dovetail connections and glue. Doing that by hand required a great deal of attention to workmanship. That was fine with me. I wanted to learn how to become the best cabinet maker possible. Kluhne didn't actually teach, so I had to learn most of what I needed from employees in his shop, but Kluhne was always there, ready to yell if I didn't produce a high-quality product in a timely fashion.

The work was grueling, and Kluhne was abusive, but I accepted that it must be that way to learn the trade. It was a price I was willing to pay in order to establish a career. One of my major problems besides Kluhne was that exposure to the sawdust and glue chemicals in his shop exacerbated my asthma problems. I knew that if I was sick too often, Herr Kluhne would become aware of my health issues, and he would kick me out of the apprentice program. Then my prospects for any successful career would be dashed. I had to hide my symptoms. When I felt an attack coming on, I would try to control my breathing as best I could to hide the wheezing. I would blame any difficulty on the strenuous work of carrying loads of lumber in from outside or moving heavy cabinets around the shop. The other workers were aware of my problem and always tried to help protect my secret.

There were no breaks and little food available. At lunch time, a cup of black coffee and a plate with two pieces of rye bread and syrup were placed on my workbench. That was all I received until dinner. I started losing weight. On Saturday evenings I would climb on my bike and ride the six kilometers back home to Lorup. Once there my mother always prepared good meals, the only ones I received all week. On Monday morning I would pedal back to my job and start the process all over again, ka-plup, ka-plup.

Mom always worried that I was too thin so every Sunday night, she would wrap up a dozen fresh eggs to take with me. I hid them under my attic bed and every night I would drink one or two of them from the shell so I wouldn't starve. I never told my father how I was treated by Kluhne. I didn't want him to get mad and do something that would get me kicked out of the program.

I continued with my training for three long years and eventually I became proficient as a cabinetmaker. Finally, it was time for my certification exam which was comprised of an all-day written test. I thought I did well but was still afraid because if you fail, you only have one more opportunity to pass or you would forever be prevented from entering the trade. You would have invested three years of hard work under brutal conditions and have nothing to show for it. Fortunately, I passed the written exam without a problem.

Then we were required to make something under the direct supervision of an outside inspector. I decided to build a chest of drawers. The observer said nothing. He just stood behind me, taking notes, and watching my every move. Doing it by hand was quite a job and all the drawer facings and dovetails were crafted by hand. When finished, I thought I had done an excellent job and the inspector passed my work. However, after he left the shop, Kluhne pulled out one of my drawers and found a small flaw in one of the dovetails. He went crazy, yelling and criticizing my lack of workmanship and how it reflected poorly on him. He threw the drawer at me. I didn't know if he actually intended to hit me, but the drawer struck me on the side of my head. It was so hard the blow cracked the drawer bottom. I was stunned but I still remember his exact words, "Maybe now you'll remember how to do it right!"

I was furious and wanted to hit him back, to punish him for how he had treated me for the past three years. God knew he deserved it. However, I still didn't have my official certificate and if I did lash out at him, he could end it all for me. The last three years of misery would have been wasted. I would have no future, so I swallowed my pride and took it. It didn't matter. Shortly after that I received my official certificate as an expert cabinet maker. Five other apprentices from different shops took the exam but only three passed. That's how difficult it was.

The day after receiving my certificate, I was free to seek employment anywhere in Germany. As I was packing my few belongings, Kluhne approached and said he was getting older. He asked me to stay in Borger to work for him. He needed someone to help run the business and promised to pay me well. I said, "Kluhne, you don't have enough money to get me to work for you. I'd rather work for the devil himself." I walked away and rode my bike home for the last time, never to see the man again, ka-plup, ka-plup.

Until I passed my exams, I had never told my dad about how Kluhne had treated me. When I eventually relayed my story, he said nothing, but I could see the rage burning in his eyes. I heard those wooden shoes tapping impatiently on the floor and I could see his jaw muscles twitching as he clenched his teeth. He got dressed, hooked the horses to the wagon, and headed down the same road I used to ride on my bike to Borger. Father never told me what had happened that afternoon, but I suspect it involved a serious conversation with Herr Karl Kluhne. When he got back home, he said nothing, but the rage in his eyes was gone. All I noticed was a little sawdust on Dad's left shoulder. I smiled. The matter was never discussed again.

As oppressive as Kluhne was, I did come away from the experience with several principles that formed the cornerstones of my professional career: always strive for perfection in everything I do, and everyone deserves to be treated with compassion and dignity.

THE COURT RULING

After escaping the grip of Kluhne, it was time for me to set out on my own career. I knew only one thing: I would never again allow my life to be dictated by any government or another man like Kluhne. I planned to be the master of my own future.

Though the German economy was recovering, there was still no work available for another cabinet maker in the small village of Lorup. I had my certificate but was not allowed to start my own company without a master's license, so I was forced to find employment elsewhere. I wound up working in the town of Herzlake, about fifty kilometers away. We built cabinets, windows, doors, and anything else made from wood. After fine-tuning my craft there, I had the opportunity to move back to Lorup and work for a Mr. Herman Eilers, a local cabinet maker. I was doing well and for the first time in my life I was making good money. It was a great feeling and it gave me a sense of independence.

By the time I finished my apprenticeship, my brother-in-law Nick Kreutzjans had already started his own construction company in Lorup. He had six men working for him and was doing rather well. He made enough money to build his own home and constructed a workshop in the back. In the winter it was too cold outside to build homes, so he used the workshop to make cabinets and wagons. Nick was earning enough to be able to buy a 98 cc Sachs motorcycle, the only one in Lorup. About three years after I started working, my brother-in-law told me that he and Marie were thinking of moving to America with their two children.

Nick had a brother, George who had established a successful construction business in a place called Fort Wright, Kentucky. After the war, George had come back to Lorup to visit his family. In spite of Nick's success in Lorup, George convinced him that he should move to America and join him there in the construction business. There was the promise of a much better life in the U.S. so after a lot of consideration, that's what Nick and my sister Marie decided to do.

Before leaving, Nick met with me and said, "Matth, you should move into my house. I rented most of it to Josef Keiser and his wife, but there's still an empty bedroom they won't be using. I'll let you stay there for free and you'll have full use of the workshop in back. I already have all the tools you'll need to start your own cabinetry business." When he threw in the motorcycle, the deal was done.

The post-war economy was beginning to thrive. More homes were being built and that was great for my new business. I started making cabinets, doors, windows, and anything else involving the interior finishing of a house. I approached my work like one would a piece of art and rapidly earned a reputation as a good craftsman. Word spread and in no time I had as much work as I could handle. I was making more money than I had ever had in my life. The sickly kid with asthma was doing well and I was proud. Life was great...perhaps too great.

It took about another six months for everything to fall apart. Technically, I needed a master's certificate to start a business on my own, but that would have involved another four years of training. I didn't have time for that. I was already doing excellent work and spending another four years in training would do nothing to enhance my abilities. Quality was what was most important, not a piece of paper. I thought I would be fine. The United States and Britain had taken over the responsibility of governing our area of Germany. I was under the impression that after the war many of the outdated laws and regulations regarding the master's certificate requirements had been relaxed to promote the development of individual small businesses. I was wrong in my assumptions. I was naive and failed to understand the politics of the situation. It was a hard lesson and a problem I would repeatedly face in the future. Government bureaucrats love to meddle in people's lives.

Someone reported to the authorities that I had started my own business without having the necessary certificate. I never found out for sure who it was, but I had my suspicions. Someone was obviously resentful of the fact that I had become so successful. I received a notice in the mail, and I was instructed to answer the charges in writing. The letter said a court date would be set for a full hearing. I realized my situation was hopeless. There was no way I could win this battle. I was certain that the decision to punish me had already been made, regardless of the hearing.

Over the past century there had been a substantial migration of Germans to the United States. The emigrants were desperate in their attempts to flee war, military conscription, government oppression, famine, and poverty. There was opportunity in America and that's why my sister Marie and her husband Nick moved there. Instead of responding to the government's letter, I wrote to Marie, "I want to go where I know I can succeed without outside interference from government. I would like to come to the United States. Do you think Nick's brother, George, would be willing to sponsor me?" In those days, you had to have a sponsor to immigrate to America. That person had to show that he could provide shelter and a job so you wouldn't become a burden to the community. The sponsor also had to demonstrate that he had enough money in the bank to provide for you just in case you couldn't secure employment and be self-sufficient.

Two months later Marie sent me a letter stating that George agreed to sponsor me and promised to provide employment. She included the necessary instructions, travel documents, and her home phone number in America. I didn't attend the scheduled court hearing and the results were as expected. I received another letter stating that I was fined 1,200 marks. That was a huge amount of money and there was no way I could afford to pay it. They also levied a four-year penalty before I would be allowed to enter a master's program, which would then leave another four more years of training before I could be certified. That meant it would be at least eight years before I could resume my business. For all practical purposes any chance for a career in Germany was over. After my experiences with Karl Kluhne, I had sworn that I would never again allow myself to become a victim of another man or government, and I wasn't going to back down from that vow.

I never discussed the court's findings with others. I didn't want anyone to become aware of my plans lest they report me before I could leave the country. The last day before I was to depart for America, I told my dad and showed him the letter. "This is what's happened, Dad. I have no other choice but to leave Germany. Make sure that once I'm in America, you send these papers back to the court with a note saying that I don't live here anymore. If they want to find me, they can come to the United States to get me."

On the day I left, my mother told me to wait for a second. She went into the kitchen and retrieved an old tin that had been sitting on the top shelf of her kitchen cabinet for years. She pried open the lid and inside was ten dollars, the same money the US Army soldier had given her in exchange for eggs and a couple chickens years ago. She cried when she handed it to me.

My twin brother Rudy, my sisters, and many of my friends travelled with me by bus to the port of Bremen along the north coast of Germany. I gave Rudy my motorcycle and all the money I had. They were Deutsche Marks and would be of no use to me in America. All I had left with me was my suitcase, the ten U.S.

dollars in my wallet, and the immigration documents Marie had mailed. I rechecked my coat pocket to be sure they were all still there.

SS UNITED STATES

Before boarding the boat, I sat in a large waiting area with other travelers. Rudy, my family, and dozens of my close friends were there. In spite of their support, or maybe because of it, I knew this would be a difficult day for me. I thanked them all and said my good-byes. I shook everyone's hand and hugged Rudy before climbing aboard. "Watch over Mom and Dad," I told him.

"I will, brother. Make sure you take care of yourself. The motorcycle will be here for you if you ever decide to come back," he replied. His eyes were red. My leaving was as difficult for him as it was for me.

The boat was called the SS United States and it was initially intended to be a trans-Atlantic troop transport, but after the war it was recommissioned as a passenger ship. At the time it was considered to be the fastest in the world. It seemed fitting that this was the first trip it had ever made to Germany. As I boarded, a Marine Band on shore played "Goodbye Forever." It sent a chill of reality down my spine. I was leaving my homeland and family, probably forever. I stood at the railing as the large ocean liner cast off its lines. I continued watching my friends until they disappeared over the horizon. I cried a little. Back there was everything and everyone I had ever known or loved. The finality of my departure was more difficult than I had ever expected.

I explored around the ship and saw a lot of wealthy American travelers returning home. I thought, *Matth what are you doing with these people? You're a simple German carpenter who can't speak a word of English. How are you possibly going to make it in the Unites States?*

I felt lost and alone. That evening I went to dinner and there was a young lady sitting at a table next to me. She had been in Germany for a while with her husband who was an officer in the U.S. Army. She was pregnant and wanted to return home to have her baby in America. Luckily, she had been in Germany long enough to pick up some of the language, at least enough that we could converse. I had found someone I could talk to, and that made the six-day trip more tolerable.

Aft deck of the S.S. United States. It was the same place where I almost drowned a day later.

By the second day we entered the North Sea and the seas started getting rough. The ship began rocking and rolling. Eating was a challenge for two reasons. First of all, the plates and utensils kept sliding across the tables and onto the floor. Worse than that was the sea-sickness. It was so severe that only about a third of the passengers ever made it to the dining room for breakfast or dinner. My mother had given me a small bottle of cognac when I left home. "Take a shot of this every morning and it'll help to keep you from getting sick on the boat." She was right. I don't know how it worked but that cognac came in handy. I was nauseated but not as bad as most people. At least I was able to eat. During our first night in the open Atlantic we ran into a January storm. I could feel the ship reeling as the wind howled outside my stateroom window. By morning the storm had become worse. The ship heaved from side to side as gale-force winds smashed into the hull. Mom's cognac was no longer working, and breakfast was out of the question. I decided to step outside onto the deck, hoping the cold air would quell the storm raging inside my stomach. It was a bad decision. I walked out and saw waves bigger than our house in Lorup. That made my stomach worse. On the way back inside, I noticed a flight of metal steps headed up to the next deck level. I wondered where they might lead and hoped things might be a little better up there, so I decided to explore a little. There was a sign next to the steps, but I couldn't read English. *What could go wrong?* I thought for the first of many times over the next several months. I climbed up and when I reached the top, the wind pummeled against me, almost knocking me over. I grabbed tightly onto the railing and looked down at the turbulent cauldron of ocean, about thirty meters below me. I was amazed by the sheer power of the storm's attack. I looked around. No one else was up there. That should have told me something.

The next thing I knew I was under water and it was freezing cold. It seemed to be an interminable amount of time but was probably only five seconds before I was able to gasp for air. I continued to hold on to the railing with all my might. If I hadn't, the giant wave would have surely washed me right off the ship to a certain death. No one would have ever known. That's when I realized what that sign must have said: "Danger. Stay Out!"

I was wet and cold, so I went back to my room to change. My winter coat was soaked. My shirt and pants were soaked. Even my underwear wasn't spared by the wave. I had purchased a brand-new pair of shoes for the trip and they were full of water. I went about the process of rinsing everything in the bathroom sink and laying them over a chair to dry. I spent the next twelve hours in bed trying to warm up and fighting the seasickness.

The following morning, I tried to put on my only pair of decent shoes. They were expensive, and I had been very proud of them. Now they were stiff as a board and covered in a white powder. I washed them off as well as I could, but when the shoes dried the following day, they were again white. All the salt water from my soaking had penetrated the leather and they were ruined. I did my best to clean them, but it was to no avail.

All I could do was to cover the salt stain with some shoe polish, but they never looked the same. It was a bad omen.

The storm passed and we spent three more days crossing the Atlantic. The weather calmed as the ship's powerful engines kept chugging across the ocean. On the seventh morning I woke up and all was completely quiet. I couldn't even hear the engines running. "What's that all about?" I asked myself. I jumped out of my bed and looked out the small porthole to see if I could tell what had happened. The boat was at the dock and in the distance, I could see the Statue of Liberty standing proudly in the mist surrounding New York Harbor. I had seen photographs of it before but never realized how massive the thing was. I just stood there and stared at it for what must have been thirty minutes. It was an amazing sight for a twenty-one-year-old farm boy from Lorup. I was mesmerized by the majestic sight of the structure, looking out over the water to welcome the new arrivals. I took at least a dozen pictures. It marked the beginning of my new life in America, a journey I would have thought impossible only a year ago.

The first thing I saw, looking out my cabin window. I was overwhelmed

NEW YORK CITY

It was January 19, 1953. Several hours after the lines were secured, I was able to deboard the SS United States. On the dock, I located my bag, a single suitcase that I had made from plywood in my own Lorup shop. It was heavy, but sturdy. All the passengers were herded into a huge clearing hall where there must have been over a thousand people waiting in different lines, all talking loudly. George Kreutzjans had supposedly paid to have someone help guide me through the process of entering the country and getting me to Cincinnati. I was instructed to look for a woman wearing a tan trench coat and a red scarf, but with all the people, I couldn't find her. I searched the hall from one end to the other but found no one matching her description.

There were many large signs where most of the boat passengers were headed but they were all written in English. I stood in the closest line, which was also moving the fastest. By the time it was my turn, I looked at the man behind the counter and said, "Matthias Toebben." He asked me a question that I didn't understand so I just looked at him confidently and repeated, "Matthias Toebben." I was convinced that he could help me, but he simply shook his head in frustration. The man repeated the question and I replied in German that I couldn't understand English. "Ich spreche kein Englisch." He pointed to the sign over the counter and said in German, "This is for United States Citizens only. You must head over to the other side of the hall and wait in the immigration line."

"Danke." I had wasted an hour in the first line and realized how much of a problem the language issue would be.

I made my way through the crowd and to the far side of the hall where I found more counters with letters of the alphabet written on signs above them. I went to the one labelled "R, S, T," and was relieved to find that the man spoke German.

"I'm Matthias Toebben," I said.

"Papers," he demanded as he reached out his hand, not even looking up at me.

I took the immigration documents out of my pocket, unfolded the papers, and handed them over. He checked the form and compared it to a list of names on a sheet sitting in front of him. He looked up and asked, "Sponsor is Kreutzjans? George Kreutzjans?"

I nodded and replied, "Ja."

"You should reply, 'Yes.'" I nodded that I understood. It was my first of many English lessons.

"And you will be headed to Cincinnati, Ohio?"

"Yes," I replied, proud that I could speak that one word of English. It was a start. After stamping my papers, he placed a checkmark next to my name on his list and looked past me toward the line. "Next!" he shouted.

That was it. I was now officially allowed to enter the United States, but I had no idea what I was supposed to do next. I waited around the large hall until five o'clock that evening but the woman with the trench coat and red scarf was still nowhere to be seen. I studied the crowd and watched what others did after finishing in immigration. They all passed through a set of large metal doors. What was on the other side, I had no idea.

I thought, *Well, Matth, it can't be any worse than just waiting around in here.* I walked through them and a second later I found myself standing on the streets of New York City. It was beyond my comprehension. There were six lanes of bumper-to-bumper traffic, everyone honking their horns at the same time. The drivers seemed to be angry with each other as they jostled for better position. We only had a couple of automobiles in Lorup, one belonging to a new doctor and the other to the police. I figured there must be more automobiles here in front of this building than in all the villages in our part of Germany. The sidewalks were just as bad as the traffic, with people scurrying about like a swarm of bees, yelling just as loudly as the car drivers. The sidewalk was a river of bodies, all bumping into each other as they rushed forward with the singular purpose of getting to wherever they were going as quickly as possible. Wherever that place was, it must have been important, too important to notice the man in a coat carrying a wooden suitcase. It was so crowded, and the people were so aggressive, I remember thinking, *What in God's name are you doing here and what are you going to do now?*

It was cold, and the evening wind was picking up, so I pulled my coat tightly around my chest. I had no idea of how I was going to get out of this place. I rested against the immigration building's brick wall and set my luggage at my feet. I tried to talk to some of the passersby, hoping someone might understand German. All I received in return were scowls. I later found out that this was typical of New Yorkers. The nicer ones just ignored me but some of them must have still been bitter about the war because they yelled "Kraut" or gave me a hard shove. I was in real big trouble and I had no idea about what to do. I realized I wasn't going to get any help, and knew I'd have to figure something out on my own. Coming to America was looking like a very bad decision.

I stood there against the building and it was getting colder by the minute. I started thinking I could freeze to death right here and no one in this city would notice or even care. I had to do something. I studied the crowd and noticed that from time to time one of the people would step to the curb and hold out their hand toward the traffic. Within a few seconds, a yellow car would pull to the curb. The individual would jump in and the car would pull away into traffic. I watched this same procedure repeat itself several times and soon understood that the yellow cars must be for hire to take people where they wanted to go. I thought, *Well, I'll try this. Things can't get any worse.* I fought my way across the stream of people, stepped to the curb, and stood tall like I had done it a hundred times before. I stuck out my hand and it worked! I couldn't believe my luck! A yellow car stopped, and the driver jumped out. He picked up my luggage and asked me something in English.

I just stood there staring at him like an idiot. I said the only English word I knew, "Yes." The driver dropped my bag, jumped back into his car, and drove away. My luck fizzled out.

I returned to my resting spot along the brick wall where it was a little warmer. It was now after six o'clock in the evening and dark shadows extended across the street. Most of the people were gone. I was so cold, I began to shiver. I knew I couldn't remain out there much longer, so I tried to get back inside the immigration building. The doors were locked. I got up my nerve, returned to the curb, and again stuck out my hand. I decided that if a car stopped, I would have to say something rather than standing there. Just like earlier a yellow car pulled up and the driver rolled down his window. He asked what I think was the same question the last driver had asked. "Matthias Toebben," I responded, and the result was the same. The driver stared at me and, after a brief second, he rolled up his window and sped away. I was again stranded in the cold dark.

About a hundred feet down the road, the driver suddenly slammed on his brakes and backed up. The guy jumped out of the car, picked up my luggage, and threw it into the trunk of his car. He then pushed me into the back seat and took off. I was on my way somewhere, but my problem was that I didn't actually know where that was. I gazed out the car window. The roads were lined on both sides by street lights and buildings the likes of which I had never seen before, so tall that constructing them would seem impossible. The driver kept negotiating his way through traffic as fast as he could. I was convinced he was some maniac who was going to crash and kill us both. He didn't. Where we were headed, I still didn't know, but we were going to get there fast. As I thought about it, I figured that there must be a lot of people like me coming into this country and many of them might be headed toward the same destination.

Suddenly the car pulled to the curb. I looked around and saw a small flight of stone steps leading up to a large building. It was a train terminal, much like ones we had in Germany but larger, much larger in fact. The driver got out, retrieved my luggage, and set it on the sidewalk next to the cab. Then he reached over to open the car door but when I tried to step out onto the sidewalk, he blocked my way. I wasn't sure what he wanted until he held out his hand. He wanted payment, so I took out my billfold and opened it. The only money I had was the ten dollars of American money my mother had given me when I left home. I gave the man the ten dollars and he gave me some money back in change. I didn't know how much but I put it in my wallet. By the time I was finished the man had already jumped back into his taxi and driven away.

When I looked down to pick up my luggage, it was gone. I panicked. Almost everything I owned was in that wooden suitcase. I knew the driver hadn't taken it, so I looked up and down the street in both directions. There was saw no sign of it. Then I glanced toward the large glass doors leading into the train terminal and there was my suitcase, in the hands of a uniformed gentleman standing in front of the building. I was concerned and wondered, *Why does this man have my luggage?* I had a bad feeling.

The plywood suitcase I made in my shop before leaving Lorup

He motioned for me to come toward him and must have seen the confused look on my face because he started laughing. I looked around and figured that with all the people milling about, there was no way the guy would try to do anything wrong. I walked up and attempted to retrieve my luggage, but he refused to give it to me. We struggled for control of the case and I thought I was about to get into a fight. I was cold, tired, and hungry but I wasn't about to allow anyone to steal my belongings. The man held out his empty hand just like the cab driver had just done a few minutes ago. He wanted money, I guess for carrying my bag up the steps. I hadn't asked for help but decided that's how they did things here. I didn't know how much to pay him, so I opened my wallet. He took what was remaining of my ten dollars. Now I was completely broke, and I still had no idea as to what I was going to do next. At least I had my wooden suitcase.

I picked it up and entered the terminal. It was so massive it looked as though half of Lorup could fit inside. A large four-sided clock presided over the center of the main hall. The walls and floors were constructed of marble and an intricate mosaic of tile work covered the arched ceilings. Just like everywhere else in New York, thousands of people walked about in a frenzy. A cacophony of conversations and loud speaker announcements echoed off the walls. I was lost. I knew I wanted to go to Cincinnati, Ohio, but I didn't even know where that was. Even if I could speak English, I had no ticket and no means with which to buy one. I went to several ticket counters and tried to explain my predicament, but no one spoke German. I was still in trouble with no prospects for a solution. Coming to America was turning out to be a very bad idea for me, one I was regretting more each minute.

Grand Central Station with its famous four-sided clock

My stomach started growling and I was hungry but had no money to buy food. All I could do was to get water from the bathroom faucets, so I drank as much of it as I could until I was full. With nothing else to do, I walked around the immense structure and admired the workmanship involved in creating the place. It was almost like a work of art. Tired and still hungry, I put my suitcase in front of one of columns, sat on it, and leaned back against the cool marble. I studied the crowd for a while, trying to come up with an idea that would help me get out of the city. I considered the possibility of getting a job somewhere in New York until I could make enough money to buy a ticket. I tried to think of what a twenty-one-year-old German who didn't speak any English could do. I had no ideas, so I decided to make the best of my situation by enjoying the architectural splendor surrounding me. I studied the marble columns, the arched ceilings, and the massive windows. I closed eyes and tried to figure out how I could ever create such a magnificent thing. It wasn't long before sleep overcame me.

I was awakened by someone tapping me on the shoulder. It was the woman with the tan trench coat and red scarf. She asked in German, "Are you Mathias Toebben?"

"Yes." I looked at the large four-sided clock directly across from me and saw that it was now one o'clock in the morning. I had actually been asleep for several hours and at this point the terminal hall was almost empty. The woman was over fifteen hours late. "Where in the world have you been?" I asked.

"We have no time for that. Here is your ticket. You only have five minutes to catch the next train to Cincinnati!" She pointed down a flight of steps and yelled, "It's the third platform on the right. Hurry!" I picked up my wooden suitcase and ran.

When I got on the train, I found a seat and a few minutes later, we pulled away from the station. By that time, I was more tired, still hungry, and disappointed with the world. The bench was hard and uncomfortable, but I was happy to finally be on my way. I fell asleep.

THE TRAIN, THE PORTER, AND THE PRIEST

The sound of the train's whistle woke me up. It was daylight. In fact, the sun was high in the sky. By now I was even more thirsty and starving than when I boarded. A porter passed by my seat. He was carrying a tray loaded with sandwiches and drinks for other passengers. When he returned, I stopped him to say that I was hungry. He couldn't understand me and all he did was to give me a small menu with prices on it. They were in dollars, so they meant nothing to me. I had no money anyway. Over the next hour, the porter made several more passes down the aisle before I made my decision. The next time he returned with a tray of food I stood up like I needed to stretch my legs. I was too hungry to care about being arrested. When he tried to get by me, I grabbed a sandwich with one hand and a bottle of Coke with the other. The sandwich was wrapped in white paper but before the porter could react, I took a huge bite of the sandwich, paper and all. A second later I took a large gulp of the Coke. It was too late for the porter to do anything about it. He couldn't exactly take the food back from me. He simply glared at me, looked down at my salt-stained shoes, and shook his head as if to say, "Man, what's wrong with you and what are you doing on my train?" I didn't care. I just stared him in the eye, daring him to try to take away my meal. I probably looked like a crazed animal, protecting its kill as I tore away another large bite of the sandwich, paper included. He turned and walked away. I knew this wasn't going to end well for me, but I was too hungry to care.

I sat back down in my seat and finished my meal. About fifteen minutes later the porter returned with another man who

I figured must have been the conductor. His black hat and jacket stood in stark contrast to his bright red face. He scowled as he walked right up to my seat. I thought, *Boy am I in trouble now! At least I'm not so hungry and the Americans probably feed you pretty well in jail.*

The conductor stood over me, pointed his finger in my face, and started yelling. He was giving me hell and I was certain I was going to spend the rest of my life in an American prison. That's what would happen in Hitler's Germany. I must have looked pretty frightened because the conductor stopped his threats. I guess he was feeling a little sorry for me. He patted me on the shoulder and said, "It's OK." He walked away without saying another word.

About twenty minutes later he returned with another tray and set it in front of me. It was loaded with grapes, soup, water, and another sandwich. I said, "Danke," and immediately ate it all. I decided that America was a great country after all...once you got out of New York City. I leaned back in my seat and again fell asleep.

The next time I woke up the sun was just beginning to peek over the horizon. Almost an entire day had passed since I had eaten the meal. It was taking much longer to reach Cincinnati than I had expected. When I looked out the window and checked the landscape, I noticed what looked like a lot of sand and brown brush. I didn't know much about Ohio but was certain there were no deserts there. I had no idea exactly where I was, but I was sure it was the wrong place. In all the rush to board in New York, the woman in the red scarf must have put me on the wrong train. *You got yourself in big trouble again, Matth. Now what are you going to do?*

I looked around the train car and noticed a priest sitting a few rows in front of me. I remembered that most of the priests in Lorup spoke English, so I hoped that maybe some of the priests in America could speak German. I got up enough nerve to talk to him. Much to my disappointment, he didn't speak any German. Regardless, he could tell I was having a problem. He motioned for me to sit down next to him. It took several minutes but eventually I was able to get him to understand that I was on the wrong train. The priest reached under his seat and withdrew a black briefcase. He opened it and withdrew a map of the United States. He pointed at it and I understood that he wanted me to show him my destination. I wasn't familiar with the geography of the country, but I did know the word Cincinnati. He pointed it out to me on the map and I replied with the only English word I had learned, "Yes."

Then the priest shook his head and said, "No, no, no." He pointed to the map to show me where our train was headed. It was

California. He got up and returned a few minutes later with the same conductor that had brought me a tray of food the day before. The two of them went over a train schedule together, trying to figure out the best way to get me to Cincinnati. The priest pulled a notebook out of his briefcase and began drawing. It was a clock with a certain time drawn on the hands. It also showed a drawing of a train stopping and its number. That was us. On the next page he drew another clock with the hands showing a different time, then another train labelled with a number heading toward a spot he identified as Cincinnati. A final clock indicated my arrival time. He had just outlined the entire itinerary for me to get where I was headed.

CINCINNATI AT LAST

Over a day later the train slowed down. I was relieved to see a large sign that read, "Cincinnati." I had travelled thousands of miles across the Atlantic Ocean and halfway across the United States and back. I was over two days late, but I finally made it. That was a happy moment.

Cincinnati's Union Terminal, a welcome sight

I finally set foot in Union Terminal and was amazed. It was a massive rotunda-shaped structure, almost as magnificent as Grand Central Station in New York. At one end a huge marble map of the United States occupied the entire wall. Five different clocks depicted the various time zones for the travelers. Along the curved interior walls hung multiple large mosaic murals depicting the history of the area and the major business that made Cincinnati prosperous. I retrieved from my pocket the papers Marie had sent me. On the bottom was written a note with a phone number. I was to call her when I arrived. I was certain she would be worried because it had taken me so long to get here. I looked around the terminal and saw an entire bank of telephones hanging on the wall. In Lorup, there were only two or three telephones in the entire village. Directly in front of me there were a half-dozen. As I stared in amazement, I saw that just to the right of the phones, sitting on a bench, was my sister, already waiting for me. She looked tired, as though she had been there for a long time. When Marie saw me, she jumped up and gave me a hug so hard it just about took my breath away. It had been years since I had last seen her. I was so happy I didn't want to let go.

Famous murals at Cincinnat's Union Terminal

"We were worried that something might have happened to you," she said in German as tears ran down her cheeks. She stepped back and looked at me with worry in her eyes. My mother used to have the same look whenever I had a severe asthma attack. "You look a little pale, Matth, and you're too thin. Are you sick?"

"No, not sick. It's been a long trip and I haven't had much to eat for a while."

"We're going to fix that as soon as we get home."

We walked out of the terminal and Marie led me to her car. It was another amazing sight.

My sister had her very own automobile, I figured her husband, Nick, must be rich. I put my suitcase into the trunk of the car and sat in the passenger seat. Marie and I talked about Germany and life in America as we headed through what she called the west side. There were warehouses and industrial buildings everywhere.

It looked pretty bad and I had expected to see a landscape that looked more like Lorup. A few miles later the scenery improved. Ultimately, we crossed a large steel bridge and I stared down at the water below. There was a boat pushing barges of coal upriver.

"It's the Ohio River," said Marie as she watched my eyes. I studied the large steel cables holding the bridge in position. They had to be at least eight inches in diameter. I had never seen anything like it before. Marie added, "It's called the Roebling Suspension Bridge because its suspended from those tall stone towers on either end. It was designed and built by Mr. John A. Roebling. Like us, he was also an immigrant from Germany."

I continued to study the impressive structure. It was an engineering masterpiece and it was constructed by an immigrant. I vowed that if Mr. Roebling could be this successful in America, I would somehow do the same.

On the other side of the river were several small cities sitting at the base of rolling green hills. The skies above them were clear blue. The sunlight was interrupted only by an occasional wispy cloud. It was a beautiful sight, a little reminiscent of Germany before the war. I was certainly better than anything I had seen in New York City.

We crossed the river and headed into the state of Kentucky. After driving up into the hills for a half hour, we entered a village she called Ft. Wright.

"Fort?" I asked.

"Yes. This entire area is referred to as Northern Kentucky. A hundred years ago there was a bloody Civil War in the United States. The southern states wanted to separate from the rest. Just south of the Ohio River the Union Army built a series of forts to protect Cincinnati from attack by the Confederates just to the south. Many of the local communities are still referred to by the names of the original forts. That's why the village we live in is called Fort Wright."

A minute later Marie pulled into her driveway. The address on the home read 2 Barbara Circle. It was a one-and-a-half story brick home with gables. It was much larger than I had expected and certainly more modern than anything in Lorup. Marie showed me upstairs to my bedroom. After she closed the door to my room I looked around and quietly said to myself, "Nick must be doing very well here. Looks like you made the right decision after all, Matth. America is going to be a wonderful country for you."

———————————— ◆◈◆ ————————————

Marie prepared a delicious pot roast dinner that night. It was the best meal I had eaten since leaving Lorup. I ate until I was stuffed. Over coffee, Nick asked, "How do you like the house?"

"Very impressive," I replied.

"Built it myself," he said with pride in his voice. "That's what we're going to do together, Matth. We're going to build houses for George Kreutzjans." We discussed everything in more detail that evening. I was excited at the prospect of working here.

Life was very good to me in the United States, so good that within the next year I grew several inches and put on twenty pounds. It was all because of Marie's great cooking.

MY NEW CAREER

I already had a job waiting for me and I was anxious to get started as soon as possible. The next morning, I got everything together for my first day but by the time I was ready, Nick had already left. Marie packed a lunch pail for me and pointed me in the right direction. It wasn't far, maybe a quarter mile down the road, so I headed out for the job site on foot. I didn't have a car. In fact, I didn't even know how to drive even if I owned one. As soon as I had walked only a few hundred yards, a man by the name of John McCormack saw me and stopped. He told me to hop in, but I had never seen the man before and I was wary. I couldn't understand English and I didn't know what he wanted. Then he said, "George Kreutzjans?"

I shook my head yes and got into the car. He took me right to the job site, a new home construction in Fort Wright. Along the way I thought, *Gosh, this guy doesn't know me from Adam and yet he's giving me a ride.* I reflected upon my experience with the priest and the train conductor from several days earlier. My opinion of America had changed a great deal since I first arrived in New York. It was a great country with many wonderful people who actually went out of their way to help total strangers.

When I arrived, I could hear the sounds of construction: nails being hammered and electric saws cutting. The familiar smell of sawdust filled the air. I felt at home. It was great to be a part of creating something again. George was giving instructions to his men when he noticed me getting out of the car. He waved thanks to Mr. McCormack and pulled me aside, "Matth, I'm building this house for Ray and Norma Mueller. I'm giving you the job of installing the cabinets and completing all the detailed interior woodwork."

It was a big responsibility but that was fine with me. My training and work experience had been in the area of fine woodwork, and I was looking forward to showing George what I could do. Several days later, I was putting the finishing touches on a fireplace mantel in the living room when Mr. Mueller came in to monitor the progress on his new home. He watched me work on the mantle several minutes before he finally said something. It was in English and I had no idea what he wanted so I just stared at him. He repeated himself but louder as though increasing the volume of his voice would overcome my inability to understand. He was talking so loudly I figured he was angry with me. He kept pointing at the mantle and I thought he was criticizing my work-manship, so I stepped back to study it. Since this was one of my first assignments, I needed it to be perfect.

It was. The proportions were correct, the wood was sanded smooth as glass, and the mitered seams were almost invisible. I finally looked at Mr. Mueller, shrugged my shoulders, and said one of the few words I knew, "George." He'd have to discuss the matter with my boss. I was worried and thought, *I've been on the job less than a week now and I've already gotten myself into trouble. I must have screwed something up somehow.* I was afraid I might have to start looking for another job.

When George came by the next day, I was afraid he was going to fire me. What he actually said to me was, "Mr. Mueller was hoping you could install an electric outlet in the mantle top."

That was all he wanted? I was relieved. That was going to be no problem and I took care of it right away. In time Ray Mueller and his wife became good friends of mine and I built a number of homes for them over the years. Several years after I first met him, he founded Comair, a successful commuter airline company flying out of Greater Cincinnati International Airport.

That initial experience of being unable to understand English made me realize just how much the language barrier could hinder my ultimate goal of becoming successful. Somehow, I was going to have to correct that problem.

Ray Mueller in later years. Seated next to him: his daughter Tansy, me and Pat Runge

One great help in learning the language was through my association with a number of new friends in the area. There was a sizable nucleus of people who had emigrated from Germany over the past several decades. Occasionally, I would be invited to attend social get-togethers at various homes where I was able to speak German and begin making a few contacts. At the same time, people would assist me with my English. It was a slow process but with each party I learned a little more. One individual was particularly helpful. His name was Bernard Lunneman. Bernie worked with me on houses at night. After about a year I became conversational enough in English to understand what people wanted, but with my heavy German accent, they still had trouble understanding me so there continued to be a significant language barrier I had to overcome. Bernie served as my interpreter with customers and that helped me a great deal. In fact, Bernie became one of my first and closest friends in America. Looking back, I don't believe I could have ever succeeded without his help.

Bernie Lunneman and his wife Eileen on the occasion of our company's 50th Anniversary. Bernie is one of the primary reasons for my success.

At some point he noticed that I always had to catch a ride to work. He asked, "Matth, why don't you drive yourself?"

"I don't own a car, don't even know how to drive one anyway. The only thing I've ever driven was my motorcycle in Germany."

"Well, it's time you learned," he insisted. Within the week, Bernie took me out in his old Ford. It was a clunker and the brakes were pretty well worn-out, so it didn't exactly stop when you wanted. First you had to downshift into second gear before you could even try to use the brakes. Then you'd have to pump them several times. Even after all that, you still had to make sure there was enough room in front of the old car to coast to a stop. We had a lot of near misses. A few weren't actual misses, but we never caused significant damage. All in all, the old car served its purpose well, and I learned how to drive.

—————————◆•◆•◆————————

Another employee of George Kreutzjans was Tony Dempsey and he did much of the electrical work. We had gotten to be pretty good friends when he said to me, "Matth, it sounds like your English is getting better."

"It's OK, but I'm still having trouble with people understanding me. It's my accent. People don't always understand what I'm trying to say," I replied.

"It might be that you're a little too formal when you speak. You need to loosen up a little and learn how Americans talk to each other."

"What do you mean?"

"Well, when you say hello to someone, you need to greet them like a friend. Then things will flow more easily for you."

"Like what?"

He told me and we practiced my greeting until we were both comfortable that others could understand me.

A few days later, Tony and I were working on a house being built for Mr. Melvin Cook and his wife on Lorup Avenue. George Kreutzjans had named the street after our hometown in Germany. Mr. Cook was a successful businessman who owned an upscale jewelry store in Covington. He was a respected member of the Chamber of Commerce, and very active in the church. I was on my knees laying the hardwood floor when Mr. and Mrs. Cook came in to check on their new home. He was wearing a charcoal grey suit with a yellow tie and she was in a nice floral dress with a string of natural pearls hanging from her neck. George followed about ten feet behind. When I saw them, I smiled, stood up, and proudly extended my hand to greet them. I was ready to show off my new mastery of the English language. "Hello Mr. Cook, you old son-of-a-bitch! How are you?" I said it just the way Tony had taught me.

Mr. Cook's jaw dropped. His wife's face turned ghost-white. I thought she might pass out from shock. I knew I had screwed up in a bad way but didn't know how. I was trying so hard to fit in. I remember thinking, *You did it again, Matth. You really stepped in it this time.*

"Whoa, whoa, whoa!" said George. "What're you doing, Matth? What're you saying to these people?"

"I'm sorry, George. Tony told me how Americans greet each other, and I thought I was being friendly."

George's face turned bright red and I was convinced he was going to fire both Tony and me on the spot. After he made amends to the Cooks, he had a private meeting with us. I never made that mistake again.

THE CHRYSLER

I enjoyed working for George Kreutzjans. He was a good man and a fair boss who paid me well. I worked hard, nine hours a day, six days a week. After a week I received my first paycheck. It was for $46. That was good money in those days, especially when compared to what I would make in Lorup. I remember writing my mother that I made the equivalent of almost 200 Marks. Later, when I was able to arrange for a phone call she said, "Matth, you wrote about how much you made in your first month of work. That's wonderful. We're all so proud of you." I chuckled and replied, "No Mom, that's how much I made in only a week. I earn four times that amount in a month." She couldn't believe it.

"Matth, you must be rich!" she said.

After thinking about it, I realized that she was right. I was rich in many ways. America was a wonderful country, full of opportunity and good friends. I was blessed to be here.

I continued to work as many hours as I could but realized that I would never accomplish what I wanted without making more. George's brother, Nick, and I were talking one evening and I told him that I wanted to do extra work. That night we decided on a plan to take on odd jobs as freelance carpenters on the side. We planned to work at night and weekends after finishing our days working for George. We made custom cabinets for homeowners and developed a pretty good reputation for excellent workmanship. Each job led to more jobs as the word spread. One day, we had someone ask us if we could install screening for their front porch. After a short while, many others asked us to do the same thing for their homes, so we got into the aluminum screen business. We stayed busy and I saved almost every penny I made.

George came up to me one afternoon and said, "Matth, I understand Bernie Lunneman has been teaching you how to drive."

I nodded yes. "It's been slow but I'm getting the hang of it."

"Then it's about time you got your own car. Come with me." He drove me to the Plymouth dealership in downtown Covington, just across the river from Cincinnati. They had a large lot outside with dozens of used cars for sale. George and I walked around to check them out. We kicked a lot of tires, apparently something Americans always did when they bought a car. I had my eye on a nice-looking Plymouth that was priced at $620. That was a fair amount for my budget, but I decided I could handle it.

George took me by the arm and said, "Come on, let's go inside and talk to a salesman." We passed by a brand new two-tone green Chrysler hard top with white wall tires. The bright showroom lights reflected off its chrome like a diamond. I had never seen such a beautiful automobile. George saw the look in my eyes and said, "Matth, it looks like this is the car you want."

I looked at the sticker on the car window and said, "I can't buy it, George. I don't have enough money."

"I'll loan you the money, but you must promise to never call one of my customers a son-of-a-bitch again." He looked serious until he started to crack a smile and laugh. I joined in, relieved that my huge SOB blunder was far behind us.

My father always told me to never borrow from another man, but in America, borrowing money seemed to be the thing to do, so I bought the car. It was beautiful and I was very proud. As I was driving it home, I wished my parents in Lorup could see me, the skinny asthmatic who couldn't even play soccer or pick potatoes was now driving a shiny new Chrysler automobile. I rolled down the window and let the wind blow across my face.

LAVERNE

Between my jobs for George and what Nick and I did at night, I was working sixteen hours a day, Monday through Saturday. At one point my sister said, "Matth, why are you working so much? You're going to kill yourself."

"I need to pay for my new car and save enough money to start out on my own."

"You've got to be patient, Matth. That's going to take time. Meanwhile there's more to life than just work. What good is that fancy new car of yours if you have no-one with whom to share it? You need to get out and meet other people around the area, more than just our inner circle of friends from Germany."

I shrugged my shoulders, to which she responded, "Listen, every Saturday night there is a dance at the Fort Wright Civic Club. This weekend you are going with Nick and me. George and his wife Barbara will join us. We'll all have great fun together. Maybe you'll meet someone you like."

I went and even danced a few times, but my partners couldn't understand a word of what I said. Any conversation had to be interpreted by Marie, making everything awkward. I felt like an idiot. One good thing Hitler did was to mandate that, in your final year of school, you had to take dancing lessons, so at least I was able to enjoy myself. It was ironic because shortly after finishing school many of those same students were conscripted into the army only to die for a losing cause. They never got to enjoy dancing.

It was my friend, Bernie Lunneman who set up my first date in America. It was a blind date with a friend of Bernie's wife,

Eileen. Her name was Margaret Bills and she was a teacher from Independence, Kentucky. She also had trouble understanding me, but she was patient and she even took the time to teach me a little more English. That was a big help.

Margaret and I would meet several more times, but the relationship never blossomed. We remained friends, however. She told me about dances that the Catholic Church sponsored at the Fenwick Club on Broadway in downtown Cincinnati every Sunday evening. It sounded like fun, so I got directions from Nick and drove there alone. When I walked in, I could hear the music playing and there were dozens of people dancing. Everyone was laughing and having a wonderful time. I thought, *Man, I've never seen anything like this before.* The music was beautiful.

I waited about a half hour before I was able to build up the nerve to approach a table of young women and asked if any of them would care to dance. It took several tries before one understood me and was brave enough to give me her hand. Her name was Anna May and she was from a community called Price Hill. She was a good dancer and we spent the entire evening together dancing and listening to music. It wasn't romantic in any way and we parted as friends with the unspoken understanding that it would never be anything more.

I had a great time at the Fenwick Club dance and returned the following Sunday evening. When I entered, the band was already playing a Tommy Dorsey number. I found Anna May standing by the punchbowl and I asked her if she wanted to dance. She held out her hand and said, "Sure."

It was about halfway through the second song when I noticed a young woman sitting at Anna's table, talking to some friends. She had dark brunette hair, soft blue eyes, and a captivating smile. She was by far the most beautiful woman I had ever seen, and I had a hard time taking my eyes off her. When she caught me staring, she blushed and looked away. Finally, I asked Anna, "Who's that girl sitting at your table, the one with the white blouse and the pearls?"

"That's my friend, Laverne Huber. She and I went to high school together."

"Do you mind if I ask her to dance?"

"No, not at all. In fact, I think you two might like each other."

I walked over and in broken English asked Laverne Huber to dance. She was very gracious and replied, "I'd love to...?"

"Matth, Matth Toebben," I said. It was love at first sight. We danced together the rest of the evening. When she spoke, her soft voice was more beautiful than the music. I didn't notice anything or anyone else in that dance hall the rest of the evening. I knew that this was the woman I was going to marry and spend the rest of my life with.

At the end of the evening I asked her if she would like a ride home. She said, "Yes," and told Anna. Laverne lived in Delhi, several miles west of Cincinnati. We talked the entire time it took to get to her home. My German accent never seemed to be a problem. Conversation between us was as natural as breathing.

Laverne and I on our first date

I couldn't wait to get together with Laverne again. The next day I called and asked when I could see her. She said that she and a few of her girlfriends were going to a place called Coney Island the following Sunday. She asked if I would like to meet her there and I said I'd love to. I asked Marie about the place and she told me it was a large amusement park. It also contained Sunlight Pool, the largest freshwater pool in the world. She told me to bring a bathing suit just in case. We had nothing like that in Lorup, just rivers and ponds. When I arrived, it was a pleasant surprise. There were a lot of people, rides, and a large lake with rowboats. We enjoyed a wonderful afternoon together.

After that, Laverne and I started dating regularly. When I first picked her up at her home, I had the chance to meet her mother. I could tell that she and I weren't hitting it off very well. I think she was a little concerned about Laverne dating a man who could barely speak English. As we continued to date, the situation didn't improve much. Because of my busy schedule, working six days a week and every evening until late, I was only able to see Laverne on Sundays. Her mother didn't feel that I was devoting enough attention to her daughter. Her husband was an established businessman who worked sixty to seventy hours a week, leaving her alone much of the time. I think she was afraid that her youngest daughter would be stuck in the same position. Laverne's father and I, on the other hand, got along well since we were both used to long hours of hard work. Laverne was extremely close to her dad, and when he saw that she had feelings for me he was fine with that. He just wanted her to be happy.

———————————— ◆◦◆ ————————————

Laverne and I were married in the basement of St. Dominic's Church in Delhi on November 19, 1955. The actual church hadn't been completed yet and that's why the ceremony was held in the basement. We were both so happy, neither of us cared. Bernie Lunneman, who had taught me how to drive, was my best man. Laverne's sister Vera was the maid of honor.

As we walked out of the church, hand in hand, we were surprised to see my sister Agnes and some of my friends from Germany sitting there. They had come all the way from Lorup to attend our wedding. I was as happy then than at any other time in my life.

Our wedding day: November 19, 1955

That evening Laverne and I hosted a reception. We partied until the wee hours of the morning and the next day we headed out for a honeymoon in Miami, Florida. That was the plan but like the old saying goes, "The best laid plans of mice and men oft go awry."

--------◆•●•◆--------

It was an unusually mild day when we headed south on US-Route 25, the old Dixie Highway. There was no Interstate system or GPS at the time, so we had to rely solely on state highway maps to get us to Miami. Fortunately, route 25 provided what I hoped would be a pretty straight shot to the south. The problem was that in many of the small-town intersections, there could be over a half-dozen road signs with different route numbers leading in a multitude of different possible directions. It was confusing and after we made our way through the Smokey Mountains, we realized we probably made a wrong turn somewhere in southern Tennessee. We found ourselves lost on an obscure road. It passed through a tiny town, so small we couldn't find it on any of our maps. Laverne and I didn't much care. It was a beautiful day with cloudless skies, and we were enjoying a wonderful time alone together, cruising down the road without a care in the world. We weren't in any hurry and knew we'd eventually find a major road again. As long as we were together, nothing else mattered.

That's when things started to go wrong. My shiny two-toned Chrysler automobile developed a ping. I knew that could be bad, so I pulled over to the side of the road. Laverne said, "What's wrong?"

"It's the engine. It doesn't sound right." I lifted the hood and could definitely hear the ping but everything looked fine.

"But you've only had the car for a few years."

"I know but I'm afraid if I don't get it checked out the engine might fail. We could be stranded out here in the middle of nowhere. We passed through that small town a few miles back and I think I saw a gas station there. We'll head back." I drove to the town which was smaller than my home village of Lorup. I found the gas station and pulled in. It had only one gas pump with a round glass Texaco sign sitting on the top. It was rusted and looked as though some of the locals had used it for target practice at one time because it was peppered with scars from BB guns. The small garage looked like it might fall down any minute. I didn't like the looks of the place, but it was our only option. The next town was at least fifty miles away and I wasn't sure the car would make it that far.

An older man in dirty overalls approached, an orange rag hanging from his back pocket. He was unshaven, and a lit cigarette hung from the corner of his mouth as he spoke. A line of ash hung precariously from the tip. "Need gas?" he asked. He smelled like a mixture of smoke, gasoline, and sweat.

"No, something's wrong with my car. It developed a loud ping a few miles back and I'd like to see if you could check it out for me."

"Ping, huh? Lift up the hood and I'll see what I can do. This might take a while."

He started the engine and spent a lot of time inspecting it. Laverne and I found two chairs in front of his store and shared a bottle of Nehi soda. I watched as he tinkered around a little and cursed a lot. Then he took what looked like a cut-off broom stick, around two feet long. He put one end against the engine block and the other against his ear and listened. It was almost like watching a doctor listen to someone's heart with a stethoscope. After a few minutes he stopped, repositioned the broom stick, and again listened. My curiosity got the best of me, so I walked over and stood next to him.

"What're you doing?" I asked.

"Listening to your engine."

"With a broomstick?"

"It's a trick my father taught me."

I seriously doubted that any cars were even around when his father was alive. How he could hear anything with that stick, I didn't know. I looked at Laverne and she just shrugged her shoulders. Finally, the man put down the stick and with great authority said, "Young man, you've got big problems here. You need a new engine."

"A new engine? How can you tell that by listening through a broomstick?"

"Like I said, my father taught me." He slammed the hood of the car down. "There's no doubt about it, though. You're gunna need a new engine."

"But my car is only two years old."

"That's how the car companies make them nowadays, roll em out as fast as they can and fix the problems later. Don't build them like they used to."

I paused to think. I didn't have any other options, so I asked, "How long will it take?"

"About five days I reckon, maybe a few more. Gotta order the engine and that could take some time."

I walked over to talk to Laverne. She had heard what he said and had a concerned look in her eyes. "What are we going to do, Matth?"

I thought for a minute. I looked up and down the town's only street and couldn't see any evidence of a hotel or restaurant. We were stuck so I said, "We don't want to hang around here for five days.

She added, "I sure don't think this guy knows what he's doing. I don't trust him."

"Neither do I. We should probably turn around and start heading back until we find where we made the wrong turn. Then we can make our way north through the Smokey Mountains. At least that way we'll keep getting closer to home if the car completely breaks down. We can even stop off and see Gatlinburg as long as the car holds up. If it doesn't, I'm sure they'll have a good mechanic there."

That's what we did and had a great honeymoon in the process. About midway through our trip, the pinging suddenly stopped and that was it. The car was fine. I turned to Laverne and said, "That old guy just wanted to make money off us. He was going to remove a perfectly good engine." I drove that Chrysler for another ten years and had no further problems with it.

AM*ST*ERDAM RO*A*D

Once Laverne accepted my marriage proposal, I realized that I was going to have to build a home for us. We wouldn't be able to live comfortably with Nick and Marie, though I was convinced that they would be more than happy to take us in. We wanted to establish our own lives, independent of others. With that in mind, I began driving around Fort Wright and the surrounding communities, looking for a lot that would fulfill our needs.

I eventually found a nice parcel of land along Amsterdam Road in Fort Wright, several miles from Nick and Marie's home. I pulled the Chrysler to the side of the road and got out to walk the property. There was an entire frontage of land with nothing on it but grass and scrub brush. It looked as though any mature trees had already been cleared away some time ago. That would make building a home a little easier. I was so involved with checking the land I didn't notice the man riding up behind me on a horse until he called out. He wasn't smiling when he asked, "Can I help you?"

I thought, *Oh man, I've been trespassing on this fellow's property and he looks mad as a hornet.*

I replied, "I'm looking to buy a parcel of land to build a home for my fiancée and myself."

The man got off his horse and introduced himself. His name was Lou Meyer and he turned out to be a nice fellow. He owned a car dealership and some bowling alleys in Covington, just down the hill. We started talking about what I needed. Finally, he said, "I was going to develop this land myself. In fact, I already had the home sites plotted out."

"Would you be interested in selling me one of your lots?"

He thought for a second and added, "OK. Sure, I'll sell you a lot."

When he said he already had the land ready for development, it caught my interest and I began to consider the possibilities. I didn't really know what I was doing but I decided to take a chance. "Would you consider selling the entire parcel of land?"

After considering my offer for a few seconds, he replied, "I could do that, but it depends upon how much you'd be willing to pay." In spite of the language issues, it only took a minute of negotiating before we came up with mutually acceptable price. I suspected it was pretty steep, but probably fair enough. I said, "Well, I don't have a lot of money, but I have saved up five thousand dollars that I can give you as a down payment."

"That works for me, son. You can give me the five thousand now and pay off the rest as you sell your homes." That was fine with me because I was still working for George Kreutzjans and I could build my own houses on the side after work. Lou and I shook hands on the deal, and he rode away on his horse. I gazed over the land and wondered about what I had just gotten myself into. I was about to start developing land for home construction and had no idea exactly how I was going to go about making it happen. I had no more money, but I had made my decision and somehow, I was going to make it work. It was exciting.

That night, I discussed my plans with Nick and Marie. "I found these lots along Amsterdam road and I'm going to start my own construction company."

"What about George?" asked Nick.

"I'm going to give him two-months notice tomorrow. That way he'll have time to train a replacement."

They tried to talk me out of it but to no avail. My mind was made up. Marie started crying. "You can't do that, Matth! You're going to go broke! You can barely speak English. How are you going to deal with home buyers?"

"I'll just push through the language problem. I can do that. It didn't stop me from doing the deal with Lou."

"What about money? You need a lot of money to start a business."

"I've worked day and night to be able to save five thousand dollars for a down payment. That's the most I can lose, so how bad can it get?"

Two days later I met with Lou Meyer to finalize the deal. I gave him the five thousand, leaving me pretty much broke with new homes to build, but I had no second thoughts about my decision.

The following Monday I told George. He was upset and didn't understand why I wanted to strike out on my own. I replied honestly. "George, my dream has always been to run my own business and I can never do that as long as I am working for someone else. If I don't take advantage of this opportunity now, I'm afraid I never will."

A month after I closed on the land, Nick came to me and said, "Matth, I don't want to spend the rest of my life working for someone else, either. What do you think about us becoming partners in this Amsterdam Road development? We can share the cost. I can do the concrete and brick work while you do all the carpentry."

Nick and I had already established our side business at night, and we had worked well together. I said, "I think that would be a great idea, Nick." We agreed to be equal partners with equal risk sharing. Nick provided an influx of some cash that we would need in the coming months.

George seemed to understand but he was still angry. I'm sure it was difficult for him to swallow considering that Nick and I were leaving after he had sponsored both of us to come to this country. If it hadn't been for George, neither of us would have been able to pursue our dreams here in America.

Things were tense between George and us for a while, but time has a way of healing all wounds. Several years later there was a going-out-of-business auction at the Janson Hardware store in Covington. I was there with Nick and another builder, Theodore Drees. George was there also. We were all bidding on items like barrels of nails and other building materials. When it was over, I asked George to join the three of us for lunch and a few Jägermeister's. We all shared stories and laughed together. The old bridges were repaired, and we went on to be good friends again. George continued to go forward as a successful builder.

I selected the first lot on Amsterdam as the site for my own home. It was October. Laverne and I were scheduled to be married in less than a year, so I had to get our future home finished. I worked on mine while Nick began work on a second one next door. About six months later, on a Sunday afternoon in June, I was working on the inside of the house when a couple came in and looked around. They were Ed Volker and his wife. He was in the banking business, and he asked me if I knew who was building the house.

"Well, I'm building the house for myself and my fiancée," I replied with my heavy German accent.

They said, "You do excellent work. We'd like to buy it from you."

"I'm sorry, but it's not for sale. As I said, it's for my fiancée and me. We plan to move in after we get married in November."

They looked a little disappointed but continued to walk around just the same, looking from room to room, inspecting the house thoroughly. From time to time they would stop to ask me a question about the construction, and finally said, "We really like this house and are serious about wanting to buy it. We've looked at a number of homes in the area, but this is the nicest one we've seen by far."

I figured they didn't understand me earlier, so I said, "That's very nice of you to say but like I said before, it's still not for sale. I could build another one for you just down the road."

He looked at me in the eye and spoke the universal language that everyone understands, money. He wrote some numbers down on a piece of paper and handed it to me. "And I'm still serious about wanting to buy your house. This is how much I'll give you for it."

I had to blink my eyes a few times to be sure I was reading the numbers correctly. It was much more than I thought he house was worth. I looked up, shook his hand, and said, "Mr. Volker, you and your wife just bought yourselves a new home."

That evening I spoke to Nick and said, "Nick, I just sold my first house."

"You what?"

"Sold it and made a great profit."

"That's great, Matth, but now what are you going to do for a home for you and Laverne?"

"We have the second lot sold with a good down payment but there's no deadline for completion. You can continue working on that one and I'll have enough time to start another for myself right next to it."

It was a great start and selling the first two homes allowed me to fully pay off the loan to Lou Meyer. I went to a savings and loan on Madison Pike in Covington and told the bank president I needed a loan for $15,000 to build my own house. I described our project and how we had already sold two homes. They gave me the money without batting an eye. I finished my home two weeks before we were to be married. The total cost including the lot was $14,500. It was small, but it was all ours. For years I referred to it as "My Little Five Room Castle."

Laverne and I were elated. She had saved a little over a thousand dollars working, so we went to Tillman's furniture store and bought the things we needed. We felt blessed and didn't realize that the blessings would continue a hundredfold over the coming years. There would also be several devastating tragedies.

Our"Five Room Castle". Laverne is standing on the front porch

FORTSIDE

Nick and I continued to build along Amsterdam Road and established a good reputation as high-quality home builders. We were almost finished with our fifth house when I received a call. It was a real estate agent and he said, "Mr. Toebben, there's a piece of property available in Fort Mitchell. It's forty acres situated at the end of Fortside Drive. It has great potential for development, and you might want to take a look at it."

I was already involved in my new construction business, but I decided to check it out anyway. The land was overgrown but it was in a great location and close to my Amsterdam Road project. The asking price was forty thousand dollars and not subject to negotiation. That was a thousand dollars an acre which was steep, but I made up my mind right there that I was going to buy it. I wrote out an earnest money check for a thousand dollars. The contingency was that I could have someone study the land before closing to see if building homes on the site was feasible.

I had met Theodore Drees once at my sister Marie's house. He was a developer in Northern Kentucky, and he had a great deal of experience in the business. I called and asked if he would do me a favor and inspect the land to see if it was suitable for home construction. He called me a few days later and said, "The land needs some site development, Matth. You're going to have to remove most of the trees and move a lot of dirt to level the hills, but you should go ahead and buy this land. I'm sure it'll be a very successful project for you."

That evening I spoke to Nick and said, "I've come across some property on Fortside Drive in Fort Mitchell and I've decided to buy it." We both knew we couldn't do the Amsterdam project and this new one at the same time. It would be too expensive, and we didn't have the manpower to pull it off. We decided to separate the business and each go forward on our own. Nick wanted to purchase more land on Amsterdam, so he would continue to develop that area while I would move my own operation to Fort Mitchell. We split up the assets and I used my share to put five thousand dollars down on the land. I signed a promissory note for the balance to be paid at five thousand a year until the loan was retired.

I was in debt again, so I needed to start building as soon as possible to establish some cash flow. That would prove to be a little more difficult than I expected but I had a little help from lady luck. The land was adjacent to a two-story house sitting at the end of Fortside Drive, just at the entrance to my new property. The owner of the home called me and asked if he could purchase the first lot I had planned to develop.

"I'm sorry but I plan to build a house on that lot."

"That's why I'm calling you, Mr. Toebben. I'd like to buy it so you don't build a house there. It would sit right behind mine and I want to preserve my privacy. I'm willing to pay you $7,500 for it."

That number was over seven times what I initially paid for the lot, so I accepted his offer. "OK, I'll sell it to you."

That put extra cash in my pocket and gave me a little more wiggle room. It gave me the extra time I needed to obtain the necessary building permits. Ed Lake was the mayor of Fort Mitchell at the time. I went to his office and described my plans, including the proposed street and sewer locations. They also specified the size of each lot. Mayor Lake looked at me funny because of my broken English. Some people perceive an inability to speak the local language as an indication that the person is not intelligent. That was what I believed he thought of me initially. He paused for a minute, staring at me, probably wondering if I was legit or not. Finally, he said that he would grant my permits, but I couldn't sell a single house until all the streets and sewers were in. That was going to be a huge requirement for me and would stretch my already limited budget, but like my father had advised me years ago, I pushed on.

I hired a man by the name of Joe Trenkamp. He was a fellow German who owned several bulldozers in Northern Kentucky. He began the process of clearing and grading the land in preparation for the streets. I was able to purchase a used Ford backhoe and began laying sewer lines all the way to the back of the property where I planned to tie into the county sanitation system along Amsterdam Road. My friend Theodore Drees lent me a street vibrator for the road construction and we started on the streets. The city engineer at the time was John Morledge and I hired him to stake out the lots. He did such a great job I subsequently used him to design the engineering plans on all my future projects.

We started construction and had the first home under roof when a fellow by the name of Harry Drugger stopped by.

Someone told me later that he was associated with the Beverly Hills Syndicate. He offered me $25,000 cash for the house, and I accepted it right there with a handshake. Once we closed, it put more money in my pocket to continue with the development. In short time I sold another house across the street from the first. Once the word spread, the demand was incredible. We just kept on selling homes as quickly as we could build them.

Ben Wessels was a friend who had also immigrated from Lorup. He had been working in Pittsburg as a bricklayer. He decided to drive down to Northern Kentucky to visit with Laverne and me for several days. It gave me an idea. "Ben, I don't really know a whole lot about brick laying and I'm already having a hard time keeping up with the home demands on Fortside. Why don't you move here? I have enough work to keep you busy for a long time."

He told me he'd consider it and about two weeks later he called me and said, "Matth, I'd like to take you up on that offer to work for you if the position's still available."

He said he could start in two weeks and when he got here, I already had two houses ready for brick work. Ben taught me how to lay bricks and we worked together for several years. During that time, he met my younger sister Agnes who had been working for a family in Indian Hills. They fell in love and married a year later. Ben decided to start out on his own, buying, remodeling, and leasing apartment buildings. He and Agnes went on to become very successful and owned hundreds of apartments and office buildings throughout the area.

———————◆◆●◆►———————

It was hard to keep up with the demand in Fortside and I came to realize that I couldn't impose on Joe Trenkamp to do my excavation work much longer. I decided that now was the time to purchase my own bulldozer, but I'd need a loan to do that. I had been working outside on one of the homes when it started to rain. My boots and pants were already muddy when I remembered I had an appointment that afternoon at First National Bank in Covington. I had no time to clean up and change clothes. I hopped in my truck and rushed down there as fast as I could. I was late when I walked up to the teller and said in my heavy German accent, "I'm Matth Toebben and I'm here to see Mr. Harry Humpert, the bank president."

She looked at me and at all the dirt covering my clothes. Then she checked out my muddy footprints leading from the front door to her counter. It wasn't a friendly look at all. I'm sure she thought the worst of me. "What time was your appointment?" she asked with an edge to her voice.

"One o'clock."

"You're fifteen minutes late."

"Yes, I'm sorry." It was a bad way to start a loan request and I was already getting the feeling I was going to have to go somewhere else to get money.

"Mr. Humpert is busy right now. He's in a meeting and can't see you."

I needed a loan for my bulldozer that day and I couldn't leave without a commitment. I looked around the lobby and saw a grouping of chairs. I said, "Well, I've got to talk to him today. I'll just sit over there and wait until he can see me."

"Suit yourself," she replied. She wasn't happy.

I sat there for around thirty minutes before a gentleman wearing a three-piece suit walked right up to me. "You must be Matth Toebben. I'm Harry Humpert. How may I help you?"

"Hi, Mr. Humpert." I stood to shake his hand but when I saw the dried mud on my fingers, I thought better of it. "I would like to borrow some money."

"Well why don't you step into my office and we can discuss it."

"Do you mind if I take my boots off first? I'm kind of muddy."

He looked at the lobby floor and replied, "I think it's a little late for that. You can keep the boots on. Most of the dirt has already dried and fallen off anyway."

I looked back and saw the trail of mud I had tracked in from the front door. I remember thinking, "Man oh man, I might as well leave right now. This is never going to work out." The bank president was very polite and told me to take a seat on the opposite side of his desk. There was a photograph of his family on top. Otherwise it was spotless. There were no stacks of papers and no reports, just that single photograph. Then he sat down in a plush leather chair and brushed a small piece of lint from his trousers. "So, what do you need money for, Mr. Toebben?" he asked.

"To buy a bulldozer."

He raised his eyebrows and replied, "We don't get many requests for that." Then instead of asking me about why I needed the machine, he wanted to know more about me and my family, how we got through the war, and how I wound up in Northern Kentucky. It was about a half hour before he even asked me about my construction business. I told him about how I had been working for George Kreutzjans.

"I know George very well. He banks here."

"He's a good man," I said and then explained how I worked all day and night to save up the money to start out on my own and how I had developed land on Amsterdam Road.

"I drove past that project a few weeks ago. It looks like you've done a good job there."

I thanked him and said that I was building a home for Art Arlinghaus in my new Fortside development. He knew Art well and we talked about him. Then he dropped that subject and asked more about me and my family. He never asked for a financial statement or facts about my income.

I realized later the he was sizing me up to see what kind of person I was. He needed to decide if I was a good risk for the bank.

All at once he said, "How much money do you need, Matth?"

"Sixty thousand dollars," I replied and expected the man to laugh in my face. That was a huge amount of money in 1956. I was nervous.

"Well, what do you plan to do with all that money?"

"I need some for the dozer. I put $9000 down, but I need another twenty to pay the balance on delivery. I have some outstanding bills for excavating and tree clearing. That's $8,000. Then I have ongoing expenses for payroll and materials to build more houses."

He thought for a minute and asked, "How much do you want today?"

"Twenty thousand today. Then I'll need twenty for each of the next two months. I expect everything to cash flow after that."

We talked for a few more minutes until he looked at his watch and said, "I have another meeting in a few minutes, Matth. I guess I'd better get you that check you need. Good luck with your project and I hope to see you again soon."

That was it, easy as can be. I picked up my check and was about to head out the door. I hesitated for a minute, walked over to the teller and said, "I'd like to open an account." She still showed me her disapproving look because of the mud, but she took care of the paperwork. Thirty minutes later I deposited my new check for twenty thousand dollars. I decided that it would be a good idea to bank with the company that was going to lend me the money. I'd probably need their help in the future.

My bulldozer was delivered several days later. It was a Caterpillar D7 with a cable blade. It was huge. I stood in front of the massive machine and said, "Good gosh, what do I do now?" I didn't have an operator because I couldn't afford to hire one. It had to be me, and I had no idea what I was doing.

As soon as I climbed up into the driver's seat and checked out the controls, I knew I needed help and needed it right away.

I went home and called the Caterpillar Company. "You better send somebody down here to teach me how to run this thing or I'm going to wind up killing myself on it."

The very next day they sent a man over and he taught me how to run it. I ran the dozer with him sitting next to me, telling me what and what not to do.

After two hours he said, "You'll be fine now."

"This big machine? I don't know about that."

"You're doing well with it," he repeated and started to leave. I think he saw the uncertain look in my eyes because he added, "I'll be back tomorrow to be sure." True to his word, he returned, and I was happy he did. The man came back two more times after that. I think he agreed I needed a little more coaching after all. He even showed me how to put in the oil and grease the track assembly. I figured I was ready to go it alone but a week later I got into trouble. It was a problem he hadn't prepared me to handle.

The Caterpillar D7 was undeniably a powerful machine. It could easily plow through a house or push over tall trees. However, it did have its weakness. It could get stuck. There was another rainy day, but I was on a tight schedule and had to keep the project moving along. There were bills to be paid, so I kept grading the lots in spite of the rain and softening ground. It wasn't long before I buried the dozer up to the top track and there was no way for me to get it out. I was in deep trouble with no good options. I called Joe Trenkamp to see if he could deliver one of his dozers to help pull me out of the mud. He couldn't. All his machines were tied up on a project the next county over. He said he wouldn't be able to get to me until next week at the earliest. I couldn't wait that long. Joe suggested that I call Bob Ratterman who owned a junkyard on the 3-L Highway. He had a couple of large tow trucks that might be powerful enough. I called Bob to see if he could help me out. He agreed, but he had to use both of his trucks before he was able to pull my dozer free. The same thing happened two more times over the next month. When I received Bob's bill for the service, I was shocked. It was an expensive lesson and I never again got the bulldozer stuck. It was much cheaper to wait until the ground dried before trying to move dirt during a soaking rain. I did get into a little bit of other trouble, however.

In the beginning stages of the Fortside development, I had to invest long hours to keep the business cash flowing. I needed to complete houses so I could meet payroll and other financial obligations. Initially I had to do much of the work myself. That meant I would typically work a nine-hour day on the houses before heading home to my "Five Room Castle" on Amsterdam for dinner. As soon as I finished eating, I would return to the job site at night, jump onto the bulldozer, and start clearing more lots. I had special running lights installed on the machine so I could run it in the dark. There was no safety canopy over the driver's seat and I was dropping huge trees. How I did that at night without killing myself was a miracle. I would operate the thing until about one in the morning, return home to sleep for a few hours, and return at first light to start the whole process over again. I did that for about six months.

One night, around midnight, the police pulled into the development with their blue lights flashing. Apparently, the noise from knocking down the larger trees was keeping some of the neighbors behind the property from sleeping. The police shut me down and told me to refrain from any more bulldozing after dark. That restriction wasn't going to work for me if I was going to be able to pay my bills.

For the first several weeks I would shut down my dozer at dusk. The police checked several times to make sure I was complying with their demands. Then I slowly stretched that time out until I was again working until 1:00 AM. I had no other choice. It was a week later when I had to push down trees in the far rear of the property, close to Morris Road. It started raining and I had to concentrate on not getting the machine stuck again. Through the rain I could see the flashing blue lights about two hundred yards away near the front of the property. I pretended I didn't see him. With all the bad weather I figured he'd never try to walk all the way to the back lots in the mud. I was wrong. About ten minutes later I was blinded when a flashlight shined directly in my eyes. The policeman was standing just ten feet away from me and he was mad. Rain was dripping off his hat and the man was soaked. His shoes were covered in mud up to his ankles.

"Shut that damn bulldozer off!" he yelled. "I gave you a fair warning a few weeks ago but now I'm taking you in!"

I turned off the dozer and left it sitting there. "You're in big trouble again, Matth," I murmured to myself as I climbed down. I seemed to say that a lot. We trudged side by side through the mud. Along the way I explained my dilemma of being a small operation and having to do most of the work myself. That's why I had to run the dozer so late. I apologized several times and offered to launder his uniform. By the time we reached the police cruiser we were both unrecognizable from the rain and mud. I think the ordeal somehow made us kindred spirits because he decided not to arrest me that night after all. He shined his flashlight in my face and said, "I'm going to let you go, Mr. Toebben, but this is the last time. You can't be out here working late at night and keeping these people awake. They have jobs and families, too."

I again apologized. He told me it had better not happen again. I promised it wouldn't and I kept my word. I decided to hire a full-time dozer operator. As it turns out, my old friend Tony Dempsey had been drafted into the service shortly after our SOB episode. While in the army he was a bulldozer operator. When he got out, he was looking for a job just at the time I needed an operator. I hired him on the spot. He stayed with me for ten years and operated every piece of heavy machinery I owned. Tony was a good man and I relied on him a great deal.

We continued building on Fortside. I made two side streets and named them after my first two daughters, Susan and Diane. Laverne and I eventually built our own home on Susan Lane. It was a nice place and I built a fifteen by twenty-foot office next to the garage. That replaced the kitchen table office in our "Five Room

Castle." We lived on Susan Lane from 1960 to 1975 and raised our five children there.

Eighteen months after coming to America, I already owned my own successful construction business. I didn't need a master's certificate and I didn't need any approval from the government. All I needed was my own skill, the promise to do good work, and the right work ethic. It was an example of the free enterprise system that made America great in those days.

At the time of the organization of this book, I realized that today, in 2019, a German immigrant could never start his own construction company here. Thirty days after purchasing the property on Fortside, I had been able to begin construction on the new project. With all the intrusive governmental bureaucracies and stifling regulations today, it would have taken years to secure the initial permits and that would have only been the first of several more hurdles to overcome.

The average home here would cost 30% less if it wasn't for excessive regulatory demands made by self-propagating bureaucracies. Meanwhile, the average homebuyer must pay the price of that burden. They must borrow an extra thirty percent to finance their new home. What do they get in exchange for that extra expense? Nothing, other than to perpetuate the same governmental agencies that have led to the problem in the first place.

It's discouraging when I think of how we have allowed our government to take so much control over every move we make. I saw the same thing happening in Germany when I was a boy. Government bureaucrats controlled everything, and the results were disastrous. I don't want America to make the same mistake. It is the major reason why I eventually got involved in politics; a change in direction was essential.

The family in front of our Fortside home on Susan Lane. From left to right:
Back row: Laverne, Susan, Me. Second row: Diane, John, Bill. Front: Elizabeth

DOCTOR REDDEN

A year into Fortside, our construction business took several leaps forward because of a few serendipitous events. We were getting busier; with that came more bills and paperwork. The responsibility of handling them fell upon my shoulders and I wasn't very adept at it. One night after Sunday dinner, I was sitting at our kitchen table that also served as my office desk. In front of me was our checkbook and a stack of invoices. I couldn't read the bills very well and my ability to write out checks for the appropriate amount was severely limited because of my continued poor understanding of English. I had an English-German dictionary sitting next to the checkbook. I would study one of the invoices, line-by-line and try to translate it into German. Once I thought I fully understood the bill, I would try to write out the check and address an envelope. It was taking an interminable amount of time. It was getting to be late at night and Laverne had already gone to bed.

At some point, she realized I was still up and walked into the kitchen to see what was going on. "Matth, what are you doing?" she asked.

"Working on the bills."

She watched as I continued to struggle, referring back and forth from the invoices to my dictionary. Finally she said, "Why don't I take a look at them?" She leafed through the ones I had completed, smiled, and said, "I think you might need a little help, Matth. Maybe I should take care of these and you can spend more of your time building the houses. I'll finish up here and you go to bed. You need some rest."

I didn't argue. From that moment on, Laverne became the company's accountant and chief financial officer. She continued to work in that capacity for over ten years. It took a huge load off my shoulders and allowed me to focus on what I knew best, building houses. Without her help, we could have never grown and enjoyed the success we had.

Another event that changed the course of the company came in the form of a phone call one evening. Laverne answered and said, "Matth, it's for you."

I took the phone and said, "Hello."

The voice on the other end said, "Mr. Toebben?"

"Yes."

"My name is Pat Redden. I've been hearing about your company. Friends tell me you've been building homes on Fortside Drive."

"That's true. We've been working there for several years now."

"I've also heard that you have a reputation for doing quality work for a reasonable price."

"We'd like to think we do, Mrs. Redden. How may I help you?"

"My husband and I want to build in the Fort Mitchell area. We would like to meet with you about the possibility of your company building our next home. When do you think we could get together?"

"Well, I work with my men all day building homes and I run a bulldozer at night, so I can't meet until about ten o'clock in the evening."

"Actually, that works out well for us. My husband, John, is a doctor and has a busy primary care practice in Covington. How about tomorrow night after ten?"

We scheduled the meeting at my "Five Room Castle" on Amsterdam Road.

When I got home from work, I laid all my brochures and plans out on the kitchen table. I'm not sure what they expected when they walked in, but from the look in their eyes I didn't think they were impressed with my little kitchen-table office. They were polite anyway and each took a chair across from me at the small table. They told me their story. They had a son, also named John, who required a wheelchair. They wanted him to be able to navigate around the entire home along with the rest of their eight children. I quickly realized that their house would have to be a single-story, ranch-style home. Special designs would be necessary to allow for wider hallways and doors to accommodate the wheelchair. The Americans with Disabilities Act was not passed until over twenty years later, so these kinds of construction details had not yet been well-defined. I had done nothing like this previously, so I would have to start from scratch on this one.

They were very nice people and we talked for a while about what they wanted. I could tell Dr. Redden was getting a little frustrated with the communication barrier. After about twenty minutes he stood up and said, "It's getting a little late and I have to make early rounds at the hospital tomorrow morning. When your father has some time to meet with us, have him give Pat a call and we can get together." When he turned to leave, his wife touched his arm and said, "John, there is no father here. Matth is Toebben Construction. He's the man who will be building the house, so you must talk to him."

Dr. Redden stepped back and looked at me. "Are you sure? You're just a kid."

"I'm the designer and builder," I replied. "I've already completed almost a dozen homes on Fortside and you're both welcome to check them out."

"I guess that won't be necessary. Pat already did her homework on this. If she's happy with you as our builder, that's good enough for me."

We sat back down at the table and continued to discuss their needs until one o'clock in the morning. I drew some rough sketches and when we were finished, he gave me a deposit check for five thousand dollars.

What resulted was a six-thousand square-foot home. It was over twice the size of anything I had built up to that point. There were thirteen rooms with five and a half baths. It included a three-car garage and a huge basement. This was the kind of home I had been wanting to build since I had started my own company. Toebben Construction slowly changed directions to become a high-end custom home builder.

Dr. Redden worked until he was ninety years old and remained in the house until 2016. We became close friends and often had lunch together. Sadly, his wife, Pat died of cancer only four years after they moved into their dream home. It was a tragedy for their entire family and everyone who knew her.

DAD

Several years after I started my business, I talked my father into making a visit to the United States to meet my family. I was surprised that he agreed and was excited at the prospect of seeing him. I made reservations for a flight to New York. When I first saw him getting off the plane, I was shocked as he had changed a great deal in the years since I had last seen him. The man who was once a strong farmer and former captain in the Kaiser's army was now frail. He could no longer stand tall, being slumped over at the shoulders from too many years of backbreaking work on the farm. His chest was round, and he could barely breathe because of emphysema, probably from smoking his newspaper cigarettes. Still, there was the same look of pride and determination in his eyes. Age had not diminished his spirit.

At the time of his visit, I had just begun work on my fifth house in Fortside. I had been excited about showing Dad what I had accomplished with my construction company. On Sunday, we drove to the site in my old rusted-out pickup truck. It was a clunker but all I could afford at the time.

When he saw it, he asked, "This is your truck?"

I didn't answer. It was more of a statement than a question. My dad simply shook his head. I could tell he was disappointed, but I was still excited to show him what I had accomplished in America. When we arrived at the job site it was quiet and looked abandoned. My employees were off since it was a Sunday. Dad got out of the truck and looked around. We were moving around a great deal of dirt to prepare for the next road extension. That involved leveling a fairly sizable hillside. We were only half finished and there was still a thirty-five-foot knob of dirt standing in the middle of the property. Most everything else was covered with bulldozer ruts and the place was littered with fallen trees.

He had never seen anything like it before. The area must have looked to him like a war zone. Dad rested on a knee and studied the project. He again shook his head and said to me, "I don't know about this, Matth. Things aren't looking so good here. Maybe it would be best if you returned to Germany with me. I think this might be more than you can handle."

Dad in front of the a hill at Fortside construction site.
"I don't know about this, Matth..."

His words hit me like a sledgehammer in the chest. I was devastated. I had been hoping to make him proud of me, to show him how successful I had become. Instead, he assumed I was a failure. In his eyes I was still that sickly asthmatic boy who would never succeed. I said nothing at the time but four months later I brought him back to the same construction site. By now, the dead trees had been removed and the land levelled. The large mound of dirt was gone. Streets were being poured and a dozen men were busy working on several of the new homes. This time my dad got out of the truck and the previous look of concern was replaced by one of amazement. He turned to me and said, "Matth, I had no idea what you were doing before, but obviously you're very successful in this construction business of yours. Congratulations, I'm more proud of you than you can imagine."

I'll never forget those words. It was one of the very few times in my life he ever said he was proud of me.

❖❖❖

After leaving the Fortside development, we were driving down Dixie Highway through Fort Mitchell. Dad looked to his right and saw a vegetable stand sign in front of a small farm. "Whose farm is that?" he asked with an excited tone in his voice.

"It belongs to Henry and Marie Kruempelman. Why?" I said.

"By gosh, I think I might know those people."

"Dad, how could you possibly know these people? You've never even been to the U.S. before."

"I had a cousin in Breddenburg. She moved to America and I remember she married a Kruempelman. It might be her."

I probably sounded a little frustrated when I replied, "Dad, there's probably thousands of Kreumpelmans scattered around this country. What are the odds that you know this particular family? Probably impossible." The look in his old eyes told me he was disappointed, so I continued, "I tell you what, Dad. I'll pull up to their front door and we can see." A smile flashed across his face.

I knocked and Mrs. Kruempelman opened the door. She looked to be in her early-eighties.

My father looked at her and knew. He said, "Guten tag, Marie."

She appeared confused. "I'm sorry. Do I know you?"

"You should know me," he answered with a smile on his face. "We used to go to school together almost every day for eight years."

She clapped her hands together and a look of recognition lit up her eyes. "My gosh, Rudolph Toebben!" She reached out and hugged him. "I haven't seen you in over sixty years. What are you doing here?"

"Visiting my son, Matth."

She looked at me and said, "The builder? I've heard about Matth, but I never connected him to you. Come in."

We sat on a couch in her living room where she served us some cookies and tea. She and Dad spent a few hours reminiscing over their childhood, telling stories, and laughing. I had never thought of my dad in terms of once being a child. He was always just Dad, stoic and serious. I don't think I've ever seen him smile so much. This was a side of him I hadn't known before and I enjoyed watching him. We stayed the entire afternoon and visited several more times before Dad returned to Germany six months later.

I remained good friends with Marie and Henry after he left. A year later, I built a home for their daughter, Libby, on Fortside. Laverne and I would stop by the Kruempelman farm every spring to buy tomato plants and flowers. On Christmas, Marie would give us a homemade smoked ham. From time to time I would visit and share a few shots of Jägermeister with Henry. He and Marie loved to talk about Lorup and our family. She had never returned to Germany after coming to America and had lost all contact with her relatives. One afternoon I told her that I was planning to return to Germany for a visit. I was going to buy a movie camera and film my family and friends. I said that if she would like, I would drive over to Breddenberg and take pictures of her relatives. She was so excited I saw tears in her eyes. She said, "Oh Matth, that would be wonderful! Could you bring back a German prayer book? Mine has worn out over the years and I can hardly read it."

The next time I travelled to Lorup, Rudy and I drove over to Breddenberg to visit with Marie's family. They were delighted to hear about her and how she was doing. We took movies and photographs of everyone. Meanwhile, my mother bought the new prayer book and a rosary. Three weeks later, I brought everything back home with me. Marie was ill, so I called her daughter Libby and told her about all the things I had brought back from Germany for her mother. Libby mentioned that Marie had been so excited about the movies and pictures, it was all she had talked about since I left.

Unfortunately, she died two months later, before she had a chance to see the family movies I had taken. She never got to use her new prayer book. It was sad, but she had enjoyed a wonderful, full life in America. Laverne and I felt blessed to have known Marie and Henry for the time we did.

Dad holding his granddaughter, Susan. My niece, Anna, and nephew, Rudy Kreutzjans

MONTE CASINO CHAPEL

Prospect Hill overlooked Latonia, Kentucky, and atop it sat the Monte Casino Chapel, small in size but paradoxically majestic in its appearance. It seemed to have been somehow transported across time from some ancient European village. The small building measured just six-by- nine feet inside and the ceiling was only eight feet high. Ripley's had it listed it as the smallest chapel in the world. Above the door was a stained-glass window with a German inscription that read, "Sehet ob ein schmerz Meiningen gliche." Translated, it meant, "See if there is any sorrow like my sorrow."

The chapel was first constructed by several German monks in 1878 and was named Monte Casino after a famous Italian monastery, recognized as the birthplace of the Benedictine Order. The surrounding seventy-six acres of land housed a small Benedictine Friary and farm where the monks grew grapes for commercial and sacramental wines. They would hold daily mass in the chapel every morning and later, in the peaceful solitude of evening, reflect upon their faith and devotion to God. In 1920, prohibition prevented the distribution of alcoholic beverages, which put an end to the winery. With no means to support themselves, the monks were forced to abandon the property. In time, the land was sold, and the farm yielded to development. Over the years, the small chapel fell into disrepair and vandalism. The door, altar, benches, the stained-glass windows, and even parts of the small steeple were lost. The inside walls were stained black from repeated small fires set by squatters. It was a tragic loss of a historical monument.

Monte Casino Chapel, vandalized and overgown.

In 1964, the owner of the chapel was found by searching through the city's tax records. He was a man by the name of Fred Riedinger, a local plumber. He decided to donate the chapel to the Covington Diocese. To be preserved, a move to a better location was necessary. After considering several options, it was eventually decided that it should become a landmark at Thomas More College in Crestview Hills. A beautiful site overlooking a lake on the campus was selected to be its new home, but the problem was going to be getting it there in one piece. The Knights of Columbus, of which I was a member, approached me about the possibility of moving the tiny church. I realized that would be a daunting task. It was small in dimension, but I estimated it weighed over sixty tons. I inspected the chapel and was impressed by the magnificent workmanship involved in hand-cutting of each stone into the perfect shapes necessary to construct the walls and arches. I decided the move would be worth trying. After the story of the project hit the newspapers and local television stations, dozens of people brought back items that had been missing for decades.

It was going to be difficult. We needed a special drag, a low-riding flatbed truck used to transport heavy pieces of machinery like bulldozers. It would have to be large enough to hold the weight of the chapel and distribute it evenly to avoid damage to the stone walls. After the spring rains slowed enough for the ground to dry, the project commenced. My cousin, Rudy Pohlabeln, and I supervised the jacking up of the structure so the drag could be backed under it. When the truck arrived, it looked a little small to me. I questioned its ability to handle the extreme weight, but I was reassured by the drag owner that the excessive weight had already been taken into consideration when selecting the truck. They claimed that the truck's bed would hold. The chapel was positioned on the drag with a bulldozer and secured with heavy ropes. As soon it had moved just ten feet, the truck's bed split in two. We all stood there in shock, fearing the worst. I expected the chapel to collapse in pieces. Fortunately, the tiny church wasn't damaged, and we were able to use the bulldozer to pull it back onto its footings.

I called Wayne Carlisle to see if he had anything big enough to handle the transport. He was used to moving extremely heavy cranes as part of his Carlisle Construction Company business. After visiting the site, he sent over a larger capacity drag. On April 7, 1965, we loaded the chapel and the truck handled the load.

A tense hour watching the drag negoitate its way between two homes.

Once on the drag, we had to negotiate our way through a fifteen-foot opening between two homes to get to the nearest road. That didn't give us much room on either side. We were concerned about the possibility of damaging the adjacent homes' foundations and caving in their basements, so we made a wooden roadway out of four-inch white oak beams. It was a tense several hours, but the chapel made it safely to the street without damaging the homes.

As soon as we got onto a solid roadway, the rain returned, and we had to suspend activity for several more days. Finally, the skies cleared, and the move was resumed. The utility companies were able to raise all their power and phone lines as the truck moved on at a cautious five miles an hour. After half a day the chapel made it to its new home at Thomas More College.

We had already poured the footings and the heavy structure was eased into position. We began the restoration process, trying to return the church to its original humble grandeur. The previous wooden door had rotted so it was replaced with a locked wrought iron gate to prevent future looting and vandalism. I was eventually able to locate the lost stained-glass transom but unfortunately it could no longer be inserted over the door. It still sits against the wall in a small shop somewhere in Covington.

Finally, on September 12, 1971, we held an installation ceremony to celebrate the placement of the chapel at its new home. The historical Monte Casino chapel was preserved for future generations. The setting in front of a peaceful lake was a perfect location where it now serves as a landmark for Thomas More University and a frequent backdrop for wedding pictures. The entire team was relieved to have finished the job successfully and we were proud of what we had accomplished.

Monte Casino Chapel in its new location

CRESCENT SPRINGS

Crescent Springs was an undeveloped community adjacent to Fort Mitchell. It was named after the multitude of natural springs dotting the area. The land was mostly comprised of produce and dairy farms. For years the only access into and out of the area was a single-lane dirt road that was marred by ruts and years of erosion. Dairy farmers would transport their milk in five-gallon cans across the bumpy road in horse-drawn wagons. By the time the milk had reached the market, much of it had become churned and hence the road was nicknamed "Buttermilk." It has since been paved and widened to four lanes, but its original name persists. Quiet Crescent Springs would eventually become the site of Toebben Construction Company's signature community.

As the I-75 interstate system was being planned for Northern Kentucky, the farm land slowly gave way to suburban development. A few of the farm owners held out and one of them was Mr. George Eubanks who owned about one hundred eighty acres along Amsterdam Road. In 1960, I met George after church one Sunday morning and we soon became friends.

Having grown up in a rural farming area in Germany, I enjoyed hunting. It was a passion and one of the means by which my father, my twin brother, and I were able to put food on the table for the family. I was talking to George Eubanks one afternoon and we began discussing how we both liked to hunt. He said to me, "Matth, would you like to do some rabbit hunting on my farm one of these days?"

I said that I would enjoy that very much. The following weekend I went out and walked his farm. It was a beautiful piece of property with orchards of various fruit trees and a fairly large lake in the back. It was a sunny but cool day, ideal for hunting. After only an hour I had shot a couple of rabbits. George had previously told me how much he liked rabbit stew, so I dropped them off at his house. He thanked me and invited me in. "Have a seat, Matth. I'd like to talk to you about something."

I took a seat on an easy chair in his living room and he sat opposite me on a couch. He leaned forward and said, "Matth, I'm getting too old to work the farm anymore and my children have no interest in it. I've decided to sell the land. With your farming background in Germany, I thought you might be interested.

I had heard that he had wanted to sell the property several years earlier for $60,000. I replied, "Thanks for the offer, George, but I can't afford to buy this farm. I purchased forty acres of land on Fortside in Ft. Mitchell and I need to save some money to continue the development."

"I'll sell it to you cheap."

That caught my attention. "Well, what do you mean by cheap?"

"Seventy thousand for the entire one hundred eighty acres."

"Didn't you try to sell it several years ago for sixty?"

"Yes, but now it's two years later and everything has gone up."

I sat back in my chair to think about the offer for a second. He was asking $330 an acre, but if I could get the price down, it might be a pretty good deal. "I tell you what, George. I'll give you the original sixty thousand you were asking but I can only afford to pay twenty thousand down now. I'll pay twenty a year for the next two years. That's the best I can do."

George stood up and said, "Deal."

We shook hands on it and that was good enough for both of us. I now owned a farm and had no idea what I was going to do with it.

The following week I again met with Mr. Humpert, the president of First National Bank. We had had a good relationship ever since I obtained financing for my bulldozer. I told him what I wanted the money for.

"I don't know, Matth. I'm not so sure this is a good idea. You certainly don't need any more land. You just purchased the forty acres in Fort Mitchell a few years ago. That should keep your company busy for the next ten years at least. Maybe you should wait."

"I know but I'm getting this property for a pretty good price and land opportunities in Crescent Springs are slowly disappearing. In ten more years there may be no more farms available. I like to hunt and that's how I plan to use the farm. Later on, I can develop the land if the construction business is still doing well. If not, I can always sell it and probably make a good profit."

George and I closed on the property several weeks later. I

had come full circle. I was again in the business of farming. I loved the peaceful openness of the land and enjoyed the idea of growing things the way our family did in Lorup. I showed the farm to Laverne and she loved it. We thought it would be fun to try to sell the fruits and vegetables by setting up a roadside stand. The problem was that people didn't want to pay. They wanted everything for free or at a severe discount. We couldn't even make enough to cover the cost of the pickers we hired. We gave up on our farming idea and decided to convert the property into a weekend retreat for the family. A large lake had been created with a dam in the back of the land. It was too shallow and overgrown to be useful. It needed some attention. We added five feet to the height of the dam and that increased the depth significantly. Then we brought in several truckloads of gravel and sand to create a beach along one side. I bought a used diving board and installed it by the edge of our new lake. We now had our own natural swimming pool. All our work must have opened the natural spring further because the water began to flow more freely. It was so clear it was almost like an actual swimming pool. It reminded me of my days as a child in Lorup where we swam in the farm pond but this one didn't have livestock just fifty feet away on the other side.

In time I built a patio and covered it with a roof. I found a fifty-five-gallon drum, split it in two lengthwise, and ran steel rods through the sides, creating a huge grill. On Sundays we would host large barbeques for friends and family. I could now reciprocate with all those who had helped me settle in Northern Kentucky and establish my business, people like: Bernie and Ileen Lunneman, Rudy and Angela Pohlabeln, Bill and Krista Gerdes, John and Helen Finken, Ben Wessels and my sister Agnes, Nick Kruetzjans and my oldest sister Marie, and my youngest brother John and his wife Judy. We all had wonderful times together for over ten years.

TRAVEL AND MOM

No matter how much time and hard work an owner invests, no company can grow and prosper without the benefit of solid management and a good workforce. Any company is only as good as the people who work within that company and Toebben Construction was lucky enough to have some of the finest, namely Rudy Pohlabeln, Jim Meyrose, and Bernie Lunneman. Rudy was my cousin and a fellow immigrant from Germany. Jim was only seventeen when he became the first man I ever hired. When he started, he was deathly afraid of heights, but after only a few years of climbing on roofs he walked around with the agility of a cat. He became a great carpenter and worked his way up through the company as it grew. I became friends with Bernie shortly after arriving in America. He's the one who taught me how to drive and he was the best man in my wedding. All three were more than capable of handling the day-to-day operations of the company. That allowed Laverne and me the opportunity to travel.

When I was twenty-seven, I made my first trip home to visit my parents. The children were still too young to travel and Laverne had to remain at home with them, so I went alone. Not much had changed in Lorup since the war. The artillery damage to the church steeple had been repaired and the bells had been replaced. Most of the craters left by bombs had been filled. The roads were a little better and there were several new buildings, but by and large the village looked much the same as it did when I was a little boy. It was as though time had passed it by.

Our house was no exception. I could still see the scorch marks and other remnants of the artillery explosion that almost took my life as I reached into the window during the Allied assault. My parents still had hogs in the back while chickens ran free around the property. It was January and the cows had been brought up to the barn for the winter. There were the same familiar smells of the animals, Mom's cooking, and Dad's cigarettes, all blended together into something reminiscently pleasing. Many of the postwar conveniences of the modern world had passed by Lorup. One thing I hadn't been looking forward to during my visit was having to brave the cold wind at night to go to the outhouse. It hadn't been replaced.

After having enjoyed the comfortable living in the United States for five years, I had forgotten just how primitive life was in Lorup. There was no central heat in the house. The first night was so cold I thought I might freeze to death. My mother had put five hot water bottles in the bed to warm it up but once they cooled down, the bed just became damp and even colder than it was when I initially got under the covers. In addition, the mattress was flat, so I tossed and turned all night trying to find a comfortable position. I didn't remember having so much trouble sleeping as a child. Finally, about two in the morning, I got up and went into the kitchen to sit next to the cooking stove, the only source of heat in the house. The problem was it had no fire because they didn't light one every day. Dad didn't want to use up all their firewood and peat until it got further into winter. For my parents the cold wasn't really that bad yet, but to me the house felt like a refrigerator. I started a fire using a peat block and sat on a chair next to it. That was better. I wrapped a blanket around myself and tried to sleep.

I must have been making a fair amount of noise because my mother got up and said, "My gosh, Matth! What's wrong? Why are you up? Why are you not sleeping?"

"It got a little cold in my room, so I decided I'd just sit here next to the stove to warm up. I think I must have gotten soft, living in America."

She felt so bad that the next day she pulled my bed into the living room and set it right next to the stove. She kept a fire going continuously until I left two weeks later.

I finally fell asleep and awoke to the smell of fresh coffee brewing. It was dark outside and still bitterly cold. Mom handed me a cup, hot and strong, just what I needed to alleviate the chill. I sipped on it as mom made a breakfast of fresh biscuits, bacon, and eggs. I had forgotten how good a German country breakfast could taste. Looking around, I asked, "Where's Dad?"

"He's outside milking the cows. Should be in when he's finished, I figure about an hour. He doesn't like to eat until that is done."

I had forgotten about Dad's morning routine. In spite of his bad emphysema, it was the animals first, then eat. I regretted not getting up earlier to help him but after a cold, fitful night, morning had come too soon. "I should have helped him," I said.

"That's OK. His lungs have been a little better lately and he enjoys his alone time in the morning. In fact, he enjoys his alone time most of the day." We both chuckled. Dad loved his family, but he wasn't known for his warm or talkative nature.

After we finished eating, Mom poured a second cup of coffee for each of us and we talked about life. Eventually I asked, "Is it unusually cold for this time of year. I don't remember winters being like this."

"Actually, it's been fairly mild so far this year."

"If this is mild, I'd hate to be here when it's really cold." We both laughed.

I thought about my childhood for a few seconds before asking, "Then how were you able to keep Rudy and me warm at night during the bad winters? As little as we both were when we were born, I'm surprised we didn't freeze to death."

"It was hard sometimes. On the coldest nights, I would wrap the two of you in small blankets and then I would hold you close to me until the morning."

I envisioned her trying to protect my twin and me from the cold. I thought about her selfless act, night after night, probably sacrificing any chance for sleep so her two babies would stay warm. I couldn't talk for several seconds as I blinked tears away from my eyes.

"How did you do everything you did, Mom? You took care of all us children, cooked, cleaned, and worked the farm. There was the war and everything else to worry about. How did you do it all?"

"In those days, you didn't have a choice. Dad and I had responsibilities. Eleven children came along, each one a blessed surprise, and we loved every one of you. We didn't plan things that way. Life just happened and that's how it worked. We had to cope and do what had to be done to survive. I guess I never thought about it much at the time. Hard work was just a necessary part of life."

I paused before saying the things I had been wanting to tell her for years. "Mom, I've never told you this before. I guess I never realized it until I watched Laverne trying to care for our own children and saw how hard you and dad have had it living on the farm." I paused for a few seconds to hold her hand and look into her eyes. "Thank you for all that you've done for us and all the sacrifices you've made." I was silent for a second before adding words I doubt she had heard in years, "I love you, Mom." She looked shocked and happy.

"I love you too, Matthias," she replied, squeezing my hand.

When I got up to hug her, she had tears running down both cheeks. Germans were not ones to display their emotions, but that didn't mean they didn't feel them. It was a clumsy hug, the kind when one person is standing and the other is sitting, but it is one I'll always remember.

Dad came in from the outside, cold and severely short of breath, but not complaining. He removed his heavy coat and sat down at the table across from me. Mom patted him on the shoulder and placed his breakfast in front of him. Dad was never a man for talking so most of the conversation came from Mom and me. Any questions posed to him were usually answered with a single word. He never elaborated.

Mom got up and I waited until she left us alone for a few minutes, thinking Dad might be more comfortable with conversation just between the two of us. I was hoping to have a discussion similar to the one I just had with Mom. I wanted to tell him how much I appreciated all he had done for me and the rest of the family over the years. I wanted to tell him how much I respected him and loved him; but like most other old German farmers of his day, Dad was a stoic man who believed any expression of emotion was a sign of weakness. Other than the single time as a boy when I had the severe asthma attack out in the fields, we had rarely been able to relate on a deeply personal level. In spite of my efforts to guide the conversation in the direction I wanted, Dad constantly deflected it toward more comfortable topics like my construction business in America or farming in Lorup. There was an unseen line that I was never able to cross. Too many generations of German culture prevented it. By the time Mom returned to the room, my opportunity had slipped by, never to return.

Despite the cold and Spartan rural life in Lorup, I thoroughly enjoyed seeing my family and friends. My only regret was never being able to have the talk I wanted with Dad. I had a bad premonition about it and later realized it was for a good reason. Dad died of his lung disease just before his seventy-second birthday. I never got to tell him I loved him.

I realize that many people aren't attracted to hunting. I respect their position, but as a boy growing up on a farm in rural Germany, it was an important aspect of my life. Hunting was an integral part of our local culture, a means by which we could feed the family. A few years after my father passed away, my twin brother Rudy called me from Germany.

"Matth, the next auction is being held in three months."

Lorup was no longer as poor as it had been under Hitler, but it was still little more than a small farming community. Other than the local dairy, there was no industry and not many businesses to generate tax revenue for the local government, so the farmers of Lorup would hold an auction every nine years to raise money. The surrounding farm lands were grouped together in parcels of around three thousand acres each and people would bid for the exclusive rights to hunt that particular section. It was expensive and generally the bidding was limited to the very wealthy from the larger cities. By now, Rudy had become a fairly successful farmer in another town, but he still couldn't do it on his own, so he called me.

"Matth, what do you think? You want to do this? You want me to submit a bid?"

I stopped to consider things for a minute. I was doing well in America and could certainly afford the cost of a winning bid. When I left Lorup, it wasn't because I no longer cared for my home village or its people. I was only pursuing a greater opportunity in America and I continued to miss my friends. Leasing the hunting rights would allow me to again see many of them by inviting them to join me in the hunt, an opportunity they could never afford on their own. "Sounds like a great idea, Rudy. Let me know how the bidding goes."

I placed the highest bid for the reserve I wanted. I asked Rudy to invite all our friends and relatives to join us, people who had been kind to our family while we all still lived in Lorup. Three months later, Ben Wessels, Rudy Pohlabeln, and I boarded a plane for Germany and spent two fantastic weeks there, hunting, becoming reacquainted with friends, and eating like kings. We repeated the hunting trip annually for the next nine years. Near the end I became too busy with the construction business and other ventures to make the trip. Rudy had a dairy farm with over seventy cows to milk every morning. When he was hunting, the responsibility fell on the shoulders of his wife, Lanie. It was too much, and she was getting overwhelmed by the amount of work. At the end of our nine-year cycle Rudy and I decided that, though it was fun, we wouldn't bid the reserve again.

◄•◦•►

Laverne and I made several trips together to Europe over the years, including those to search for her family roots. Once the children were old enough, we took them with us, but it was always a challenge with the five of them. The last one was a trip that changed the direction of our business significantly. We spent a week in Lorup so the children could see their grandmother. After that it was a driving tour through the rest of the European continent. I particularly remember Holland. We all loved that country. Amsterdam, its canals, the windmills, and the tulip fields were spectacular. Acres of flowers were in full bloom and extended as far as we could see. They had large dairy farms that served the finest cheese I've ever tasted. When we returned to the country years later, we were disappointed. The cities were no longer as clean. Crime was more prevalent and we didn't feel safe anymore. I suspect it might have been due to their liberal attitude toward drugs. We haven't been back to Holland since.

While in Switzerland, we were at a restaurant and noticed a woman and her daughter sitting at the table next to us. They were talking in English and Laverne struck up a conversation with them. They complimented Laverne on how well her children were behaved and she beamed with pride. As they were leaving, the woman invited us to come and visit their winery the following day. That was a wonderful surprise. The winery must have been hundreds of years old and was the most beautiful one we had ever seen. They gave us a personal tour and served lunch with samples of their finest wines. In just two days we had become great friends. They gave us their address and phone number but somewhere between Switzerland and France, we lost it. I felt bad about that.

Our next destination was the south of France. By the time we arrived in Nice, it was late and we didn't have reservations anywhere. They were having their annual flower festival so finding a room was all but impossible. The children were tired and crying so I stopped at the first hotel I saw.

"I'm sorry sir, but we have no rooms available," said the clerk. "In fact, I doubt there are any rooms available in all of Nice right now. It's the flower festival."

"I'm sorry also, but I have a wife and five tired children in my car. I'm not leaving here until you find a room for us. If you don't, we're going to spend the night right here in your lobby."

Flustered, the clerk made several frantic phone calls and five minutes later said, "I've booked a suite for you in downtown Nice, but it's going to be pretty expensive."

"I'll take it."

We arrived at the hotel twenty minutes later and I reserved the room for the next four nights. When we woke up the following morning, we looked out over our balcony to see the old city of Nice and the entire flower festival below us, extending along the avenues in all directions. It was a sea of varying colors and the smells of a hundred different food vendors. Laverne and the children were having a great time walking through the old town and shopping. We ate at little sidewalk cafes and had dessert at a few of the many patisseries.

The following morning, I woke up and was just lying in bed and looking at the ceiling, thinking about nothing specific, when it felt like something was crawling on my stomach. I dismissed it until I definitely felt another something running across my chest. I threw back the sheets and jumped out of bed. There were three large bugs under the covers. Laverne and the kids started screaming and that was the extent of our visit to Nice. We packed our bags as fast as we could. On the way out, I stopped at the reception counter just long enough to pay our bill and drop off the keys.

It was a few days later, on a Saturday morning, when we were heading back through Germany along the Autobahn. I noticed I was getting low on gas. I pulled into one of the rest areas along the highway. It took about fifteen minutes of waiting in line before I reached the pumps. As I filled the tank, Laverne and the children went into a convenience store to use the bathroom and buy a few snacks. The rest area had everything a traveler would need: gas station, grocery, restaurants, and even a hotel. I thought of all that traffic heading in both directions along the Autobahn and an idea sprung into my head. I had to set it aside for now but as soon as I got home, I planned to look into it. That idea turned into one of my most successful business ventures.

<hr>

Marie and I had tried on several occasions to get our mother to come to America for a visit. Mom was having none of it. When I tried to push the issue, she replied in a firm voice, "Matthias, I was born in Lorup, I grew up and worshiped in Lorup, I married your father in Lorup, and raised my children in Lorup. I spent my entire life here and this is where I am most happy." That was the end of that. I flew to Germany to talk to her in person. She had not yet seen her grandchildren and that became a good selling point. After some pushing on my part, she finally relented.

The main hurdle was to get her to agree to fly on an airplane. The only planes she had seen were the ones that came crashing out of the sky over Lorup during World War II. It left a huge impression on her that God did not want people to fly. That was the real reason for her refusal to travel to America. With a great deal of cajoling and handholding on my part, I eventually got her on a plane. She was surprised when she saw how nice it was on the inside and sat in the seats. They were more comfortable than any chair she had ever owned in Germany.

As the plane was speeding down the runway, she was holding onto the armrest so hard I was convinced she would break it off. After we were airborne, she continued to hold on so tightly her hands were turning blue. I finally patted her shoulder and said, "It's OK, Mom. We're in the air. The hard part's over. The plane isn't going to crash."

She took a deep breath, relaxed her death grip on the armrest and enjoyed the rest of the flight. She made four more flights to America after that. She had four children living in America, each with their own family--mine, Marie Kreutzjans, Agnes Wessels, and my youngest brother, John, so we were able to keep her pretty busy. She also had a number of grandchildren in America and she thoroughly enjoyed meeting them. She kept track of each after she returned home. She was enjoying the fruits of her labor, raising all us children in Lorup.

One of Mom's trips to Kentucky was on the occasion of her ninetieth birthday. I realized that hers was on the exact same day as Henry Stark, a good friend of mine who had also been a builder. We were both members of Summit Hills Country Club. Since he was a widower and also ninety, I called and asked him what he was doing for his birthday. He said, "Nothing special, Matth. Why?"

I'd like you to join Laverne and myself for dinner at Summit. By the way, I have a date lined up for you."

"A date? What are you taking about, Matth?"

"Well, my mother is visiting, and her birthday is on the same day as yours. We'll all celebrate together."

I could tell Henry was excited at the prospect of going out. "That sounds great, Matth. I'm looking forward to it."

That Friday we all met at Summit Hills. They had a band playing and it was a beautiful evening. Mom and Henry couldn't speak to each other without me translating but both seemed to be having a wonderful time. Finally, Henry asked my mother to dance. I don't think she had done that for decades. At ninety years of age they both enjoyed themselves tremendously on the dance floor. I reminded me of the first time I danced with Laverne at the Fenwick Club in Cincinnati. It brought great joy to my heart watching my mother having so much fun that evening.

Mom's last visit to see us was at the time of her ninety-third birthday. We had a birthday celebration at our home. Being a devoted Catholic, she was proud to have the Bishop Ackerman of Covington attend. For her it was a great honor.

Mom's 93rd birthday celebration at our house. From left to right:
Laverne, Me, Marie Kreutzjans, Nick Kreuitzjans, the Bishop's driver, Father Smith, my
mother Anna, Agnes Wessels, Bishop Ackerman, Ben Wessels, Judith Toebben, John
Toebben

The last time I saw my mother she was ninety-seven years old. She was still strong for her age but was showing signs of her advancing years. Life had taken its toll but hadn't taken anything away from her indomitable spirit and stubborn determination. We went to the St. Marian cemetery to visit the graves of my father and my siblings. As we walked along, side-by-side, she held my arm for support. Though her mind was sharp, physically she wasn't as strong as she once was. Her feet tended to shuffle a little. When we reached Dad's grave, we stopped to say a small prayer.

Cemetery along the side of St. Marian's Church where my siblings and father
are buried

I asked her, "Mom, what's it like to have been around so many years, to have seen so many incredible changes take place in Germany? Has it been a little sad for you?"

She reached over and brushed a few leaves off Dad's headstone and patted the cold surface gently, just as she patted his warm shoulder on many occasions in the past. There were no tears, but I could tell by the look in her eyes, she still missed him terribly. Theirs was a quiet, enduring love not disrupted by the many outside influences of modern life. After a minute, she answered my question. "Sad? Sometimes, I guess. I've seen my share of both good and bad over the years, Matthias. I've lost a lot of friends and family members along the way. Mostly it's been good, though. I still see every day as a blessing from God." She paused for a second, looked at Dad's headstone once more, and added, "I'm looking forward to enjoying another blessing tomorrow."

The statement pretty much reflected the inner strength of spirit that was so typical of my mother, always seeking the positive in each situation. She was very much like Laverne in that regard. Mom left this world three years later, just a couple months shy of her one-hundredth birthday. I miss both her and Dad still. They had an uncommon strength of character and resolve which I can only hope to ever achieve.

GENEALOGY

After seeing where I had grown up in Germany, Laverne realized that she didn't know much about the Huber family history. She only knew that their ancestors had emigrated from somewhere in Germany, but had no idea about what city or region it might have been. I believed it was important for us and our children to know about her roots. It helped to establish one's identity, so Laverne and I hired a genealogist to outline her family tree. She discovered that their original family was from Wilfingen, near the Black Forest area of southern Germany. The genealogist compiled a report that contained some general information, but the only actual name the report provided was a man by the name of Adam Huber. We needed to know more so I called the mayor of Wilfingen and explained that I was looking for the family of Adam Huber.

"Huber, Huber, Huber," the mayor kept saying as he tried to recollect. All at once he said, "Yes, I've heard of him. There were two brothers who went to the United States in the early 1800s. One went to Indiana somewhere and the other wound up in Cincinnati. No one had heard much from them since." In those days, travel across the Atlantic was treacherous and involved six weeks on a boat with poor living conditions. That's why people seldom returned to Germany once they left.

I was shocked that this man was aware of the history of a family that had left his small town over a hundred years ago. I guess it was so small, the travels of anyone adventurous enough to brave the difficult journey became part of the local folklore. I told the mayor that my wife and I would like to travel to Wilfingen to find her relatives. I told him I would appreciate anything he could do to help us out.

Laverne's parents Pearl and Adam Huber, on the day of our
daughter Susan's First Communion

In 1955, my friend Ralph Drees and his wife Irma joined Lavern and me as we flew to Germany. We rented a car and drove through the Black Forest, a place as mysterious as it was beautiful. When we arrived in Laverne's family's home town of Wilfingen , I stopped in front of a local church and spoke to an elderly man who was walking along the side of the road. I figured he was old enough to know something about the history of the families living there. "Have you ever heard of a family by the name of Huber?"

"Why, yes. They live right there," he said as he pointed to a lovely old farmhouse directly across the street. It had to have been built in the early part of the nineteenth century. I couldn't believe our luck to have found Laverne's family this quickly. We parked the car and knocked on the home's front door. An elderly woman answered and looked stunned to see several strangers standing before her. She didn't invite us in. After I explained why we were there she replied, "I married into the Huber family years ago. I'm not aware of any other Hubers living nearby. I'm not even sure we are the family you're looking for. Huber is a pretty common name in Germany, you know." I could tell the woman didn't trust these four strangers standing on her door step.

Laverne and I in Wilfingen, tracing the Huber family roots

"Yes, I'm aware of that but my wife and I were just hoping you could help us. She would like to learn more about her German ancestry."

The elderly woman paused to consider my request. She said, "My husband will be home in several hours. Maybe you can return later and perhaps he can help." She closed the door and locked it without saying another word.

We left to find a place for lunch and tour Wilfingen. We returned a little after three that afternoon. A man in his sixties with thinning grey hair greeted us at the front door. He was more gracious than his wife and invited us to come in and have a seat. I took a few minutes to explain why we were there.

"Give me a minute," he said and disappeared up a flight of wooden stairs. We could hear him rummaging around on the second floor, apparently moving boxes around. When he came back, he was carrying an old book. He set it down on a small coffee table with the gentle care someone would give to a rare artifact. It smelled musty and the leather binding was worn. "This is a history of the Huber family. It goes back several hundred years." He carefully opened it and I could see the pages were yellowed with age. They looked so brittle that they might disintegrate if touched. He did so with respect for the history that was contained inside. He looked up and asked, "Now when did you say those two brothers left for the United States?"

I told him as much as we knew, and he again began to leaf through the pages. He paused on one and read more closely. "Yes, yes! Here they are: Joseph and Herman Huber. They left Germany in April of 1843. The family lived directly across the street, right next door to the church. It's a vacant lot now but it used to be a farm. The only remaining brother inherited it but never married. When he died, the home fell into disrepair and the house was torn down." He searched through the book for several more minutes and said, "There are a few more names here but I'm afraid that's all I have for you. There is no mention of an Adam Huber."

I wrote down the names. Laverne and I continued with our search, but we had hit a dead-end and it was time to return home. We were both disappointed, but we weren't about to give up. Using the names the man had given me, I continued to make calls to Germany from the U.S. and finally found what we were looking for. It was a family that knew all about the history of Joseph and Herman coming to America. I made arrangements to meet with them.

———————————————— ◆•◦•◆ ————————————————

The following year Laverne and I returned to Wilfingen. We drove past the same house where we had spoken to the elderly couple the previous year and proceeded to an address that had been given to me by the mayor. It was several kilometers away, through farm country. We crested a hill and had a panoramic view of a lush green valley laid before us. In the distance, we could make out a large group of people standing in the roadway.

"I wonder what that's all about," said Laverne.

As we drew closer, we realized it was Laverne's family, waiting for us to arrive. There had to be fifty of them, each waving a small American flag. Laverne was so happy she started to cry. They welcomed us into their homes and fed us as we all shared stories about life in Germany and America. One of the girls was getting married the following day and we were invited to attend the wedding. All the guests were anxious to hear about America. We spent hours talking to everyone, while I served as an interpreter. It was difficult for Laverne because she couldn't speak German very well but, regardless, we all had a wonderful time together with her family. It was comforting for Laverne to finally discover her history. She tried to remain in touch with many of them over the following years.

COUNTRY SQUIRE ESTATES

Over the next decade I purchased more land around our Crescent Springs farm until I had accumulated over three hundred fifty acres. I-75 was being completed. That brought more home buyers to Northern Kentucky, but the old single-lane Buttermilk Pike couldn't handle the load. It was widened to two lanes, but it wasn't long before it was again becoming too congested. Fortunately, Governor John Y. Brown and the State of Kentucky decided to widen it to a four-lane highway. That and its proximity to the interstate made Crescent Springs one of the most ideal places to live in Greater Cincinnati. It was within ten minutes of most desirable features in downtown, but without the associated traffic and social problems of a large city. Fortside was pretty much half complete so we decided it was time to start development of Country Squire Estates, our most ambitious project to date. It gave us the opportunity to begin my dream of constructing larger, more elaborate homes on generous-sized lots, much like we did for Dr. Redden ten years previous.

The entrance road was constructed in the early seventies and we named it Rosewood Drive. The engineer outlined lots, each containing around two hundred feet of frontage along the road. The first house was designed to be a showcase model home. It was a single-story, eight-room house with three bathrooms. I went to California to purchase a large heart-shaped bathtub. The walls behind the tub were mirrored while a large crystal chandelier was suspended directly over it. The overall appearance was stunning, and the people of Northern Kentucky had never seen anything quite like the home before. We opened it up for a public showing and on the first day it was purchased by a man named Robert

Tarvin. My sister Agnes and her husband purchased the second lot and I believed that Country Squires Estates was well on its way.

When things are cruising along too well, life has a tendency to throw a few speed bumps in your path. The Toebben Company was no exception. Our elation over the initial success in our new development soon dissolved over the following several months. We had an extra-large lot situated behind a lake on Rosewood. A gentleman from Cincinnati contracted with us to build "One of the biggest homes in the Northern Kentucky." He wanted it to be a ten-thousand-square-foot, single-story ranch with a maid's quarters over an attached three-car garage. The basement would contain its own bowling alley and entertainment area. Everything was to be "first-class." Once the architectural drawings were complete and approved by the buyer, we began construction. We worked on that house day and night for months to get it finished on schedule. By the time it was finally under roof, I had already invested a substantial amount of money into the project. It was time for the owner to pay his next construction draw. The check didn't arrive, but I was patient because I knew the man's background and believed he was good for it. After several more weeks, I started getting a little nervous but continued to wait. By then the costs kept accruing and I was spending more money every day the keep the project moving forward. Before long, the man owed me a huge amount. When I tried to call him on the phone, he didn't answer. That was a bad sign.

I kept calling until finally, he picked up the phone. It was early afternoon, but he sounded drunk when he said, "I just filed for bankruptcy this morning and I can't pay you." He hung up the phone and that was it, no explanation and no apology. I was left standing there, still holding the receiver in my hand. When I tried to call back, he refused to answer. It was like someone had just punched me in the stomach. I was devastated. Here I was with a substancial amount of my own money already invested in the largest home in the area and had no prospective buyer for it. The prospects for finding one were slim. The cost would be prohibitively more than most people could afford.

That night I didn't sleep a wink. I tossed and turned and eventually got up and started thinking about the problem. Our company had done well in Fortside, so we had a little financial cushion. Just the same, failure to sell this house would be a huge drain on our bottom line and would set a bad precedent for Country Squire. I couldn't allow it to be thought of as the community so expensive, it bankrupted the home buyers. I struggled to figure out a way to get myself out of this mess. I remembered what my father had always told me when I faced serious problems with my asthma as a child. He said, "Don't let anything stop you, Matth. When you're down, just stand up and push forward." I considered the situation for a while and that's what I decided to do, push forward. I wasn't just going to try to minimize my losses. I was going to turn this mistake into a success. This house wasn't going to be a problem for me anymore but rather it would become an opportunity. I simply didn't know how I was going to make that happen yet.

The following month I went to the Home Builders Convention in Las Vegas to try to get some ideas. It was a huge show and there were vendors from all over the country. They were showing things that had never been seen before in the Greater Cincinnati area. I spoke to other upscale builders from around the country to see what they were doing. That's when I learned that a builder couldn't make a name for himself simply with superior workmanship and larger homes. People wanted more, so I decided to recreate the entire home buying experience. I planned to establish a culture whereby a home was more than just a house. It would be an extension of one's personality, a reflection of one's own status in the community. That meant I had to spend a lot more money to create a dramatic showcase. I purchased all the newest high-tech conveniences to finish the kitchen and bathrooms. Most people wanted glitz and that's what I was going to give them. The master bath was adorned with large mirrors and gold fixtures. A huge crystal chandelier was hung in the dining room. We raised the entrance foyer ceiling several feet and accented it with ornate moldings. We hung another chandelier in there, creating a grand entrance space when prospective buyers walked in. Then we invested a huge amount of money to furnish the rooms and staged the home to look like a Hollywood estate. Even the maid's quarters were decorated with the finest furniture. With its setting behind the landscaped lake, the house spectacular.

I also realized that the opening had to be turned into more of a prestigious social event because this would set the stage for the construction of future estate-style homes. We wanted to set the bar far above what anyone had previously done for a home show. Formal invitations were sent out to hundreds of individuals, professionals, corporate CEOs, and real estate company owners. Advertising was purchased. On the day of the scheduled showing, my staff served wine and cheese to the guests. We had music playing in the background. The turnout was well beyond our expectations. Within a half hour, a corporate executive and his wife from Cincinnati approached me and inquired how much I was asking for the home. I gave him a price that I thought was an exorbitant amount, thinking that we would negotiate down from there. Without hesitating, he accepted the offer, pulled out his checkbook, and handed me a sizable down payment. We closed within the month. We had interest expressed by over a dozen more potential buyers. My gamble to invest more into the house had paid off. I learned that people were willing to pay top price not just for superior quality, but also image. It was a great day. Country Squires Estates was again back on track and demand for our custom homes exploded. It was the Toebben Company's signature project that would continue to keep us busy for the next forty years.

———————————◆◦◆———————————

Laverne and I enjoyed our beautiful home on Susan Lane in Fort Mitchell, but our family had grown to five children. Some were teenagers and that made things a little tight. We decided to set aside eight acres on Rosewood in Country Squire to build again. This would become our final dream home where we would raise our children to be adults. I designed a nine-thousand-square-foot house with five bedrooms and six bathrooms.

Our dream home in Country Squire

The front door was shipped to Uruguay where a local craftsman hand-carved the Toebben Family crest into the outside facing. I wanted to replicate the German feel of my childhood home in Lorup, so I arranged to have large wooden beams installed in the ceilings of the kitchen, foyer, family room, and my study. The wood was rough when it was delivered so we proceeded to hand hew each one of them in the garage. It was a great deal of work but well worth it. We installed detailed custom wood cabinetry in the kitchen and bathrooms. Swarovski Strass crystal chandeliers were ordered from Austria and an antique marble fireplace was imported from an old German castle along the Rhine River.

The front door showcasing our family crest

There was a double-door walkout to a large patio and pool. Along one side, I built a shuffleboard court and a gazebo. Laverne and the children loved the pool during the summers. Our children were still young when we moved in, so our house eventually became a social gathering place for their friends during their teen years. That was fine with Laverne and me because we always knew where they were. They were all great children, but it was nice not having to worry about them.

On the Fourth of July every year we would hang a large American flag in front. We'd have a family picnic in the back yard and watch fireworks. At Christmas, we held a Christmas celebration, an annual tradition until 2014. Laverne and the children would decorate the house in traditional German style. I can still smell the food cooking in the kitchen and the sounds of laughter filling the house. The screams of my grandchildren while they opened their gifts warmed my heart. My youngest daughter Elizabeth would play the piano while we all gathered around to sing Christmas carols. They are all sweet memories.

Laverne and me in front of our gazebo

COMMERCIAL DEVELOPMENT

We first entered the commercial development business at about the same time we started Country Squire. There was very little opportunity for any kind of shopping in Crescent Springs and the residents needed places to purchase groceries and other necessities. I thought it would be a good idea to build a nucleus around which other businesses could grow. I purchased four older homes on the corner of Buttermilk Pike and Anderson Road. The houses were torn down and we constructed our first shopping center. It contained a bank, drug store, restaurant, and other businesses. The center was an immediate success and became the springboard for the official formation of our commercial/industrial division that would eventually be managed by one of my sons. Over the subsequent years we continued to build shopping centers and professional buildings in Kentucky and throughout the Tri-state area. We now lease over eight-hundred-thousand square feet of space to over two hundred and sixty businesses. Eventually we purchased an old school building on Buttermilk Pike. Using it as a shell, the new five-story Toebben Building was constructed. It has housed a multitude of different businesses and offices as well as serving as our main corporate headquarters ever since.

One of the key factors in the growth of a community is the creation of jobs and nothing does that better than an influx of corporate development. When companies invest in a region, employment opportunities are created. This results in an increase in population and a proportionate increase in the demand for further businesses and construction. Development is the financial lifeblood of any community. Working under the direction of the regional Chamber of Commerce, the city of Florence, and the officials of Boone County, over one thousand acres of land near Mt. Zion Road were set aside for development. The result was the creation of the Florence Industrial Park, one of the largest such projects in Northern Kentucky at the time. The Toebben Corporation purchased an original two hundred acres and subsequently added more until we had four-hundred-fifty acres of land. Georgia Pacific committed to the first forty acres and FedEx wound up using a hundred acres. The result was an influx of multiple other companies, large and small. All in all, thousands of new jobs were created in our region.

Toebben Corporate Offices

I served two terms as President of the Northern Kentucky Home Builders Association and also served on the Board of the Northern Kentucky Chamber of Commerce. As a result of our company's ongoing growth in the construction sector, I was fortunate enough to be honored with the Spirit of Construction award in 2005. What made it so special for me was that the award was voted upon by my peers in the construction business from throughout the Tri-State area. I fully realize that any such recognition could have never occurred without the help of everyone at Toebben Construction who contributed so much to make the company achieve a level of success that was well beyond my expectations.

Ground breaking ceremony for the Toebben Industrial Park in Florence, Kentucky

BLINDSIDED

Like much bad news, it came in the form of an unexpected phone call. I was in the on-site construction office, a trailer in Country Squire, when the phone rang. It was Laverne and her voice sounded a little shaky. I knew she had a doctor's appointment that day, so I was a little worried when she said, "Matth, we need to talk. Could you come home?"

"I'll be right there." The office was only a few minutes from our house, so I dropped everything I was working on and jumped into the car. I was worried but Laverne was only thirty-seven years old, so I figured how bad could it be? When I opened the door and saw her face, I knew it was bad.

"The doctor found a lump in my breast."

"A lump?" I paused for a second to process the information. "Does he think it's cancer?"

"He can't tell for sure, but he's concerned enough that he wants to arrange for a biopsy and some tests."

That was the beginning of a four-and-a-half-year emotional rollercoaster ride. The procedure was performed by a surgeon at St. Elizabeth's Hospital in Northern Kentucky. When we met with the doctor to discuss the biopsy results, he confirmed that the lump, was in fact, cancer. The word seemed to suck the air out of our lungs. Laverne and I were both so devastated, we didn't hear half of what the doctor said for the next few minutes. It was important information, but we missed it. The doctor understood. He had seen the same reaction many times before with other cancer victims, so he was very patient with us.

"Where do we go from here, doc?" I asked. "Surgery?"

He paused for a second and I could tell from the look in his eyes that it wasn't good. "Like I said, the tests show that the tumor has already metastasized throughout the body. I'm sorry but I'm afraid surgery isn't an option in this case. The cancer is too widespread to remove. The only thing I can offer is chemotherapy."

"But you can cure it, right?"

"I'm afraid not, Mr. Toebben. It's incurable."

Laverne and I were beyond belief. We were speechless, searching for some small amount of good news. There would be none.

Finally, Laverne asked the obvious question. "How long do I have?"

"With the chemotherapy, I'd estimate about six months."

Laverne is normally a strong, upbeat woman, but this was too much. We both got teary eyed and I can't remember much about what was said during the rest of the visit. Once you hear the word cancer, things start to blur. We both felt helpless. When we got home that day, she looked at me with tears in her eyes. "Matth, what about the children? How are we going to take care of them?" That was typical of Laverne. Her first thoughts weren't of herself but her children. I hugged her hard and said, "We're going to get through this thing. I'm going to take care of this somehow. I promise you." I prayed to God for help.

I have always been a problem solver, the one who could make things happen, but now I was powerless and didn't know what to do. I didn't know how I could possibly keep my promise to her. We needed a miracle. I decided to call a few of my physician friends. I had built homes for many of them, and Dr. Redden was the first to call me back. He asked me what the problem was, and I explained everything to him. He said, "Matth, I'm sure you already realize how bad this situation is. There's only one suggestion I can give you, and that is to take Laverne to the MD Anderson Hospital in Houston, Texas. They have some of the best cancer experts in the world."

John called them and made arrangements for us to get in to see one of their specialists right away. The doctors reviewed the biopsy slides, did a lot of CT scans and X-rays. Several days later a group of them met with us. They agreed with the doctors at St. Elizabeth. It was widely metastatic breast cancer and there was no hope for a cure. They also estimated that she probably had only six months to live. Laverne and I were devastated all over again. We came here with a glimmer of hope, only to see those hopes dashed.

Then one of them said, "We could try entering you into one of our research programs."

Laverne and I looked at each other, confused. We talked to them for a while to see what their program was all about. They said it was strictly an investigational protocol that would involve some aggressive chemotherapy combinations that had not been tried on actual patients thus far. They warned that it would be unpleasant and somewhat risky because of the potency of the medications. There was even the risk of death. Laverne and I discussed it together and decided a little hope was better than no hope at all. They began the treatments several days later. It was tough going and the drugs made her terribly ill. After Laverne received the first series of agents she was allowed to return to Kentucky. The doctors spoke to the oncologists at St. Elizabeth and instructed them on the details of the protocol. She received the treatments twice a week. The hospital was close to home, but the process was still very hard on both of us. I hated to see her going through all the pain and vomiting. She didn't complain, though. That's the way she was, always tried to be positive.

She almost immediately lost her hair. Like most women, that upset her more than the treatments. I did a little research and found a store in Florence that sold wigs. I said, "Let's drive there and see what they have." We found the place and the lady was a big help. Laverne selected two wigs. When we got home, she tried them on and looked in the mirror. "Oh my gosh, Matth. That looks pretty good. In fact, I think it actually looks better than my normal hair." She thanked me and gave me a hug. It felt good to see her happy again.

We continued to travel back and forth to MD Anderson multiple times over the next twelve months. She had already lived six months beyond what they had predicted, and I could tell they were surprised to see Laverne doing so well. From time to time, they would adjust her treatment regimen depending upon the size of the tumors in her body. The entire process continued to be extremely painful. Her left arm swelled to twice its normal size. Regardless of her condition, she tried to maintain a positive attitude. She remained as active as possible and participated in a number of charity and community programs for the next four years.

MD Anderson sent a letter saying it was time for another follow-up battery of tests. Traveling back and forth to Houston was getting to be too difficult for Laverne and we were going to have to wait several months before everything could be scheduled. We spoke to her local oncologist at and asked if the tests could be performed here. They agreed.

Afterward, we met with the oncologist at St. Elizabeth. She sat us down in her office and said, "We have some great news. We can't find any evidence of cancer anywhere in her body."

"Are you sure?" asked Laverne.

"Absolutely. It's almost a miracle given the extent of her original disease. We should probably schedule some follow up tests in another six months, but as long as you continue to do so well you won't have to return to Houston."

It was, in fact, the miracle we had prayed for. We both wept tears of joy. Laverne was so happy that now she would be able to see her children and grandchildren grow up. That was a great moment in our family's life. You never appreciate someone as much as you should until you face the possibility of losing them. We could now look forward to growing old together. We didn't realize then that there would be a price to pay down the road.

INTERSTATE INVESTMENT

When I returned from our last trip to Europe with the children, I remembered my experiences on the Autobahn. It was the precursor to our own interstate system in the United States. Once on the road, there were few chances for travelers to get gas and food. I thought about this for a short while and decided it might present an excellent business opportunity. A few weeks later I drove to the Ohio Department of Highways in Lebanon. I met with the regional director and asked him about my idea. I wanted to build areas for gas stations and restaurants along the Interstate Highway, just like I had seen along the Autobahn in Germany.

He said, "Sorry, Mr. Toebben. We're not planning to do things that way. We will construct occasional rest areas with bathrooms, but we have no plans for what you have in mind."

I thought for a second and said, "Well, how are all those people traveling along the expressway going to get their gasoline and food?"

"They can simply get off on one of the interchanges and drive to the nearest town or wherever else they can find what they need."

He kind of burst my bubble and I set my ideas aside for a week or so. I couldn't get one thing off my mind. If you construct an interstate expressway system to promote rapid travel between cities, why force people to drive miles out of their way just to get gas. That made no sense to me, but I learned that the government seldom did things in the most logical or efficient way. It kept eating at me, so I decided to drive back to Lebanon to study the proposed sites for I-75. It was all public information, so the plans were readily accessible. I learned that the highway department had already staked out the route from Cincinnati to Dayton. I noticed that, on average, twelve hundred feet on either side of the proposed center line would be owned by the government and that's where they would build necessary fences. The state of Ohio was in the process of buying up the land for the project, leaving the land on either side as private property. I made note of the locations where the interstate would intersect existing roads and made my decision.

I went back to my banker, Harry Humpert, president of First National Bank. I explained what I wanted to do.

His response was, "Matth, this could be expensive. Are you sure you want to do it?"

"Absolutely," I replied. "This is going to be one of the most successful business ventures I've ever undertaken."

"Well you've never failed before Matth, and you certainly have the reserves to cover the loan. How much do you need?"

"I want a hundred thousand now to purchase options and then more as I actually close on the properties. If I'm wrong about this, I can pay back the loan."

We talked a little bit longer and Harry wished me good luck. The necessary funds were in my business account the following day. Every Thursday after that I followed the map of the proposed expressway and looked for the surveyor's flags. That indicated the center line. Then I would step off the twelve hundred feet and I would find out what farmer owned that land along the future exit ramps. I would knock on his door and try to buy up to ten acres. The land was selling for around $600 an acre and that would eat up my one hundred thousand in short order. Instead I purchased options to buy and that allowed me to avoid tying up too much cash until we closed. I did this all the way up from Cincinnati to Dayton, Ohio. I eventually extended my searches for land into the surrounding states.

I spent the entire $100,000 and controlled just over two hundred options to purchase almost any significant interchange land along the entire I-75/71 corridor in Ohio and Kentucky and I-64 in Indiana. I expected the future value of the land to be a hundred times that amount, but I was still taking a substantial risk. If the state decided to change the proposed interstate route, I would sustain a loss. Is was during this process that I met Mr. Harry Martineau. He was the founder and sole owner of M&M Realty, one of the largest real estate companies in Ohio at the time. He had facilitated the purchase of a piece of land for me along Reed-Hartman Highway in Blue Ash, a community just north of Cincinnati, but he was unaware of my reasons for the land acquisition. Several years later, I got an interesting call from my friend Harry. "Matth, I finally figured out why you were interested in buying up land options. You're working on the proposed expressway system. I think it's a great idea. I've sold

M&M and have some time on my hands. I'd like to learn more about what you're doing."

I told him we should get together for lunch and discuss it. We met at the Carrousel Restaurant in Cincinnati and I explained my plan. He said, "Matth, do you mind if I tag along with you on your Thursday trips looking for land? I'd like to learn more about it and maybe I can offer you some advice."

"Sure. It'll be nice to have someone to talk to while I'm traveling around the state." Every Thursday after that we would meet for breakfast and then head out to follow the backroads searching for any that might cross the future expressway. Harry helped me buy a number of properties and we got to be good friends. We stopped at a restaurant in Dayton for lunch one day and I explained a problem that had developed. "Harry, I've exercised a number of my options and things are going pretty well, but some them are about to expire and I'm not sure what to do. Should I just let them lapse?"

"Matth, you ought to sell those properties while you still control the options. Right now, they should yield a pretty good price. Once they expire, the land will be worthless as far as you're concerned."

"Yeah, you're right Harry, but I don't have the time to do that. I have a construction business to run."

"Selling property is what I used to do, Matth. I was good at it. You want me to try to take care of them for you?"

"Wow, that would be great, Harry." I wasn't expecting much because there was only a four-week window before the options expired. Two weeks after our lunch in Dayton, Harry called. "Matth, I sold two of your properties and I have interest in several more."

I realized this guy was a good salesman. I hadn't paid him anything. He just enjoyed the action in real estate sales. I thought about it for several weeks and decided Harry would make a great partner, so I gave him a call. "Harry, I know I haven't paid you for all the work you've done thus far. I have an offer for you."

"What's that?"

"Running this interstate business is turning out to be too much for me right now. I have my construction business to manage and now I'm about to get involved in something else. I want to give you half of my interstate venture but in exchange I'd like you to manage the sales and leasing."

"I'd love to do it, Matth. I've been kind of bored ever since I sold my company."

We formed our partnership and it was working out just as I had hoped. We still went out most Thursdays to search for property, but it was getting to be more difficult. We had already purchased every attractive piece of land available within fifty miles of Cincinnati and we had to travel farther to find opportunities. We had been interested in a two-hundred-acre farm along the proposed route of I-70, north of Dayton. It was owned by Lucas and Debbie Vanpelt. We only needed about ten acres of the land, but they were insistent on selling the entire farm as one unit, and they were asking a high price for the land. We tried to purchase an option for the land, but they weren't interested. We visited them on several more occasions, but they stayed firm in their demands. Realizing the upside potential of the property, I made the decision to buy the entire farm. Harry and I drove up there for the third time to close the deal. When we walked in, they had us sit with them at their kitchen table. I began, "You struck a hard bargain, Lucas, but we've decided to buy your whole farm for the price you're asking."

Lucas had a serious look on his face when he replied, "I'm afraid you're a little too late, Mr. Toebben. We sold the property just last week to the Shell Oil Company."

I was shocked. Word must have gotten out and now we were competing with the big oil companies for land.

Harry asked, "Have you closed on the sale yet?"

"It's scheduled in two weeks. Why do you ask?" said Lucas.

"I'm just curious," replied Harry. "Do you mind if I take a look at your contract?"

"Certainly, but we already cashed a sizable security deposit. I'm afraid it's a done deal."

Harry interrupted him. "I've been in the real estate business in Ohio for over thirty years and I think I know the law better than many lawyers. I've never seen a contract I couldn't get a client out of. We might be willing to give you more money for the land than Shell offered."

I stopped him. "We're not going to do that, Harry. If they have a signed contract and have been given earnest money, then that's it. They have a deal. I'm not going to ask Lucas and Debbie to go back on their word." We left their home on friendly terms realizing that the oil companies had a lot more people on the ground. Harry and I were going to have to work twice as fast if we hoped to secure any more land.

There was another property I had to buy outright and after our VanPelt experience, decided we'd better jump on it immediately before any of the oil companies beat us to the punch. It was a two-hundred-acre farm where I-71 crossed State Route 73 near Wilmington, Ohio. Another nearby intersection of State Route 380 made the land twice as valuable. The land would offer sites for multiple exit ramps creating over a half-dozen corners for future gas station, hotel, and restaurant development. We wanted the property and were willing to pay whatever it took to get it. The owner's name was Emmet Bailey, a man who had been in the restaurant business for years. His family was pressuring him to get rid of their land. Just like the Vanpelts, they wanted to sell the entire farm, not just one parcel. That was going to be tough because I didn't want to commit that much money to the sale until I could be absolutely certain the government would not change the location of the interstate at the last minute. I asked Mr. Bailey how much he wanted for the land and he replied, "$1,000 an acre."

"A thousand dollars an acre! That adds up to two hundred thousand dollars total. That's twice what land is worth around here," I responded, trying my best to sound indignant. I had already decided we would buy the land even at twice that cost. It was too valuable to pass up.

Mr. Baily said, "That expressway is going to pass right through my land and that makes it worth the price. The government will be willing to pay a pretty hefty sum for the right-of-way." As we continued to negotiate, I could tell he was sizing me up. Because of my heavy German accent, he probably didn't think I knew what I was doing and that I couldn't possible afford his asking price.

"That's still a lot of money Mr. Bailey."

"I figured it might be too much for you."

I sat back and acted like I was thinking about things. I didn't want the man to raise the price if he thought I was too anxious to do the deal. At the right moment I said, "I'll tell you what. How about I give you five thousand dollars today and if I can't close in ninety days, you can keep the money."

From the look in his eye I could tell he didn't think there was any way I could close on a deal that size in three months. He was confident that he had just made an easy five grand on this immigrant. I didn't want him thinking about the issue any more, so I looked at Mr. Baily and said, "My partner Harry has a lot of experience in real estate. Why don't we have him draw up a purchase agreement? Your secretary can type it up and we can get it signed today."

We all signed the document and it was legally binding. Within the following sixty days Harry and I secured a commitment from Chevron Oil to buy one acre of the land for $76,000. Standard Oil committed to buy a site across the road for ninety thousand. I received the right-of-way payment offer from the Department of Highways for another forty. That put $206,000 in our pocket so I called Mr. Bailey and told him I was ready to close. I think he was a little surprised. He didn't believe I could come up with that kind of money so quickly, but I bought the entire 200 acre parcel of property for the agreed $200,000 without a dime coming out of my own pocket. Later I was able to sign long-term property leases with several more gas station chains. Except for the initial three acres of land right around the exchange, we still own that farm today. At closing, Mr. Bailey realized what I was doing. He went on to start purchasing interstate property on his own and became one of my toughest competitors.

I continued to sell or lease sites to oil companies, restaurants, and hotels along the Interstate throughout the Tri-state area. It turned out to be one of the most lucrative business ventures I had ever undertaken. I believe some individuals might have been a little jealous of that success. A few people, including some reporters, suggested that I might have had illegal access to confidential information prior to buying the land options. The local newspaper published a front-page story claiming that I had profited from what was tantamount to insider trading. They hadn't even spoken to me to get my input before the article was published. It was an outright lie and I called the newspaper to complain. They wanted the involved reporter to talk to me on the phone to clarify the story. They said they wanted to give me the opportunity to tell my side of the story. I had had enough experience with reporters in the past to know that the call would be a setup. They had a way of twisting information so that the words fit into the predetermined narrative they were trying to sell to the public. I refused to be interviewed over the phone, but I did offer to speak to the reporter on one condition: we had to meet face-to-face in my office. I wanted to be on my own turf and to look him directly in the eye.

A week later, the reporter showed up at my office as scheduled. He brought another person along for support. I think they might have been a little concerned about liability issues. That was good. I wanted them a little off balance. We all sat down at the table in my conference room, me on one side and the newspaper people on the other. I allowed them to grill and cross-examine me for about thirty minutes. It was difficult to hold my temper, but I had learned that it was best to smile and be friendly until you had to fight back.

By the time they were finished, they had nothing because there was no story there. I had successfully defended myself with facts. Then it was my turn. I leaned back in my chair and said, "Now if you are interested in the true story, here is what happened." I explained how I got the original idea while driving on the Autobahn in Germany. Then I explained how I was able to access everything I needed. "There was no inside information. Everything I uncovered about the expressway system was the result of my own research and was in the public domain. You check it out and you'll find out I'm right." I looked at the reporter in the eye and added, "It's something you should have done before you wrote your article. That was sloppy reporting. You'll find that the interstate information had been there for years and has been available to anyone who wanted to take the time to look into it. Nobody did because no one else thought about the business potential. Now, that's the story you can print. If you continue making your false and unfounded accusations, I'm going to sue you for malicious libel."

The reporter turned pale. He stood and said, "Thank you for your time, Mr. Toebben." He and his companion left without saying another word. They never retracted the story. I've never known a newspaper to openly admit it was wrong. It was a painful lesson for me. Newspapers and other media are protected by our constitution but too many of them abuse that right by sacrificing the truth in exchange for stories that generate increased subscriptions or ad revenue.

There is a sad note to the interstate leasing story. Harry Martineau and I got to be very good friends over the years. We would frequently confide in each other. Though Harry sold his M&M Realty company, he maintained a small real office on Harrison Avenue in Cincinnati. It was on one Thursday evening, when I noticed he was upset and distracted. "What's wrong, Harry?"

"You know about the office I've been keeping on the West Side?"

"Sure, you've mentioned it a few times."

"Well, I only have a staff of two people: a manager and a secretary. I found out that my manager has been embezzling money from me over the past year."

"That's horrible. How much did he steal?"

"Around $25 thousand."

"That's a lot of money, Harry. What are you going to do?"

"I already fired him, but I don't want to see him go to jail. I told him that if he paid back the money this month, I wouldn't report him to the police, but he said it was already gone. Then he warned me not to talk to the police."

"He threatened you?"

"That's the way I took it."

"Are you going to report it to the police?"

"I don't know, Matth. I just don't know."

A week later I received a call from Harry's wife. She said that she and Harry were eating breakfast a few days earlier when he received a phone call from his secretary. Someone wanted to meet with him about a farm they intended to sell on the western outskirts of Cincinnati. It was a sizable piece of property and was projected to be sold at a high price. It would generate a sizable commission and Harry was excited at the prospect of securing the listing. He was to meet his secretary at the Western Hills Shopping

Center and from there the two of them were supposed to drive to the property together.

Harry left for the meeting but never returned that night. His wife called the police. When they interviewed the secretary, she began crying. It only took a few minutes before she broke down and confessed to what had happened. She was romantically involved with Harry's office manager who had embezzled the money. She was driving Harry down River Road ostensibly on their way toward the property. Harry was in the passenger seat when she said she needed to pull over for a minute. Before the car came to a full stop, her boyfriend jumped out of some bushes and into the back seat of the car keeping a gun pointed at the back of Harry's head. Poor Harry had to know what was about to happen. It must have been terrifying.

I found out later that the boyfriend had three witnesses who stated that he was with them at the time of the murder. He was never successfully prosecuted for the killing but was convicted later of an unrelated crime. The girlfriend claimed that she didn't know what was going to happen. She said she was afraid for her life. No one was ever held accountable for Harry's death. The episode reinforced one unfortunate fact in my mind. Though our country has an excellent justice system, justice is not always served.

CARROLTON

Once Country Squire development was well underway, we had to give up our farm retreat. Laverne missed the weekend get-togethers with family and friends, while I missed the hunting opportunities. We shared many fond memories of those days and talked about ways to resurrect them. The answer came in the form of those unexpected phones call one afternoon in my office.

"Mr. Toebben, my name is Walter Peterson," the voice said.

"I'm afraid I don't know a Walter Peterson. What can I do for you?" I asked.

"I believe you own some land at the junction of I-71 and Route 227 near Carrolton."

Carrolton was a small city about sixty miles from Cincinnati at the confluence of the Kentucky and Ohio rivers. Interstate 71 runs through its southern border. "That's correct. I bought ninety acres there as an investment some years ago."

"Well sir, I'm calling to see if you would be willing to grant me permission to hunt deer on your land."

"I'm sorry to disappoint you, Mr. Peterson but there are no deer to hunt around there."

"You're probably not aware of this because I doubt anyone has asked your permission to hunt the land before, but there were three good-sized bucks taken at that exact location just last year. I've seen a lot of deer activity around the land, but I didn't want to trespass without your permission."

I was stunned to hear this. My friends and I had been traveling all the way to West Virginia every year to hunt and now this man was telling me that there were plenty of deer right on my own property, just sixty miles away. "I appreciate your call, Mr. Peterson but I'm an avid hunter and if the deer population there is that plentiful, I plan to hunt the land myself. You're welcome to join me and some of my friends if you like." He appreciated the offer but declined. I figured he might have felt like an outsider. "Well, the invitation is open if you ever change your mind," I said before ending the call.

A few weeks later, I put together a group including, Ben Wessels, Rudy Pohlabeln, and Gordon Martin. We had a great time together hunting the land that morning. That got me thinking about the possibility of accumulating more land in the area. The following weekend I decided to explore the region and after pulling down Whites Run Road, I saw a "For Sale" sign. It was a seventy-acre parcel of land and they were asking a fair price, so I bought it. About three months later another gentleman called me saying he was interested in selling seventy acres directly adjacent to the land I had just purchased. I bought that one and now owned one hundred forty acres in addition to my original ninety acres near the expressway. The week after closing on the land, I walked the property line and discovered many deer trails and rubs where bucks had been scraping trees, marking their territory. There were a lot more deer here than I had anticipated. I organized another hunt with several friends and family members. It was good day, but we heard a great deal of gunfire on the land next to mine. It was a little too close for comfort. I was concerned about all that shooting going on nearby and not knowing who they were or if they knew what they were doing. The wrong shot in the wrong direction could be disastrous.

I did some research and found that the land in question was a six-hundred-acre parcel owned by Mr. Ridley Stout, a banker from Carrolton. I called him and told him who I was.

"Are you the Matth Toebben from Northern Kentucky?" he asked.

I don't know how he knew me, but I replied, "Yes. The reason why I'm calling is that I purchased a hundred forty acres adjacent to your land and I would like to lease your property during the hunting season."

There was a pause before the man replied, "I'm sorry, Mr. Toebben but I can't lease that land to you. I run the Carrolton Bank and half the city hunts that property. If I lease that land to you, I'm afraid I'd upset too many people and lose many of my customers."

We talked for a few minutes about hunting and farming until he finally said, "I really don't want the property anymore. I can't take care of it properly. What I can do for you is to sell you the land outright. That way my customers can't complain."

I hadn't been expecting this, so it took me a few seconds to consider his offer. "What are you asking for all six hundred acres?" He told me, and it was too much.

"I'd love to buy your land, but I really don't want to spend that kind of money just to hunt." We ended the conversation on good terms, and I gave up on the idea.

About two weeks later Mr. Stout called me back. He dropped his asking price, but it was still much too high. I again declined and said, "Why don't you just go ahead and lease the land to me? That'll put some cash in your pocket, and you get to maintain ownership. I can't imagine your friends and customers could be that angry at you for leasing your own property."

"I'm sorry, Matth. I still can't do it. You don't know the people around here. After all these years of hunting the land they feel entitled to use it. I'm afraid that the only way you'll be able to hunt there is if you own the land outright." I stood my ground, but we still ended the call on friendly terms.

It took another six months before Mr. Stout called me for the third time. He cut a large amount from his asking price. Now it was an attractive proposal, and it presented an opportunity to own a substantial amount of land in the region. I said, "Why don't I drive down there and we can discuss this over lunch." I wanted to see the property, so after eating we walked around the land for a while. Mr. Stout couldn't point out exactly where the property lines were located, but there was no doubt, it was a large tract of land. We negotiated a little and I agreed to purchase the land. That increased my holdings in Carrolton to 740 acres. After that I kept purchasing surrounding farms until Laverne and I owned fifteen hundred acres of beautiful land. One of the farms came with an existing house, several barns, and twenty head of cattle. I hired a farm manager to help organize everything.

Most of the land was heavily wooded and the rest had been cleared for raising crops. The problem was that the property had been neglected for over twenty years and was now overgrown. The previous owners had failed to follow proper crop rotation schedules so most of the top soil had eroded away. I shipped a bulldozer down there and spent six months clearing the land, so we could plant clover, grass, and other food for the deer and livestock. We constructed roads, several equipment sheds and more barns, one with a concrete floor so we could hold parties after a long day of hunting.

One of our annual hunting trips in Carrollton with family and friends

I had a special double wide trailer home shipped in from Indiana and placed it on a concrete pad. Directly in front of the home we created a large lake by means of a thirty-foot-tall dam. Before the lake filled with water, we built a twenty by fifty-foot swimming pool area with concrete along one side. It was separated from the rest of the lake with a galvanized pipe fence. A bridge leads to an island with a gazebo for fishing. Much to my surprise, my new lake soon sprung a leak and wouldn't fill completely. The soil was too rocky, and the water kept finding a way around the stone, so I had a 100 by 200-foot rubber mat made and tucked that in along the dam as a barrier. The leak problem was solved.

Weekend family fun at the Carrolton farm

The Carrolton property became the new gathering place for the Toebben family and our friends. We had grill-outs and picnics almost every weekend just like we had done on the Crescent Springs family retreat. Laverne and I enjoyed endless hours hiking with our grandchildren and watching them fish in the lake. As they all grew older, they developed an interest in four-wheelers, so we carved miles of track through the woods and fields for them to ride. The trails also provided access for fence maintenance.

Riding horses with my daughter, Elizabeth, and John's daughter, Hannah

One of the older barns was about to collapse so my two sons John and Bill decided to build a saloon out of the lumber. It has a stone fireplace, a bar, and swinging doors just like the saloons you see in old western movies. They even bought an old piano to place inside. Just across from the saloon they constructed a cabin and a big stone pit for grilling. The boys held some grand grill-outs of their own.

The Moose Saloon built by John and Bill. Sitting on the porch: Laverne and Irma Drees

When I first purchased the land there was a great deal of timber on it. Over half the trees were ash. I hadn't planned on harvesting the timber until I read an article in a farming trade magazine. There was a huge problem with something called the emerald ash borer. It was a small beetle than wound up coming to America through the importation of infested lumber from Asia. The females laid their eggs in the tree bark and then the hatched larvae would feed on the wood underneath. The result was a dead tree and at the time there was nothing that could be done about it. The magazine report stated that the infestation was following the interstate system as contaminated lumber was being transported along the highways. We were less than a mile or so from I-71 so I was looking at the impending loss of thousands of trees, some of them so big a bulldozer couldn't knock them over. I walked the land and thought, *I just can't let all of this go to waste.*

I discovered that a new saw mill had just started up only about a mile from my land. When I told the owner that I had over twelve hundred wooded acres of land that close, he jumped at the opportunity to log the farm. He put three crews in there and they worked two full years, harvesting the ash trees. They didn't cut anything with a trunk size less than ten inches in diameter. Those trees were left behind and, as expected, all have fallen victim to the ash borer. Hundreds of trees died and now fall over without warning, creating a dangerous situation. I'm just thankful that I stumbled across that article. Otherwise, more trees would have died for nothing.

While surveying the damage a year later, I was astonished to see how the woods had already begun to replenish themselves. Every few feet a new sapling was springing up. It illustrated how life has its own way of recovering from almost any devastation. It'll be interesting to see if the new ash trees survive the infestation in the years to come.

PAINTSVILLE AND THE MINE

The interstate venture left the Toebben Company with a great deal of surplus cash in its accounts. I was only 39 years old and I was looking for something to do with the extra money. I still enjoyed designing residential homes, but the building business had become automatic. It almost ran itself so there wasn't the same level of challenge as when the business began. In addition, the Toebben Company was solely involved in the real estate world in one way or another, be it construction or the leasing of land and office space. It made us somewhat vulnerable to anything that might adversely affect that business sector, such as sharp increases in interest rates or the price of building supplies. Essentially, all our eggs were in one basket. I decided it would be a good idea to diversify so when the possibility of an entirely new business opportunity was brought to me, I was excited at the prospect. It looked like it could be a long-term source of cash flow for the family, and I had always been a long-range planner. In retrospect, I wish I had stuck with what I knew best.

I receive a call from Bob Appelman. I knew him fairly well because he had done a lot of trucking and excavating work for me in the past. He said, "Matth, I'd like to have lunch with you this week. I have something I want to run past you."

"Sure," I said, curious as to what Bob had in mind. We met for lunch at Frisch's restaurant and after a little small talk about business and families, I said, "Bob, what did you want to talk about?"

"I'm looking for a partner to join me in the coal mining business."

This caught me by surprise. I replied, "A partner for what?"

"Coal mining. I need somebody with money because I'd like to buy this coal mine operation in Paintsville. I think it would be a great opportunity."

He described everything to me over the next hour. The proposal was to purchase the White Ash Mining Company in Paintsville, Kentucky. It was reasonably profitable business owned by a man named Willard Castle and his two brothers. They reportedly had a good reputation as coal mine operators. The purchase included three thousand acres of land with one deep mine operation. There were multiple superficial coal seams of varying thickness. They had not yet been mined. Most were so thin the only way to effectively work them was through an approach from above ground.

I told Bob I needed to think the matter over for a few days, knowing that this could be the source of diversification I was looking for. However, I knew absolutely nothing about the mining industry, and I wanted to do some homework. After a few phone calls and several days of background research, I called Bob and said, "Maybe we can do this, but first we have to look into it some more."

The mine was about 130 miles southeast of Cincinnati, so we decided to drive down there to check things out. We met the owners, the three Castle brothers. Willard was the head man who ran the deep mine. He seemed to be an honest and forthright guy. He told us about the mine and showed us around only a small section of the three thousand acres because much of the land was inaccessible by road. The coal under the land was a good, high-quality bituminous product. The mine had its own rail siding and tipple operation for separating the coal by size and loading it into railroad cars. The railroad siding could handle twenty-five rail cars at a time which was a great deal of coal being shipped out every day. I was concerned that operations would be a problem, but Willard Castle agreed to remain with us to manage the day to day business.

Tipple Operation

We returned home where I mulled over the coal mine proposal in my mind for a few weeks. I considered the upside advantages and downside risks. With the present price levels of coal, it looked like an excellent investment, but it only made sense if we could mine the shallow veins. One problem was that neither Bob nor I knew anything about mining. The good thing was that we would have Willard to run things locally while I could monitor the bottom line from my Northern Kentucky office. That way, the mine wouldn't take time away from my family and other business interests. I decided to do it, but first I had to have another look. I returned and spent two more weeks going over their operation and reviewing their books with my accountant.

Everything looked to be legitimate and in solid financial condition. The price of coal at the time was stable at nine dollars a ton, and at that price we could make a decent profit. One factor that made the purchase more attractive was that it included the surface ownership of the three thousand acres. The land was almost completely covered by white oak trees which produced a beautiful lumber. I could envision the future of white oak logging on the land. That would help us recoup some of the purchase price. After several weeks of negotiations, we agreed to buy the mine for four million dollars in cash. It would turn out to be one of the biggest mistakes of my life.

◆◦◆

We had about two hundred men working on the deep mine, but to make any decent profit we had to retrieve the coal from the shallower seams. The only practical way to access them was through strip-mining. We went through the lengthy process of securing the necessary engineering studies and permits from the state, but we didn't have the equipment we needed for stripping. I secured a loan for six million dollars from GE Capital and used the money to purchase large bulldozers, front loaders, and other heavy mining equipment. We set up a company that owned the machinery and then leased it to White Ash Mining so everything would cash flow. We were making decent money with just the deep mine operation. It provided the highest quality coal and kept us in a positive cash flow position while we continued to work on the strip-mining permits.

My previous belief that I could run the company from home turned out to be a wrong assumption. Within a year of closing the deal, the Federal Government enacted the Federal Mine Safety and Health Act. It seemed like a fair bill to protect the miners. That was fine with us and we fully expected to meet its provisions, but shortly afterward I got an urgent call from Bob Appelman. "Matth, they're shutting down our operation!"

"What? Who is 'they'?"

"We were visited by a number of federal inspectors yesterday and they shut us down until we can make the required changes in how we do things. It's the new Federal Mine Act."

"Well, we already plan to do that, but it'll take time. That's time we can't afford to lose. Why can't we continue running and bring everything up to par while we continue to operate?"

"I asked them that and they said no. I offered to make any and all changes to bring us into compliance with the new law as soon as we can, but they won't agree. They're shutting us down today."

I didn't know which way to go. It didn't make any sense to me. The government was going to put over two hundred men out of work. The bill was supposed to protect the miners, not starve them out of their homes. The more government bureaucrats get involved in things, the more they can mess up people's lives. It's like President Reagan used to joke, "Some of the most dangerous words in the English language are, 'I'm from the government and I'm here to help.'"

I looked into it and finally realized the problem. We were a non-union operation and most of the inspectors were former union miners. I believe they had an agenda above and beyond enforcement of the new federal regulations. They wanted to make an example of us, so they decided to completely shut down our deep mining operation. They needed to strangle us into submission until we became unionized. The problem was that because of the actions of these government officials, all our men were at risk of losing their jobs. They had families to feed and the bureaucrats were taking away their only source of income. I felt horrible about that and I had to do something for them fast. I couldn't wait a year for us to meet the new regulations. The men and their families would be devastated.

I called Congressman Gene Snyder who was a good friend of mine. When I described the situation to him, he said, "Listen to me, Matth. You need to fly to Washington right away so we can fix this messGene set up a meeting with an official from the Bureau of Mines. He was a reasonable man. I told him my story and how all those men were going to lose their jobs. Within a couple days, we had the official approval to reopen.

⟢•●•⟣

While we waited for the government to finalize the authorization, Bob Appleman and I decided to begin the process of surveying the land for strip mining and possible logging. We met with Willard Castle and he spread the topical maps of the three thousand acres across his desk. At one point I asked Willard, "What's this area?" It was a sizable section, at least a few thousand acres that appeared to be isolated.

"Not sure. I've never been in there myself. It's heavily wooded and as far as I know, nobody else has been there for as long as the mine's been in operation. That must be more than thirty years."

We studied the map until I said, "I'd really like to see what's in there but there are no roads into or out of the area." I looked more closely and said, "There is a railroad track. Has the mine ever used that?"

"I know for a fact that we haven't shipped any coal across it. Must be very old."

I turned to Bob and said, "I'm curious. We ought to check it out and see what's up there. Maybe there's a road running along the track."

Bob and I jumped into an old pickup truck and drove for over an hour until we found a dirt road that intersected the track. The rails had been overgrown with scrub brush and saplings, and we almost missed it. There was no road following the track, so we decided to drive down it, one wheel between the rails and the other in the brush. It was a tough drive and we had to plow through a lot of vegetation as we bumped across the ties. We were about to give up and turn around when we approached a small clearing. In the middle, only about twenty feet from the tracks was a house. It was old and the paint on the boards had blistered away long ago. The roof along the far side was sagging in a foot or so. I figured it was probably abandoned, that is until I saw some movement inside.

"What do you think this is all about?" I asked.

"Not sure, but I think we should just try to back out of here. I don't like the looks of it," replied Bob.

I studied the building through a window and saw what looked like a child running around. I decided to get out of the truck and investigate further.

"I think this is a bad idea, Matth," Bob warned.

I approached the house anyway. The air was filled with a pungent, chemical smell. The front door was wide open, and I saw several more children, barefoot and half-naked inside. A woman dressed in a tattered dress came to the door. She stared at me for several seconds and said nothing. Looking over her shoulder, she yelled out, "Levi, there's a stranger here!"

A minute later, a large man filled the doorway. He had a scruffy beard, matching dark eyes, and an expressionless face. I noticed he kept his right hand hidden behind the door frame and I pretty well knew what that meant. I realized Bob was right. I should have stayed in the truck with him. The man spit on the ground and didn't take his eyes off me when he said through rotting teeth, "This here's private property. Whatta ya want?"

What I wanted to do was get the heck out of there and fast, but I was afraid that if I turned and ran, I'd probably get a back full of buckshot. If I didn't run and tried to confront, him, I might get a chest full. I was in a pickle and my mind raced for something to say, something that wouldn't further agitate the man. "Sorry to bother you, mister. We just purchased the White Ash Mine a few miles away and we're trying to find an access road to the backside."

I figured that if he realized that I was the mine owner, I'd be missed if he shot me and dragged me back into the woods. People would know where I was headed today. If I didn't return on schedule, someone would organize a search party and the trail would lead directly to his front door and whatever he was making around here. I was hoping the guy was smart enough to understand, but he didn't look very bright. I was afraid I could be dead any second, but he didn't shoot. I watched him closely and could almost sense the wheels turning inside his head as he considered the situation. He looked back at our truck and could see Bob sitting behind the wheel. There was no way this guy could tell if Bob was armed or not and I doubted he wanted to get into a firefight with his family inside.

He again spit and said, "Can't get anywhere through here. This here's a dead end. You and your friend in the truck best leave."

That's what we did. No further discussion was necessary. I slowly backed away toward the truck. I didn't want to turn around for fear he just might change his mind about shooting me. Bob and I drove back down those tracks so fast I thought I might lose a kidney along the way. We never explored the land again. This was dangerous country where the people lived by their own set of rules.

———————— ◄•●•► ————————

A few days after the train track incident, the government officially allowed us to open the mine while we made the necessary changes. It took eight men, working seven days a week for a year, but we did it. Finally, we were back on board and had the mine running to full capacity, all thanks to the level-headed intervention of Congressman Gene Snyder. We were able to hire back the deep mine employees, and everything was running well. It didn't take long before we had another problem with the union.

After the inspectors had failed to shut us down with overly harsh enforcement of the Miner Safety and Health Act, the United Coal Miners decided to try a more aggressive approach. They still wanted to force us into shutting down the mine until it became a union facility. Willard Castle approached me one day and said, "Matth, you probably ought to get out of Paintsville for a few days."

"What? Get out? I don't understand. Why?"

"There's a rumor spreading that a group of union organizers from West Virginia is planning to shut down our operation."

"Again?" I was mad. After going through all the trouble of getting the mine reopened, now they were going to do this to us.

"Matth, this could become very violent and you don't need to be around here for that. Let us take care of it ourselves. We know what to do."

A few days later, several cars of union men from West Virginia arrived. They placed a barrier across the train track access to our tipple. They planned to shut us down and believed the White Ash miners would join in their effort. They stood behind the barricade and hung a sign that warned: "DO NOT CROSS OUR LINE" They were armed with ax handles and pieces of steel pipe. It looked like they meant business.

So did our men. Led by Willard Castle, they marched forward on the barrier carrying rifles and shotguns. Willard had faced this kind of situation before and was not afraid of the union thugs. Our men tore down the barricades and walked forward until they were nose-to-nose with the outsiders. The other guys blinked first. They must have decided that our small operation wasn't worth getting shot over. They got back in their cars and hightailed it back to West Virginia.

I believed our union problems were finally behind us until I received another call from Bob Appleman a few weeks later. "Matth, we have another problem. They're shooting up our bulldozers."

I leaned forward in my chair. "Shooting? Who's shooting?"

"Can't say for sure because it's happening late at night. I suspect it might be the unions trying to stir up trouble again."

"Are you sure?"

"No. Like I said, it happens at night, but who else has a reason to shoot up our equipment three nights running."

"How much damage has there been?"

"Mostly dings, nothing major yet, but it's just a matter of time before they destroy one of them."

"We have six million dollars' worth of equipment sitting down there. You should call the police before they wind up killing someone."

"They aren't going to be on our side."

"Then call Willard. Tell him to do what he has to do. Be careful. I don't want us shooting at some teenage boys just letting off steam."

I wasn't there but Willard told me what happened. He stationed about a dozen men with high powered rifles near the dozer area. As expected, the shooters showed up after midnight and again started firing on our machines. It was dark, but their muzzle flashes gave away their positions. Our men returned fire about twenty feet over their heads. The skirmish was over in seconds. We didn't have another incident at that mine. It was further confirmation of my belief that when dealing with thugs, sometimes you had to get down to their level before they understand you're not going to back down.

A year later we took another hit, but this one came from another direction. The price of coal plummeted from nine dollars a ton to three dollars in less than four months. We were behind the eight ball. I was told that the power companies had stockpiled huge reserves so the demand for coal was low. That seemed strange to me because when I drove by several power companies, their supplies looked pretty low. That flew in the face of what I had been told about excess reserve buildup. It seemed to me that someone was playing games. I couldn't figure out who, but I believed someone, or some group of people, might be trying to squeeze out the smaller mines. It was something I could never prove. The prices were so low, we were losing money with every ton of coal we produced. You almost couldn't give the stuff away and there was nothing I could do but cut overhead and try to weather the storm. Any profits from the Interstate property business were diverted to the coal mine to keep it afloat. We were losing fifteen thousand dollars a day. That forced us to abandon the strip mine operation and cut the deep mine from two shifts down to one. Though we were losing money, we had to keep the mine open because if we didn't, the tunnels would fill with water and we'd be finished.

Again, men were laid off and their families suffered. I felt so terrible I couldn't sleep at night. I was stuck between a rock and a hard place. There were no good options. I didn't like laying off all those men but if I didn't, the entire company would fold, and everyone would lose their jobs. I had the responsibility to keep everything from collapsing, but we were getting desperate. I infused more money from the Interstate business, but I couldn't keep doing it indefinitely. I called First National Bank to secure a loan for another couple million dollars. Harry Lowe, the president at the time, said, "Matth, you're already pretty deep into this thing. I'm going to have to present your request to the entire Board of Directors."

"That's fine," I replied. I arranged for my accountant to send Harry updated copies of my financial statements. I guess they didn't need them because several hours later, Harry called back. "Matth, I canvassed the board by phone, and they voted to approve your request. I'll have the money transferred into your account later today."

That extra cash gave me a little more breathing room in my attempts to keep everything running. The problem was that I was going to have to head down to the mine to personally supervise things. I drove to Paintsville fully knowing that this time I would have to stay there for quite a while. Laverne was left alone to raise the children and she was getting frustrated with the situation. It was hard leaving her and our family like that, but it was my responsibility to turn this disaster around. I had no other choice. I had to keep White Ash Mining alive and get the men their jobs back. Bob and I spent a great deal of time working on it. The price drop had already forced many of the other small coal mines to fail. We didn't want to become another statistic. I had to keep returning to Northern Kentucky for a few days every week to monitor the construction business. I was getting stretched thin.

———————◆◆◉◆◆———————

It happened late on a Friday afternoon while I was sitting in my Northern Kentucky office. The pain bore into my chest like nothing I had ever felt before. I became weak, like I might pass out any minute. I remember thinking, "I'm having a heart attack! I better get out of this office or I'm going to die alone inside here!" I didn't understand. I was only forty-five and I didn't smoke. My blood pressure had always been fine, but I knew the signs of a heart attack and it sure seemed like that's what was happening.

I collapsed outside my office door and my secretary called for an ambulance. They took me to the emergency room where the doctors did an electrocardiogram, chest x-ray, and an entire battery of blood tests. The doctor examined me and reviewed all the lab results. He looked up and said to me, "You're fine, Mr. Toebben. There are no signs of an infarction."

"Infarction?"

"Sorry, I mean heart attack. You haven't had a heart attack."

I figured all the stress associated with Laverne's four-year struggle with cancer, plus the impending coal mine failure had taken a toll on me. The next morning, I was shocked when I looked in the mirror. I thought, *Good God, Matth, you look terrible! You must do something to get your life under control! It's destroying you and your family.* It was then that I made my decision. It had to be done for the sake of my family and my health, but I couldn't stomach the thought leaving the coal mine business as a failure. As soon as I could turn things around and make it profitable, I was going to sell White Ash Mining.

It took several more months, but finally I heard some good news on the radio. The price of coal went up two dollars a ton that day. If it continued to increase, we would soon be back in the black. It wasn't long before it hit eight dollars. The bleeding stopped, and we began to recover. We were able put all the production processes back on line, rehire the miners, and start making money again. Two weeks later coal made its way up to twelve dollars a ton. That was like a day of sunshine after months of dark clouds and rain. We were out of the woods and I was able to recoup much of the money I had diverted from the Interstate business. I spent a half million dollars paying overdue bills and had cash left over. With the patient understanding of Laverne and a great deal of praying for God's help, we had weathered the storm. It wouldn't be long before I could sell.

As the price of coal kept improving, it was tempting to keep the mine, but it was still demanding too much of my time and it was sucking the life out of my family.

I let it be known that White Ash was for sale and I received a call from a Mr. George Martin who was a banker from Charleston, West Virginia. He said, "I understand your coal mine operation in Paintsville is for sale."

"That's true," I replied.

"Well, I'd like to buy it. How much do you want?"

"Eight million, excluding the heavy equipment. You'll continue to lease the machines from me." I replied. That would cover much of my initial investment while leaving Bob and myself with a respectable profit.

"Eight million! That's way too much. I'm not paying that!"

"Well that's fine but that's what I want for it. You don't have to buy it. We're making good money, so I don't have to sell." I was bluffing. In fact, I did want to get rid of the mine as soon as possible.

After he hung up the phone, I decided to do a little background check on Mr. Martin. I didn't like what I discovered. The man might have been a bank president, but he was a bully and a crook who had a habit of loaning people too much money at interest rates well above market. When they couldn't pay the exorbitant fees, he would force them into foreclosure and seize their property for himself. He wasn't someone I wanted to do business with unless I had a tight contract in which all the "t"s were crossed and the "i"s were dotted.

Because of the previous low prices of coal, a number of the smaller operations folded and less overall production was the result. White Ash had been dangeroulsy close to being in that group, but now the power companies were scrambling to replenish supplies. That resulted in even higher prices. The following month, the price of coal jumped another four dollars a ton to $16. Mr. Martin called me back and asked, "Is that mine of yours still for sale?"

"Yes, it is."

"Well, I still want to buy it."

"You can, but you can't get it for the old price any more. The number now is ten million and you still have to lease my strip-mining equipment until that loan is retired."

He went through the roof and unleashed a string of profanities I won't repeat here. He hung up, but an hour later he called back and said, "I'll take it." I had my lawyers draw up all the necessary papers and made sure they went over all the contracts with a fine-toothed comb. We closed on the sale, but I still didn't trust the man and was afraid he might try something fishy. My instincts were correct. It was a good thing I was careful.

The first shenanigan he tried didn't affect me personally. He started selling coal right out of the tipple and all the transactions were in cash. I suspected he was skimming and not paying taxes on those profits. It wasn't my problem, but I was certain the IRS would eventually become interested in what he was doing.

The second one did affect me directly. He was still leasing the surface mining machinery from me. Since Mr. Martin bought the mine, the demand for the equipment skyrocketed and so did the prices, making my used machines more valuable. That's when I discovered what he had done. He took my 992 wheel-loader and sold it. I paid a half million dollars for the machine and he sold it for $750,000 like it was his to sell. It wasn't. He was leasing it from me.

I was furious when I called him. "You took my 992 Caterpillar loader and sold it! That's illegal! I still owe loan payments on it. Not only that, you cost me over a hundred thousand dollars in tax consequences."

He said, "Boy, when I want to talk to you, I'll call you." That was it. He hung up on me. I called back and said, "Mr. Martin, I'd like to discuss this matter in a business-like fashion. I don't appreciate the way you hung up on me."

"You heard what I said." Bam, he hung up on me again. He was used to getting his way by bullying people around but this time he picked on the wrong person. It was time to go to battle. I again called him and said, "I will see you in court!" That was all. I was the one who hung up before he could reply. I had my attorneys file a couple of lawsuits several weeks later and the fight was on. I knew Martin was an extremely wealthy man with a lot of resources at his disposal, so I knew it would be a tough battle. The suits were filed in Charleston, which was in his backyard, so I was at a distinct disadvantage.

Our attorney was a man named Will Ziegler. He was good, but he and his partners felt that I needed to hire someone with a lot more expertise in this area. I said, "I want you to get me the best attorney you can find. I don't care what it costs. I've got a solid case here. He's hurt a lot of people and I'm the one who's going to stop him."

Will called back a week later and said, "Matth, I've found the man you need. His name is Stanley Prizer."

"Great, where's he from?"

There was a slight pause before he replied, "Charleston."

"Charleston! We can't have an attorney out of Charleston! George Martin owns half the town. I won't stand a chance."

Will responded, "That's not going to be a problem. Stanley knows all about George Martin. He's hurt a lot of people in Charleston, including a number of Stanley's close friends. He's been wanting a piece of this guy for a long time."

Will Ziegler and I flew to Charleston so we could meet this fellow in person. When I walked into Stanley's office, I was impressed. I had never seen a lawyer's office like it. It was as plush as the Oval Office in the White House. I figured this Stanley Prizer must be very good at what he does. I also realized he was going to be expensive. We sat down in his office and I relayed my story.

"You have a very good case, Mr. Toebben. I'll take it on for you."

I said, "Thank you, but what's it going to cost me?"

"Write out a check to me today for $100,000 and I'll bill you the balance when we win."

I noticed he said "when" and not "if." That was a good sign. I was impressed but it cost me a hundred grand to get out of his office. All in all, it was money well spent. By the time we went to court, George Martin had already sold two more pieces of my equipment. He was getting into deeper and deeper trouble. I don't think he cared because he was used to bullying others into submission. During the trial Stanley spoke for forty-seven minutes and covered hundreds of figures, never once looking at his notes. He was the most brilliant mind I had ever seen in a courtroom. George Martin's attorneys spoke for only fifteen minutes and appeared befuddled.

We broke for lunch on the final day of arguments and Stanley took us to an upscale local restaurant. It had personal telephones at every table. Ours rang and Stanley picked it up with a knowing smile of his face. He listened to the caller for a minute, looked at me and said "George Martin would like to settle. He's offering a million plus compensation for your equipment."

"No," I replied. Stanley said, "No deal," and hung up the phone. We resumed our lunch and five minutes later the phone rang again. Stanley said, "They doubled their offer." I figured George Martin realized he was in big trouble, so I again said, "No deal. I want to nail this guy against the wall."

"Rejected," said Stanley and hung up. The phone rang a third time and George Martin had decided to ante up his offer to four million in addition to the cost of the equipment he sold.

"Deal," I replied and that was it. All we had to do was sign the necessary legal papers and my involvement in the coal business was over. It wasn't the end for George Martin, however. The trial had drawn a great deal of interest from the IRS. Agents had been in the court room the entire time, taking notes. It seems they were planning on having a serious discussion with Mr. George Martin.

In retrospect, a part of me wishes I hadn't sold the company. I had invested a huge amount of time and, with the help of Willard Castle and Bob Appleman, we had worked our way through the worst of it. The company was again on solid footing. Profits were excellent and that allowed us to rehire all the people who had been laid off. The company added additional men to the payroll, creating even more job opportunities for the local community. In time the price of coal continued to increase. White Ash profits went through the roof, so in that way I regretted the sale. It wasn't the best decision from a business standpoint, but it was from a personal aspect. I knew that if I had continued to hold on to the company it would continue to consume more and more of my time, time that would come at the expense of my family. After all was said and done, it was the right thing to do.

UNIONS

When I owned the White Ash Mining Company, the unions tried to shut us down by trying to bully our men in to walking off the job and shooting up our heavy machinery. Once out of that business, I didn't expect any further violent union confrontations, especially in Northern Kentucky. It was a wrong assumption.

I have never had any problems with the original concept of labor unions. They were an integral part of America's history. In their early days, they accomplished a great deal for the average American worker through collective bargaining agreements. The unions became a major contributing factor in the establishment of a solid middle class. The problem was that, in time, the unions became too powerful, and with that power came corruption. The organizations' tactics started to become uncomfortably reminiscent of the German Sturmabteilung who suppressed the expression of all opposing views and dissent through extreme violence. The unions became infiltrated with a thug mentality and began intimidating non-union workers to join in order inflate their ranks and increase membership dues. Some union leaders even sold their members out in exchange for obtaining lucrative deals from business for themselves.

That's one of the reasons why I formed all my companies as non-union and supported "Right to Work" laws. I paid all my employees well and treated them with respect. They didn't have to pay union extortion to get a fair wage from me. They weren't forced to pay money that was used to support politicians that didn't necessarily share their own personal views. Too many unions became just another form of big business, but their product was nothing more than membership growth at all cost. Increased enrollment translated into more union dues and fatter paychecks for the union bosses. Anyone or any company who successfully opposed them posed a threat to their bottom line and power structure, so the ultimate union goal became the intimidation of non-union businesses.

It happened in the construction sector in Northern Kentucky. I had a contract to construct a building in downtown Covington. It was for a liquor store on Pike Street, next to the C&O Bridge. We were waiting to have a concrete foundation poured. The owner of the concrete company kept stalling me and I kept calling and complaining. Finally, I met with the owner at his office and said, "Why haven't you poured my foundation? You've promised me three days in a row that you'd be there, and it still hasn't been done. This is costing me money. What kind of operation are you running?"

His response was, "Matth, I'm getting sick and tired of your complaining. If you think you can do any better, why don't you just buy my company? Then you can do whatever you want!" I think he was trying to bluff me into backing down because he started grinning. The smile faded when I responded.

"Well, what do you want for it?"

He gave me a price and the next day I was in the concrete business. We finally got the foundation pour for our building on the schedule. At the same time, the rodbusters, whose job it was to lay the rebar reinforcing steel rods for the foundation, decided to go on strike. We already had the foundation excavation complete and were ready to pour. I was concerned that if we didn't get our foundation completed soon, it would fill with water, which would be a big problem. Our men decided to do the rebar work themselves. Shortly afterwards, members of the iron workers union came on the job and tried to shut us down. They warned, "Keep your hands off that steel. That's our job."

My foreman, Pedro, a two-hundred-fifty-pound giant of solid muscle, refused to be intimidated by anyone. He walked up to the union leader and said, "You guys aren't doing the job so we're going to do it ourselves. We have a schedule to keep." Fearing a nasty battle, everyone stopped working and Pedro called me, "Matth, I need to talk to you in person. We have a problem."

"Come on over."

He walked into my office an hour later and described what had happened. He said, "What do you want me to do?"

I replied, "We need to get that foundation poured. We're already a month behind schedule. Do what you have to do to get it done. I'll back you no matter what."

The following day, at about eleven o'clock, I pulled into a parking lot adjacent to the work site to see how things were progressing. The Ironworkers Union was still picketing but my men were on the job anyway, busy installing the rebar. A big black

Cadillac pulled up to the site. Three big union thugs stepped out, ready to start knocking some heads. Pedro had been waiting for them and was ready. Earlier in the morning, he had cut several two-foot-long sections of the steel rebar rods and had a pile of them sitting at his feet. As the thugs approached, he picked up a couple of the rods and held them in his right hand. One of the union men made the mistake of getting in Pedro's face and threatening him. Pedro grabbed the guy's shirt with his left hand, hit him in the head with the rod, and threw him to the side like a bag of garbage. The other two started running back to their car. Pedro picked up several more rods and started throwing them. One stuck right in the side of that big black Cadillac. The union bullies jumped into the car and sped away, the rod still sticking out of the door. We never heard from them again.

* * *

Several years later, we were involved in a project at Ft. Mitchell Country Club. They demolished their old clubhouse and we won the contract build a new one. Being a non-union builder, we soon started being harassed by the construction union leaders. It was almost a daily event. By the time we had the building under roof, problems escalated, and that's when Laverne started receiving phone threats. One guy in particular kept calling her and saying, "Is it worth your husband's life to keep building that country club?" He would call almost every other night, right after dinner. On one particular evening I was the one who answered the phone. The man hesitated for a second before saying, "You're never going to finish that job."

"Watch me," was all I said, then hung up the phone.

There had been a recent bombing at another company's construction site, so I took the threats seriously and decided to post two armed guards around the Ft. Mitchell Club property. I warned the men that the unions would use a number of tactics to distract them. As if on cue, the next evening, after the construction crew left, a new white Cadillac pulled down the entrance drive. The driver was a well-dressed, attractive woman wearing a short white dress. When she got out of the car one of the guards remembered my warning. He ran inside and looked out the back window in time to see a man dressed in jeans and a black hoodie, sneaking up to the rear of the building. He was carrying a gunnysack and it was loaded down with something heavy. The guard yelled and startled the man. He ran out of view to the side of the building, dropping his pack in the process. The guy disappeared just as the lady in the white Cadillac sped away. When our guard inspected the sack, he found that it contained dynamite sticks and fuses. We called in the police and doubled our security.

We never had another union threat after that, and we have since developed a good working relationship with multiple union sub-contractors.

THE LAKE

For those not familiar with Kentucky, Lake Cumberland is a huge body of water in the southern part of the state. It was created by the Army Corps of Engineers when they built an earthen dam across the Cumberland River in 1952. It served as a means of flood control and the production of hydroelectric power. What resulted was a pristine, deep-blue lake with over a thousand miles of heavily wooded shoreline. The crystal-clear water serves as a popular destination site for water recreation and camping. The lake hosts two state parks, thousands of waterfront homes, and a multitude of boat docks. It is where one of our family's worst disasters occurred.

It was the summer after my oldest son, John, graduated from college. He, my daughter Diane, and a group of their friends had driven down to the lake for a weekend of boating and waterskiing. They put in at the Grinder Hill Marina, a remote dock along the southern shore. It was a sunny day and they were enjoying a wonderful afternoon on the water. Thousands of other boaters were there taking advantage of the weekend. The water was rough from all the boat traffic and the resulting waves made things unsteady.

John had just finished his turn at skiing and signaled that he was ready to stop. He was making his way back to the swim platform, pushing his ski along in front of him so his friends could pull it onto the boat before he boarded. They put the engine in neutral but didn't turn it off. That failure turned out to be a catastrophic mistake. While trying to load John's ski, the wake of another boat hit them broadside, causing one of the boys to stumble. He fell against the throttle, and the boat lunged backward at full speed. John had just enough time to turn away before the prop hit him. He tried to escape but the reverse rotation of the prop pulled him further into the blades.

Grinder Hill Marina

John was knocked unconscious. His shocked friends struggled to pull his bleeding body from the water. He was hemorrhaging profusely. Fortunately, one of John's friends was a nurse. She and another friend immediately put towels over the wound and began applying pressure. They frantically tried to rush back to the dock, but the impact had been so severe the engine stalled out, and they had difficulty getting it restarted. Even after it turned over, the ride was hampered by the damaged prop, and it was a painfully long way to the dock. In all the confusion, they made a wrong turn and got lost. With each tick of the clock, John's life was ebbing away. By the time they got there, he had already lost a critical amount of blood. The towels they used to pack the wound were soaked, and large pools of red filled the bottom of the boat.

The south shore region was so remote, there wasn't an ambulance, so John was transported to the nearest hospital in a hearse. It was a bad omen. At the Albany Hospital Emergency Room, John's blood pressure was critically low. They started two intravenous lines, one in each arm. Immediately, two nurses each forced blood in as fast as they could by squeezing the bags. He received a total of thirteen units but still wasn't stable. He was taken to surgery where the doctors worked furiously to control the bleeding. Once he was somewhat stable, they performed a diverting colostomy to prevent further wound contamination.

━━━━━━━━━━ ◆◆●◆◆ ━━━━━━━━━━

It was later that day and I was enjoying a relaxing Sunday afternoon at home with friends when I got the call no parent wants to receive. It was one of John's friends and he told me what had happened. I could barely comprehend what he was saying. They were all just going down for a weekend of fun. How could this possibly be? All I could say was, "Is he alive?" I was afraid to hear the answer.

"Yes, but it's bad, Mr. Toebben. Real bad. The doctors said you should get here right away."

That meant they didn't think John would survive. I knew I had to get there immediately but didn't how was I going to do that. It was at least a five-hour drive to the south shore of Cumberland and I couldn't wait that long. I didn't know if my son would still be alive by the time I got there. I called my friend Ray Mueller, the owner of Comair Airline. He arranged for me to take a private plane out of the CVG airport to a small regional airport near Albany, Kentucky.

It was only a one-hour flight. I prayed the entire way, begging God to spare my boy. By the time we approached the area it was already dark. For some reason the small regional airport's runway lights were off and we couldn't see it from the air. I was in a panic. I had to get to my son. The pilot radioed the air traffic control center in Atlanta and gave them our coordinates.

"You're just about on top of it," they replied.

"Roger that." The pilot initiated a rapid descent and seconds later he could see the runway in his headlights. We came in hot and hard, bouncing several times before coming to a stop. I wasn't afraid. The only thought in my head was the vision of my son, lying alone on a stretcher somewhere, barely clinging to life.

There was no terminal like one would expect to see at a major airport like Greater Cincinnati. There were a few hangers and a single office. All the lights were out, and no one was around. The pilot made a slow three-hundred-sixty-degree turn, shining his lights on the surroundings, trying to find something or someone who could help us. We saw a perimeter fence that ended in a gate next to one of the hangers. I got out of the plane to look around and found a small opening in the fence. I was relieved to find a payphone on the outside wall of the hanger. Five minutes later I was riding in a cab, on my way to Albany, wherever that was.

Rushing through the emergency room door, I asked the first person I met where John Toebben was. She took me to see the doctor.

"How is he?" I asked.

"He's out of surgery but it's pretty bad. We've called for a priest."

"A priest!" The words just about ripped my heart out. "Where is he? I need to see him!"

"He's in recovery. They stopped the bleeding and they're about to place some dressings on his wounds." He paused for a second before adding, "You might not want to see him yet. Like I said, it's pretty bad and not something you want to subject yourself to."

"I don't care! I want to see my son. I can handle this. Please take me to him."

The doctor led me to John's bedside and there was no way I could have been prepared for what I saw. The prop had torn away most of the skin and muscle from his low back to his upper legs. Bones and tendons were exposed. The sight almost dropped me to my knees in anguish. I wanted to do something, anything for him, but I was helpless. I turned to a good friend, Dr. George Miller who was a Northern Kentucky surgeon. After I described the situation to him, he asked, "What's his blood pressure, Matt?"

I told him the numbers the nurse had given me, and George replied, "It's still too low. They need to work on making it better before we do anything. Once it's been stable for a while, you need to arrange to fly him out of there. He needs to be treated in the nearest trauma center." He arranged for a Medevac helicopter transport out of St. Mary's Hospital in Louisville. When I told the local doctor about the plan, he warned, "Your son will be dead before that helicopter is ten feet off the ground." It was another stab at my heart. Uncertain of what to do, I called Dr. Miller back. He said, "He's right, Matth. Transport is definitely risky, but if he remains there it'll be even more risky. The local hospital simply isn't equipped to handle your son's case. You need to get him to a trauma center as soon as possible. With the severe low blood pressure, he's at risk for multiple organ failure. The wound is already infected from the contaminated lake water and bowel contents. Once that infection spreads, he could become septic. There are no good decisions here, Matth, but getting him to St. Elizabeth's in Crestview Hills will give him the best chance for survival."

I decided to proceed with the Medevac transport and I'm glad I did. The local doctors did a magnificent job, but he needed to be in more experienced hands. A doctor and nurse kept him stable during the flight to Northern Kentucky. When he arrived at the hospital, the surgeons at St. Elizabeth started him on IV fluid replacement and massive doses of intravenous antibiotics. They began an aggressive series of surgical procedures to remove all infected and dead tissue on a daily basis. John was placed on a Circle Electric Bed which allowed the nurses to rotate him regularly to prevent pressure sores and to allow better access for bandage changes. They used what they called "wet to dry" dressings. That meant they placed gauze soaked in antibacterial solution on the wounds. Once the dressings dried several hours later, the gauze was removed and with it any remaining infected tissue. It was extremely painful.

I was walking down the hall on my way to John's room when I heard his blood curdling screams. Though he was unconscious, he still felt the pain. It caused regular oozing of blood as the old dead tissue was torn away. I could tell the nurse was in a hurry as she pulled off the dressing. I understood that she was overworked and had too many other patients to care for, but I couldn't allow John to be subjected to this level of pain. I studied exactly what she did and soon asked her, "Do you mind if I change his dressings from now on? I plan to be here most of the time anyway so I'm more than happy to take care of it."

She agreed and from that moment on I took care of things myself, every two hours, every day. Before removing the old bandages, I would dampen them first and then gently tease the old gauze off. It took longer and still hurt but it was less painful than just ripping it off.

In time, John gradually regained consciousness. Fortunately, he didn't remember much of the accident. He did understand the severity of his problems. John's first concern was whether or not he could have children in the future. During a visit one afternoon he said with tears in his eyes, "Dad, if I can't be a man anymore, I want you to let me die."

That was just one of many painful moments during his ordeal. I had to hold back the tears when I replied, "I know that things aren't looking very good from that standpoint right now, but we're going to fix this thing, son. I promise. For now, you just worry about getting better and soon the doctors are going to take care of everything." I was lying. I didn't know if the doctors would be able to help or not, but John still wasn't out of the woods and had other matters to worry about, like surviving. I wanted him to focus on the task of recovering. Then we could worry about everything else. That was over thirty years and three children ago.

Dr. Joel Kreilein a local plastic surgeon began the process of replacing the lost skin with grafts taken from his thighs. Several weeks later they began a series of operations designed to recover the damaged areas by rotating flaps of muscle tissue from the back of his legs. Then it was months of physical therapy, most of which he did at home. He had a specific regimen to follow but did a lot of extra things on his own. I was working on the Country Squire property one afternoon when I noticed out of the corner of my eye, someone climbing a small hill a couple hundred feet away. The guy was on his hands and knees. Once he reached the top, he would slide down the hill and start climbing up again. I walked over to check it out and found John, his shirt soaked with sweat and dirt, struggling up the hill, over and over. He was determined to push through the pain and regain his muscle strength any way he could.

The recovery was a slow and grueling process, but John prevailed. A year to the day after his disaster, John kept a promise he had made to himself after the accident. He returned to Lake Cumberland with the same friends that had been with him on the day of the tragedy. They drove a boat to the same location on the lake and John jumped into the water. They threw him a rope and a pair of skis. He was determined to do it again. He got up and though he didn't get very far, he did it. They all celebrated together with a bottle of champagne. It was a heartwarming day for everyone.

COLLUSION

After getting out of the coal mine business, I was again looking for a chance to diversify our portfolio. Since the coal eventually rebounded so well, I had a renewed interest in the energy sector as long as it didn't take too much time from my personal life. A neighbor of mine, Judy Phillips, approached me with a business idea to get into the propane gas business. It looked like an attractive proposal, so we formed the Kendow Energy Company and sold propane on a wholesale basis to customers throughout the Tri-State area. The company's profits were adequate, but the business never took off as well as we had hoped. It would eventually serve as the foundation for a new venture that we would establish several years later.

In 1938, the natural gas industry became heavily regulated on both a state and federal level. The belief at the time was that gas was a natural resource under the public domain and prices could be better controlled through government supervised monopolies. If companies wanted to raise their rates, they would have to file a petition and hold hearings with input from the community. Theoretically the program was projected to provide lower, more stable prices for the consumer, but the process became so inefficient and cumbersome, the opposite resulted. The government simply can't run business as well as a free market system that determines the true cost of a product based upon supply and demand.

President Ronald Reagan and his advisors realized this fact. They saw the beneficial results of a free-market system when they deregulated oil in 1981. The result was an immediate sharp increase in the price of gas, but this was soon followed by a dramatic decrease over the long term. Buoyed by his success in managing the oil situation, Reagan proceeded to deregulate the natural gas and electric industry in 1985. This opened the markets and presented an excellent business opportunity for interested entrepreneurs. I did a great deal of research on the prospects of again investing in energy supply. I didn't want to be caught off guard like I was with the coal company problems. It looked like a solid idea.

In 1984, Judy Phillips, another friend Robert Robinson, and I started a new energy supply business. Together we formed the Stand Energy Company to compete with the major energy providers. Our business plan was to purchase natural gas and electricity directly from suppliers and sell it at a discount rate to businesses that utilized great amounts of energy. Robert would serve as president, and Judy as vice-president, while I would become the secretary/treasurer and chairman of the board. We decided to fold the former propane company, Kendow Energy, into Stand. I secured financing for our start-up expenses and we established an office in the Rookwood Building in Mount Adams. Judy possessed a great deal of business expertise and on her recommendation, we hired Larry Freeman, who helped managed the day-to-day operations and marketing. He now serves as Executive Vice President of the company.

Judy Phillips and I

Stand Energy enjoyed excellent success right from the start. We recruited more and more companies as clients until we were selling millions of dollars of gas and electric every month in thirteen states. Stand Energy did so well that we received an award as one of the fastest growing businesses in Cincinnati.

Then, things started to turn south. It was like the entire White Ash Mine fiasco was playing out all over again. Thousands of other companies like ours had sprung up around the country competing with the large utility companies. Most were successful...perhaps too successful. Our costs to purchase electricity began escalating. They were jumping every day: $50, $100, $300 a unit while we still had long-term contracts to provide electric at $19 a unit. It was killing us and there was nothing we could do about it. We lost over $42 million in just over two weeks!

I remember wondering how could prices increase so quickly like this? There was no significant weather change, natural disaster, or anything else that could affect the supply and demand models. I again reviewed in my mind our business plan and the extensive research we had done. I could find nothing wrong with our thinking. What had happened? We were hemorrhaging large amounts of money with no end in sight. The crisis was beginning to affect the entire Toebben Companies' bottom line. There seemed to be no other solution but to terminate business activities of Stand Energy and declare bankruptcy. That left a sour taste in my mouth. Bankruptcy was tantamount to admitting failure and that was a hard pill for me to swallow.

I was forced to schedule an emergency meeting with some bankruptcy attorneys in order to prevent collapse of our entire company. The night before the meeting I couldn't sleep. "How could I have possibly been so wrong? What did I miss?" I kept whispering to the darkness of the bedroom. I prayed to God for guidance until I eventually fell asleep and dreamt of my father. It was of the time when I was a little boy in Lorup. We were working in the fields and I had to stop because I was having one of my severe asthma attacks. I was sitting on the ground and crying because I was a failure and couldn't do anything. That's when my father said, "Son, when life gets hard and there appears to be no solution, you stand up straight, put your chin out, and push on. You keep pushing until you see a light at the end of the tunnel."

I woke up in a start. Dad was right. An idea popped into my head. I hadn't missed anything at all. There was absolutely no reasonable explanation as to why our costs were increasing so dramatically. The most important thing was that it wasn't just one supplier that suddenly raised their rates. It was a multitude of utility companies across the board, all doing it simultaneously. Someone or some group was playing games. I decided to fight them. I jumped out of bed and started making notes.

It was ten o'clock on Monday morning when we met with our team of lawyers at the Rookwood offices. The lead attorney said, "Your only option is to proceed with the bankruptcy, Mr. Toebben. Dozens of small utility companies like Stand have already collapsed around the country. Stand is going to fail and if you don't seek bankruptcy protection, it's going to bring down the rest of your companies with it." The other lawyers nodded their heads in silent agreement.

I looked at them and said, "Well, I have another idea. We're not going to file for Chapter 11. Stand did nothing wrong. This entire situation was orchestrated by some of the large utility companies in an effort to drive us out of business. That's not going to happen without a fight. I'm going to sue."

"What?" they all replied in unison. "You can't sue here. Who can you possible sue?"

"I think I can." I explained to them my reasoning. "This rapid change in prices didn't occur by happenstance. It's impossible that so many different utility suppliers would decide to raise their costs in unison over such a short period of time. This had to be a willful plan. We were eating into their profits and they didn't like it. They have tried to eliminate the competition by colluding to destroy the small independent companies like Stand. That's illegal and I'm going to sue all them."

I had made out a list of all the involved utility companies and gave it to the lead attorney. "First thing tomorrow, I want you to file suit against every one of them for recovery of our losses."

He looked at my list and shook his head. "Matth, you can't do this. You're dealing with some big boys here and they are powerful. They have billions of dollars backing them. Do you know what's going to happen to you? They're going to chew you up and spit you out."

I looked at him and said, "What do I have to lose? I'm already down forty million and we were going to file bankruptcy anyway. I want to fight them."

The youngest attorney then spoke up, "I think Mr. Toebben might be on the right track here. We should head to court and face them. We can probably get all the information we need through discovery. If everything falls into place, we can win this!" They filed all those suits the next day and all hell broke loose.

If I was going to keep the company going instead of declaring bankruptcy, I would need an infusion of cash. I knew George Schaefer, the president of Fifth Third Bank. I hadn't done much business with him up to that time, but we were acquainted through the Chamber of Commerce. I called him.

"What do you need, Matth?"

"I need $18 million today."

"What's this all about?" he asked. I explained everything to him.

"Come over right now," he said.

When I arrived, George met me upstairs in his office and escorted me to a conference room where four people were already sitting on either side of a large table. George took a seat at one end and I at the other. George introduced me and said. "Tell us your story, Matth."

I explained to them my suspicions and what we planned to do. One of the people at the table interrupted me and said, "I don't think we've ever done business with you before, Mr. Toebben. Why are you coming to us now? Why not use your regular bank?"

I had been expecting this and I told them straight up. "I've been dealing primarily with Key Bank up until now. They have been getting a little nervous because I had withdrawn ten million in cash from my accounts there."

George then interjected, "How do you plan to get your money back Matth? How do you plan to pay off this loan if we give you the money?"

I continued to tell them about how I believed the different utility companies had colluded to destroy Stand and similar small utility companies across the country. I explained my reasoning behind everything and discussed our plans to sue each of the major companies separately. I reinforced our attorneys' belief that we had a solid case. We all talked for another hour and a half, them asking questions while making notes, and me giving honest answers. Finally, George Schaeffer stood up and looked at his watch. "Well it's almost lunch time and I have an appointment."

That just about sucked the air right out of my lungs. I was thinking, *I lost this battle before it even started.*

I watched George walk away and with him any hopes of ever keeping Stand Energy alive long enough to follow through on the suits. After three steps he turned around and said to one of his people, "Don't forget to cut that eighteen-million-dollar check for Mr. Toebben. See you later, Matth. Good luck. Keep us posted."

We completed all the paperwork and I agreed to sign on the loan personally. They gave me an extra line of credit for fifteen million just in case we would need it. That took Stand off life support while our lawyers pursued each lawsuit, immediately sending out interrogatories and aggressively scheduling depositions.

About a month after filing our suits, I received a call from Washington. They wanted to send a representative to talk to me about a few issues. We scheduled the meeting for the following week. When he arrived, the man introduced himself as being from FERC.

"FERC? I asked. "I've never heard of it.

"Sorry. I'm afraid we use too many acronyms in Washington. It's the Federal Energy Regulatory Commission. We're a division of the U.S. Department of Energy," he replied. He was polite and well-spoken as he continued to explain the function of what they did. It took about ten minutes of small talk before he got to the actual reason for our meeting. "Mr. Toebben, I understand you've filed lawsuits against some of the largest utility suppliers in the Midwest."

"That's true."

"Why would you ever want to do that?"

"They have been colluding with each other to artificially

raise the unit cost of electricity. It's all part of an effort to drive small companies like mine out of business. Many of them have already folded."

"If you plan to make that kind of accusation against highly-respected corporations, you'd better be able to prove those charges."

"I understand."

"Well how do you plan to do that?"

It was then that I realized the true purpose of this man's visit. He was on a fact-finding mission. I suspect that many of the larger utility companies got together and twisted a few arms in Washington to find out what I had on them and how I was going to prove my case.

"How I do that, sir, is for me to know. Tell your supervisors and anyone else who sent you here that if they want to know what I have planned, they're going to have to find out in court." That was the end of the meeting. I shook the man's hand and escorted him to the door.

We owed one utility company from the Michigan area over nine million dollars. Of that, about nine hundred thousand was based upon the original $19 a unit cost. The remaining eight million was the result of their own price manipulation. Within two months of filing our suits, the Michigan company called and after we talked for about ten minutes, they wanted to settle the case. I told them we weren't interested in a small settlement. They offered to forgive the $8 million. That would leave us only responsible for the original $900,000. We refused to settle because of all the extra costs we had incurred. They countered with an offer to forgive any and all debt, including the legitimate $900,000 charge. We signed the agreement. After that, it was like dominoes falling. Almost all the remaining companies agreed to settle with similar terms. They all began to realize that they were vulnerable. Their plans would be exposed in open court and they didn't want the negative publicity associated with a trial.

The only exception was Cinergy, the local company based in Cincinnati. I don't think they liked the fact that Stand was in their backyard. The battle was prolonged and outrageous legal costs were accumulating on both sides. Finally, I again approached George Schaefer, the president of Fifth Third Bancorp. The CEO of Cinergy was on the bank's Board of Directors and I asked George if he could facilitate a meeting between us. It was done and our final lawsuit was settled out of court. Stand still had to pay a small fraction of the inflated charge but it was an overall victory for us.

Within eighteen months the entire matter was behind us. Stand paid off all its loans to Fifth-Third Bank and was back in business. That was three decades ago and Stand is still a thriving corporation, selling gas and electricity in eighteen states.

Stand Energy 30th Anniversary Christmas Party

HIGHLAND CROSSING

At times life offers us solutions to problems long before they actually surface. After we had established a significant presence in commercial development, I was approached by a group of several investors and their attorney from Lexington. They wanted to discuss a project with us, so I scheduled a meeting in our corporate office building. The group had purchased twelve acres of wooded land in Fort Wright, next to the existing St. Charles nursing home. They wanted to contract with us to construct a three-story building to serve as a for-profit retirement home facility. The plans called for a structure with 144 individual apartments, a main kitchen, common eating area, social area, and outdoor sites for recreation. It was to be marketed to self-sufficient senior citizens who no longer wished to assume the responsibilities of owning a home. It seemed like a good idea, but I didn't have a lot of contacts in Lexington, so I was a little wary of the group. The attorney did present a letter of credit from a bank in Lexington and the project financing appeared to be guaranteed. The estimated cost after the land purchase was about three million dollars. I insisted that the deed on the property be signed over to me in order to protect myself in the event of a default on their part. It would be transferred back to them after reception of their final payment.

Our terms were accepted, and we began construction a month after the group's million-dollar deposit cleared the bank. As soon as the building was under roof it was time for the investors to pay their next construction draw. It didn't arrive by the date stipulated in our contract. I waited two weeks before calling their attorney and said, "You're two weeks overdue on your next payment."

"They're having a little trouble with the bank."

"What do you mean they're having trouble with the bank? You led me to believe the project was secured with a guaranteed letter of credit."

"I'm afraid it was withdrawn. My clients need more time to secure different financing."

I replied, "I have bills to pay."

"Like I told you, there is no money right now, but my clients are in the process of rectifying the problem."

I didn't like the way this sounded. I had a contract but the cost of suing for non-performance would be costly and time consuming. I decided to work with them. "I'll agree to give you another two weeks to restructure your financing, but all work will cease until that happens. If it doesn't, I'm going to take over the entire project. The lawyer protested, but after ten minutes of discussion he relented.

As I was afraid, the group was unable to obtain financing, so the land and uncompleted retirement facility were mine. At least I was in possession of the deed. The problem was that I didn't want to tie up too much more of my own money than I already had in it. It was going to take another two million to finish the job, so I began recruiting investors at one hundred thousand dollars a share. Fifteen put up the cash and served as limited partners while I functioned as the general partner. A year later the building was complete, and the Highland Crossing Retirement Center was open for business. I hired a manager and staff and began advertising in the Greater Cincinnati papers. There was a good response but the best I was able to do was 82% occupancy. Our breakeven point was 90% so we were losing money every month. I covered the shortfall on my own, hoping things would eventually turn around, but they never did.

I remember by experience from years ago when I had a customer fail to pay for completion of a huge home in Country Squire Estates. At that time, I went to a builder's convention in Las Vegas to see what people were doing in upscale home construction. Using what I learned there, I turned a failure into a profitable success. I decided to use the same approach on the Highland Crossing situation. I found a retirement home trade journal and discovered that there was a national meeting being held in Phoenix the following month.

I made arrangements to attend and found out what I needed within the first two hours. One of the initial speakers stated that people deciding to move into a retirement center wanted assurances that the next level of living accommodations would be available if their health deteriorated. The elderly are less likely to leave the security of their own home if they have no place to go when they develop Alzheimer's Disease or some physical ailment that would require on-site care. He said that any retirement center should designate at least 30% of its apartments as assisted living if it expects to be profitable. That was my mistake. I had no such options available for our tenants. I needed actual nursing home beds.

I flew back home that evening and the following day held a meeting with Highland Crossing's resident council. It was a group of representatives chosen by people who lived there. Its purpose was to give the residents a voice in what was happening in their little community. I presented my idea and initially there was some resistance. However, when faced with the possibility that they might someday require assisted living accommodations themselves, they relented. I promised to minimize any inconvenience for them. All residents of the third floor were moved to equivalent apartments on the lower floors at no personal cost.

I hired an architect to draw up the necessary plans. The entire third floor would be converted to thirty-five assisted living apartments with their own eating area and separate elevator, capable of handling wide wheelchairs or stretchers. It would be staffed with full-time professional personnel experienced in assisting those who required special care. When the changes were complete, we advertised the new facility and within two months enjoyed 100% occupancy with a waiting list. We were in the black.

I, along with my fifteen limited-partner investors, continued to own Highland Crossing for another fifteen years, but it was demanding a fair amount of my time. None in my family members were interested in taking over the business so I eventually decided to sell it. I approached Sister Luann who was the director of the nearby St. Charles Nursing Home. I offered to sell it to them for $3 million. At that price it was a gift, but her Board of Directors felt that the cost was excessively high. I was forced to advertise in the national trade journals and within six weeks I received a dozen substantial offers. I wound up selling to the Atria Corporation, a national assisted-living company out of Louisville. They paid $11.3 million.

The limited partners and I enjoyed a handsome profit from the sale, and I was comfortable knowing a respected company had taken over. The residents would be well cared for. One benefit that I wasn't yet aware of wouldn't become apparent until years later. It might have been a coincidence or maybe it was planned by some divine will. I prefer to believe the latter.

TRIPLE T RANCH

Though I had left Lorup over thirty years earlier, farming was still in my blood, especially when it came to raising livestock. We had a few cattle on the Carrolton farm, but my dream hobby was always to be in the prize cattle business. I was most interested in raising registered Black Angus so when a friend called and asked me if I'd like to go with him to a Black Angus cattle auction in western Kentucky, I jumped at the chance. I had never seen championship quality cattle before and when I got to the farm I was impressed. We were in Kentucky horse country, but these animals were groomed as well as the finest thoroughbreds. The ranch was a top-notch operation with grounds that were meticulously manicured and surrounded by black fence boarding perfectly aligned along the perimeter. The barns were more organized and cleaner than some homes. I remember thinking, *Man, what a place. This is exactly how I would want to do it.*

The auction began at 10 AM and I had had no intention of bidding. I was there with my friend just as an observer. The first animal sold for $9,000 and I thought, *Wow, that's a fair amount of money for a cow!* The second went for $18,000 and the third $24,000. It was very exciting and as I followed the bidding on each one, I got caught up in the process. I thought, *My gosh, I've been wanting to do something like this my entire life.* What are you waiting for Matth? Dive in! I did just that. Before I knew it, I had purchased the next thirteen cattle, not even thinking about the total cost and what in the heck I was going to do with all of them. Suddenly, I was in the champion Black Angus business.

They were going to deliver my cattle the following week and the only place where I could possibly keep them was our 1,500-acre family retreat in Carrolton. It was certainly big enough but after seeing the auction farm, I knew it wouldn't be of sufficient stature to run the kind of operation I wanted. I housed the cattle there temporarily and began looking for a more suitable place to raise championship-caliber animals. It took several months but eventually I ran across a three-hundred-acre place for sale on Rice Pike in Boone County, just thirty minutes from my home. The land was called Caintucky Acres and was owned by the Rodney Cain family. "Biz," as he was called by his friends, was the owner of Wiseway Electric and I had known him for some time through the Chamber of Commerce. I checked into the local land prices and he was asking a reasonable amount. I was in a hurry, so, without much negotiating, I purchased the land.

They had a tenant farmer living there and I think he let it deteriorate over the years. The land needed work, so I spent a year bringing it up to the standards expected for a successful Black Angus ranch. I brought in bulldozers and cleared out all the old rotting fence posts and scrub brush. I had the original home remodeled and built two new ones for the help. The wire fences were replaced with new board fencing. Several first-class barns and grain silos were also erected. Once roads were constructed, the entire land was reseeded. A year later we proceeded to move my small herd of cattle from Carrolton to their new home, the Toebben Triple T Angus Cattle Ranch.

Through a friend of mine I was able to find Kevin Gallagher, an experienced farm manager. He and his wife, Susan, had recently sold their ranch in Texas and were looking for jobs. I hired him along with three other men who also had extensive cattle ranch experience. Kevin helped guide me through the process of establishing our product reputation. To be successful, it was essential that you include prize bulls and cows into your herd, and Kevin knew where to look for the best of the best. We travelled to California, Wyoming, and Colorado in search of specimens we needed to build a superior herd. We worked on that for a year.

Kevin Gallagher and his family.

One evening Kevin called and he sounded excited. "Matth, there's a cow in California and I'd like to bring her into our herd. She'll provide an excellent opportunity to enhance the blood lines." I asked him the name of the cow and who was selling it.

"The cow's name is Lucy and her owner is the Julio Gallo Wine Company," he replied. "She's to be auctioned off with some other cows."

All good cattle are classified in trade books, so I asked Kevin about Lucy's blood lines. I looked it up and her genealogy was promising. I said to Kevin, "What do you think the price is going to be?"

"It's hard to say for sure but I'd guess around $25 to $30 thousand. It all depends upon who's doing the bidding."

"That's not too bad given her history. Why don't we fly to California to take a look at her?"

The Julio Gallo Estate was a beautiful ranch situated in the middle of thousands of acres of grapes. They extended in all directions as far as I could see. The company was started by Julio and Ernest Gallo after prohibition, when Ernest was only seventeen years old. They grew it into one of the largest wine companies in the world.

The first cow we approached was surrounded by a small group of potential buyers. She was standing on a display pedestal and was groomed so beautifully she almost looked like a painting. She was a premier specimen and obviously would be an expensive one. I looked at the ear tag and, as I suspected, it was Lucy. After walking around the cow and studying it for several minutes, I turned to Kevin and said, "Thirty thousand, huh? I don't think so." I knew she would fetch much more than that. We walked around and inspected several other animals, but none were of the same caliber as Lucy.

I met Ernest Gallo's son-in-law, Joe Kohlman, who managed the ranch. He was a very cordial guy and was nice enough to arrange a personal tour. They had their own glass bottle manufacturing company. Next to it was a rail terminal where they were loading one car after another with thousands of bottles of wine. Joe took us to see the family's personal wine cellar. We sat at an old wooden barrel with a polished top that had to be twelve feet in diameter. He told us that after World War II they had purchased cuttings from the best grape vines in Europe and had them delivered to California to be cross bred with the larger, sweeter American grapes. The result was the creation of some of the finest wines in the world. Joe opened several bottles for us to try. I suspected that maybe he might have been trying to soften me up for the bidding. Actually, he turned out to be just a nice guy with a passion for the wine business.

When the auction began, the first cow fetched a price of over $30 thousand. As suspected, I was going to pay much more for the cow I wanted. The bidding for Lucy was already at $60,000 before I had even started. Finally, I entered the battle and wound up buying Lucy for $70,000. That was one of the highest prices paid for any cow in the United States that year. A reporter for one of the cattle trade magazines ridiculed me as being a naïve newcomer who spent much more than Lucy was worth. He made me a laughing stock, but I was determined to make him eat his words.

One of my prized bulls from Lucy's embryo harvest

About a week after the sale I called Joe Kuhlman and I said, "Before I put Lucy through the stress of transporting her to Kentucky, I'd like to breed her."

"We can do that. What bull would you like me to use?"

My ranch manager Kevin had already done some research on it and told me which bull to select. When I informed Joe of my choice he replied, "Excellent choice, Matth. I can tell you've been getting some good advice from Kevin."

"I certainly have. I wouldn't be able to do any of this without his help."

"I assume he also advised you to have the embryos flushed out before she's shipped."

"Exactly." That would have made us one of the first programs in the country to use embryos to establish quality blood lines.

"We should be able to harvest around four or five of them and each will be worth about ten thousand dollars. That should cover over half the cost of Lucy."

"That's what I'm counting on, Joe. Let me know when you have the embryos."

Joe bought a semen specimen from the bull we selected, and Lucy was inseminated. A month later he called me and sounded very excited on the phone. "Matth, you've got to be one of the luckiest men alive. We harvested nineteen embryos from Lucy. Can you imagine that, nineteen from only one breeding? It's unheard of. I've never seen anything like it in my life."

We now had nineteen potential calves from the most renowned cow in the business. Some embryos were frozen for later use. One was implanted into a recipient cow that served as a surrogate mother. She gave birth to an excellent calf nine months later. The following year we held our first auction. We planned to sell the calf, one cow with another implanted embryo, and one of our frozen embryos. All sold for a great price and I more than recouped all the money I had invested in Lucy. We still had seventeen embryos remaining, either already implanted or still frozen. Purchasing Lucy turned out to be an excellent investment. Word of our success spread throughout the industry and made it back to the gentleman who had written the scathing article about me the year previous. He was forced to eat his words after all. He had to write a follow-up article about me. His reluctant headline read, "How Lucky Can You Get!"

The entire industry now knew about us and our program. We became recognized as one of the top breeders in the country. In fact, the National Cattle Breeders Association awarded us the "Best Cattle Breeder Award" for the entire United States. We were all extremely proud of that accomplishment. We continued to breed and sell the Black Angus for years. It was my passion but like some wise person once said, "All good things must come to an end."

After many years of success, I had to sell the Triple-T cattle herd. Laverne became quite ill and I needed to spend more time with her. She was more important to me than anything else, so I made the decision to sell our prize cattle. When we announced that we were going to liquidate one of the finest herds in the country, we had responses from breeders all over the United States, Canada, Mexico, and South America. So many people attended the auction we almost ran out of parking places on the farm. When all was said and done, we made over a million dollars more than we had anticipated. It was a sad day for me, but it was something that had to be done. Laverne came first. She was the center of my life and without her I would be lost.

Looking back, I was happy with my Black Angus experience. I was able to pursue one of my dream hobbies and in the process met many wonderful people along the way. Some of them are still friends to this day.

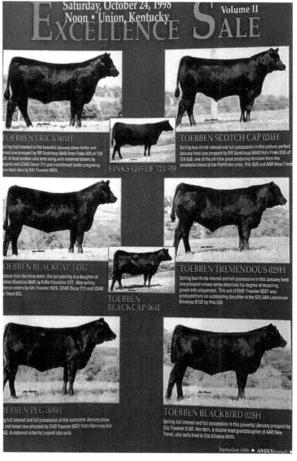

Brochure listing some of the black angus cattle Triple-T had up for auction at our first sale

RIGHT TO FARM ACT

There is an important side-story associated with our cattle business. On our Triple T Cattle Ranch, three creeks ran through the back of the property. They joined together to form a bigger one that ultimately made its way to the Ohio River. Over the years, erosion had caused rocks and debris to wash down from the smaller creeks and dam up the large one. During heavy rains the water would overflow the banks and flood the land. Top soil washed away and the grazing land for my cattle herd was being destroyed. My solution was to remove all the obstructing material that was blocking the normal flow of water through the creek. I wanted to restore it to the way it had been a hundred years ago when the land was more pristine.

I had a bulldozer delivered to the site. On the weekends I drove down and ran it until I was able to push the rocks back up onto the bank. I opened the creek bed until it was about twenty feet wide and five feet deep in the middle. It would no longer back up and flood my land. I took great care to shape the banks to make everything look natural. After all, this was to be the showplace for my future prized Black Angus herd, so everything had to be perfect. The area looked beautiful and I believed I had done a good job. My land no longer flooded, and the grazing lands were successfully restored.

All was well until several months later when I received a call from the Corps of Engineers in Louisville. The gentleman said in an arrogant tone, "Mr. Toebben, several weeks ago you were on your farm on Rice Pike with a bulldozer. What was your purpose in that?"

My first thought was, *How does this fellow know what I'm doing on my own land and why is he calling me about it?* I found out later that a neighbor of mine who worked in Cincinnati turned me in for "damaging the environment." He wasn't man enough to discuss the matter with me personally, so he called in the government.

I explained to the caller that the creek regularly ran over its banks and was destroying my land. I was taking the necessary measures to prevent further flooding. "It's good farm management," I said. "You should know this."

"Your problem, Mr. Toebben, is that you have violated federal and state laws because you didn't get a permit. That's illegal."

His confrontational attitude started to drive up my blood pressure, but I remained calm...at least as calm as could be expected under the circumstances. "Illegal? It's illegal for me to manage a problem on my own farm!"

"That's correct, Mr. Toebben."

"I just can't believe that! Who are you to tell me I can't improve my own land?"

"Sir, what you did was wrong. I must insist that you restore the land to the way it was."

That angered me even more and I'm sure my blood pressure was going through the roof. I said, "Well, I don't know about that. I improved the land and I'm not interested in putting those rocks back. That's just not going to happen. It'll cause my top soil to erode again." The battle lines were drawn, and I didn't intend to lose.

He got upset with me because I wouldn't cave in to his demands. He was one of those pesky bureaucrats just like some of the ones I grew up with in Germany. They get into a position with a little power and it goes to their head. His next words were, "Well, Mr. Toebben, we have a meeting scheduled in Louisville next Monday and you need to come to that meeting to defend your actions."

I paused for a few seconds before replying, "Sir, I don't need to defend anything from anyone. What I do on my own property is my business and I'm not going to attend your meeting."

"Mr. Toebben, you're not understanding me. You're in violation of state and federal law. As of right now you will be fined twenty-five thousand dollars a day until you comply with our demands. Put the rocks back."

"The government takes most of my money anyway, so you might as well take some more, but it won't make any difference. I'm still not putting the rocks back. It's my land and I'll do what's necessary to protect it." We had reached the insurmountable point of no return and the conversation abruptly came to a halt.

Two weeks later my phone rang, and it was the same man from the Corps of Engineers. He was a little more polite when he asked, "Could we meet at your farm?"

"Sure, just name the date and time. I'll be there." I was a little concerned. Twenty-five thousand a day was a large amount of money. I was hoping that maybe the government wanted to settle but I was ready to fight them if need be. I wondered, *If they can push me around like this, what do they do to small farmers? Those people don't have resources with which to fight back.* I decided I would challenge these bureaucrats no matter the cost. What they were doing wasn't right.

The meeting was scheduled, and they showed up on the Rice Pike property. There were five of them: one from Boone County, two from the state of Kentucky, and two from the Corps of Engineers. They were accompanied by an attorney. They were all dressed in suits and nice shoes. I was wearing boots and jeans. I was alone, except for my secretary. She was there to take notes. We shook hands like we were all good friends. After introductions, the first words came from their attorney, "Mr. Toebben, where is your attorney?"

"Attorney? Attorney for what? Why would I need an attorney?"

"You probably need one, sir. As you were told previously, you have violated section 404 of the Clean Water Act. That's a violation of federal law." It was obvious they weren't here to settle. Their goal was to intimidate me.

"Well if I ever feel like I need one, I'll be sure to get one. In the meantime, my personal secretary will take notes of exactly what is said here today." They looked at each other and I could tell they were a little uncomfortable with her taking notes. They expected me to cave.

We all decided to walk down to inspect the creek and they all got their nice shiny shoes muddy. I chuckled to myself. It was a small victory.

The site looked well-manicured and beautiful. There was nothing for them to complain about. They stepped aside to confer with each other. After a minute the lead attorney said, "Mr. Toebben, we'd like to get this situation resolved. We will forgive the fine, but we still must insist that you return the rocks to their original position. In addition, you must replant any small trees you disturbed."

I considered their offer which was really no offer at all. I was right back to where I was several weeks ago. They only planned to forgive the fines which were unjust in the first place. I needed to buy a little time, so I replied, "I'm still not sure I want to do that. I need to think it over." The meeting concluded without resolution and the suits with the muddy shoes returned to their cars.

The entire episode didn't make any sense to me. How could a government agency be allowed to bully farmers like that? The following day I called Senator Mitch McConnell who was a good friend of mine. I had been an early supporter of his 1985 bid to unseat the incumbent Democrat Senator Walter D. Huddleston.

It was part of my commitment to do what I could to help make Kentucky a red state. Laverne and I had held a large fundraiser for Mitch at our home in Country Squire Estates. He wasn't the Senate Majority Leader yet, but he still wielded a fair amount of influence. When I explained what had been happening to me, he said, "Let me see what I can do for you, Matth."

"Thank you, Senator, but I don't want you to handle this. I want to take care of it myself. What they are doing to the farmers isn't right and I going to try to fix it."

"So, what can I do, Matth?"

"I need a copy of the original Clean Water Act as passed by Congress. I want to read it myself."

"That won't be a problem. I'll send you a copy right away."

———◆•◆•◆———

A few days later I was sitting in my office, reading the act. It was long and complicated. It wasn't until I reached the final pages that I found what I was looking for. I grinned and said to the empty room, "Gotcha!"

The state still wanted to settle so I arranged to meet them at the farm a second time several weeks later. They were looking pretty confident, but I had an important piece of paper in my back pocket. They again offered to forgive my fines, which by now were almost a million dollars. They thought they had me over a barrel and were still insisting that I return the rocks and plant new trees.

I walked over to their lawyer and said, "I'm not going to do that."

The lawyer was shocked by my refusal and was obviously upset with me. "Then the fines are still on the books and accumulating late penalties. We're going to keep fining you daily until you comply."

"Then you'd be breaking the law," I replied.

"What?" said the incredulous lawyer. "Us? Breaking the law?" He laughed and added, "You don't know what you're talking about."

That's when I pulled the paper from my back pocket. "I want you to read this."

He looked at the title page and said, "I'm not going to stand here and read through the entire Clean Air Act. I already know it.'

"Then maybe you can just skip to the last pages and read the sentence I highlighted. Read it out loud so everyone can hear."

His face turned pale as he read the sentence. He said, "Oh, this changes nothing. There's a counteraction to this."

"No there isn't according to Senator McConnell." I grabbed the paper from the attorney's hand and read the sentence myself. It basically stated that all farms were exempt from the Clean Water Act regulations. I looked at each of them and added, "You've been illegally fining innocent farmers. Maybe you should all consult an attorney before they decide to sue you." They all looked at each other and didn't say another word. They simply drove off. That battle was won but I wasn't finished. There was still a war to be waged.

I requested that the people in Frankfort send me copies of any and all farmers who had been cited or fined under the same circumstances. The state charged me five cents a copy. The list contained almost five thousand individuals. The names were there, but the addresses and phone numbers had been redacted. I had my attorney call them back and ask why they had deleted some of the requested information. They didn't have a legitimate explanation. He insisted that they send a new list including all the phone numbers and addresses they had omitted. He threatened legal action if they failed to comply. Within the week I finally got what I wanted. I notified many of the farmers who had been cited that they had recourse against the State of Kentucky.

After that I decided those poor farmers needed more help. They didn't have the wherewithal to protect themselves. I consulted friends with the Kentucky Cattlemen's Association and various other Kentucky farming groups. With their help and that of others, I crafted the outline of a bill we called, "The State of Kentucky Right to Farm Act." I sent copies to all those farmers on my list. That got everyone motivated to call their representatives.

The bill was scheduled for a hearing in front of the combined Senate and House Committee on Agriculture in Frankfort. I was asked to speak. As a former president of the Home Builders Association, I had already testified in front of a number of legislative committees. I was familiar with the process and was comfortable doing it. The morning turned out to be anything but comfortable, however.

I got there early, at 7 AM, and was first to sign in on the agenda sheet. There were five other individuals behind me. They also had bills to discuss. I took a seat and waited for my bill to be presented, fully expecting it to be the first matter on the agenda. Before long the room was filled to beyond capacity, almost as though it had been packed with bureaucrats. At the time, Kentucky was very much a blue state run by Democrats. The senate and congressional majority leaders were Democrats, the governor was a Democrat, and the committee chairmen like the one in front of me, holding the gavel, was a Democrat. For some reason I never fully understood, they were opposed to the Right to Farm Act.

I waited patiently as those who had signed in after me had their bills presented and voted on. Though I had spoken to him the previous day, the chairman never called my name. After several hours, he closed his folder and announced, "Meeting adjourned."

He wanted to stonewall my bill. I was angry, so I jumped up and yelled, "Mr. Chairman, my name is Matth Toebben and I'm here to present the Right to Farm Act. I was the first to sign in this morning and yet you decided to pass over me. Why are you doing that? Why won't you let me testify for the farmers of Kentucky?"

The Republicans on the committee started looking at each other and asking, "What's going on here? This isn't right."

The chairman felt the pressure, and he reopened the meeting. "I'm sorry Mr. Toebben, it was a simple oversight on my part. You may proceed." I knew he was lying.

I had my huge stack of names in front of me as I said, "Mr. Chairman, the farmers of Kentucky are being bullied and abused by the same government that is supposed to protect them." I proceeded to tell my story about my personal experiences and read the official statute given to me by Senator Mitch McConnell. I added, "The same thing has happened to every farmer on this list. There are almost five thousand individuals here and that doesn't include those cases that have been swept under the carpet." I continued for another fifteen minutes. When I was finished, you could hear a pin drop. All of the sudden, the ranking Republican member on the committee stood up and said, "Mr. Chairman, I request an immediate vote on this issue. The Kentucky farmers have been ignored long enough. It's time they be heard." Nobody wanted to challenge him. Within thirty seconds the chairman called for a voice vote and that was it. The bill was sent to the House and Senate where it passed with little opposition.

From there it went to Governor Paul Patton's desk to be signed. I already knew him pretty well. There was a great deal of opposition to the bill from the Democrats, but this issue was too hot to ignore. He signed the bill and it went into law. That was about fifteen years ago and it remains one of my proudest accomplishments.

EDUCATION

Laverne and I have had a keen interest in education ever since our children attended Covington Catholic and Villa Madonna Schools. She and I began supporting students by funding a half-dozen annual scholarships at Thomas More University. In addition, we set up various endowment funds for needy students at Covington Catholic, Notre Dame Academy, Springer School in Cincinnati, Holy Cross School in Covington, and the Gateway Community and Technical College, in Florence.

Though we have long appreciated the importance of a good education, we came to realize that it wasn't always available to some children in the community. One example involved a member of our own family. My middle daughter, Diane Marx, had a son, Brent. He was a thoughtful and wonderful child. Every afternoon he would ride his bicycle over to our house to visit Laverne when she was ill. He would sit next to her and talk for a while until he would say, "I'm sorry, Grandma, but I have to go now." She greatly appreciated those small opportunities to see her grandson.

I noticed that there seemed to be a gradual change in his personality. He became difficult to handle and wasn't doing well in school. He became short-tempered and appeared frustrated. Diane and her husband Scott were beside themselves with concern. They didn't know what had happened.

One evening, Diane called me. She was crying when she said, "We had Brent tested and he has a problem."

"What is it?" I asked.

"He's dyslexic."

"Dyslexic! I've never heard of someone being dyslexic. What is it?" I was fearing the worst. Diane described the entire problem to me. It explained all the recent changes in his personality. My first response was, "How do we fix it?" That's what I did, fix problems.

"He needs to be in a special program for learning. Our problem is that there are no schools in Northern Kentucky equipped to handle this kind of difficulty, but there is one in Cincinnati. It's Springer School and they specialize in teaching children with learning disorders. I'm going to enroll him there." That was one of the wisest decisions she ever made.

Brent excelled in the school. Years later, he was getting ready to graduate. Diane invited Laverne and me to attend. We took a seat near the back and waited for the ceremonies to begin. The master of ceremonies announced that one of the speakers for the evening was Brent. I was shocked at the change that had taken place in our grandson. The same person who had struggled so much as a boy was now an articulate young man. He spoke with confidence about his affliction and how he had been unable to keep up with the other children at his regular school. He was afraid that he wouldn't ever amount to anything. It was the same fear I had when I was a young boy suffering from severe asthma in Lorup. Brent stated that his life had been completely changed by the Springer school. He expressed his appreciation for all they had done for him and the other students. Laverne and I were beaming with pride at his speech and his ability to have overcome so many obstacles. After the ceremonies I began to wonder just how many other children were hampered by dyslexia and how many futures were affected. It was at that point that Laverne and I started a $100,000 endowment fund at the school to help pay tuition costs for dyslexic children who couldn't afford the special attention they needed.

It was about a year later when my oldest daughter Susan called to tell me that she had transferred her children to the Holy Cross School in Latonia. She loved the school and the teachers there. She said the principal mentioned that they would like to start a school for children with learning disabilities, similar to the Springer School in Cincinnati. "As you know, there's nothing available for children with dyslexia in Northern Kentucky," said Susan. Then she asked, "Do you think there's any way you could help them out?"

Since I had a grandson with a learning disorder, I was interested and asked Susan to explain a little more about their plans. We talked about the matter for a little bit and I said, "Would you set up a meeting with the principle so she and I can discuss her plans in detail?"

The Toebben House

We met and a month later I purchased a large home directly across the street from Holy Cross and deeded it over to the school. With the help of a great many volunteers donating both time and money, the new center for learning disabilities was established. It was named "The Toebben House For Academic Achievement." Children with all types of educational problems now had a place that could meet their special needs. Bishop Joseph Foys officiated the grand opening on August 30, 2009, and the school has enjoyed great success ever since. Laverne and I were so moved by the school's accomplishments we established another $100,000 endowment fund to support its ongoing efforts.

Bishop Roger Foys officiating
the dedication ceremony

Having been in the construction industry for over five decades, I became painfully aware of the shortage of people with necessary skills in the workplace. Our federal government had been so preoccupied with the concept of promoting four-year college degrees they failed to consider the need for skilled people in the blue-collar workplace. Too many students were graduating fromcollege with heavy student loan debt and no marketable skills needed to obtain a job with sufficient pay to cover their loan responsibilities.

Though I agree with the concept of a four-year degree, it's not for everyone. Obtaining an education that results in well paying jobs is often more important. It is for this reason that I have been a staunch supporter of Kentucky's community college and trade school programs. Plans had been drawn up to construct a branch of the Gateway Community and Technical College in Florence, Kentucky. They had acquired most of the necessary land but did not have sufficient funds to construct an adequate roadway to serve as an entrance to the new college. Toebben Companies owned much of the surrounding land and the right-of-way as part of our Interstate property acquisition efforts. Knowing this, Gateway approached us to see if we could help. In response, we deeded over the necessary land to Gateway and agreed to pay the entire cost of building the access roads at a total expense of one million dollars. Gateway has successfully educated thousands of students since its opening in 2002.

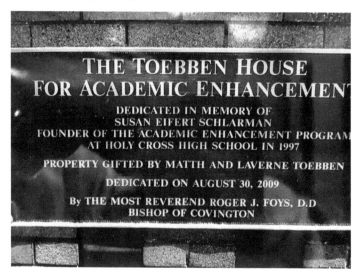

LOST CAR, LOST LIFE

I was sitting at my office desk when the call came. It would change my life forever. It was Laverne. "Matth?" I could tell from the tone in her voice that something was seriously wrong. I knew she had been shopping at the Fort Mitchell Kroger's and wondered what could have possibly happened.

"What is it Laverne?" I asked.

"Someone stole my car while I was in the store."

"Stole your car? At the grocery, in broad daylight?"

"Yes. I was only inside for an hour or so and when I came out it was gone."

I told her to call the police and drove right over. It was a large parking lot and when I found Laverne, the police were already there talking to her. I could tell she was frantic and almost on the verge of tears. When I spoke to the policeman, he asked me, "What kind of car is it, Mr. Toebben?"

"It's an off-white Cadillac Eldorado like, like..." I kept looking around for something similar, and added, "Just like that one over there." He and I walked over to the car and I read the license plate number. It was Laverne's missing car, sitting in the next aisle just a hundred feet away.

Laverne's face turned red. "I'm so sorry for making you drive over here, officer. I'm sure you have more important things to do than helping a woman find her lost car."

"That's OK, Mrs. Toebben. We get calls like this from time to time." I think he said that just to make her feel better. We both thanked him for his help and watched him drive away.

"Oh Matth, I'm so embarrassed. I don't know what happened."

"Don't worry, Laverne. We all do things like this. How many

times have I misplaced my wallet and panicked until you found it for me?" We shared a laugh at some of the forgetful things we do sometimes, and drove home, thinking nothing more about it.

Several weeks later, I came home after a particularly difficult day at work and went directly to the family room to gear down and read the paper. Laverne came in and asked me something, I don't remember what, but it was nothing important. I answered her, and she returned to the kitchen to make supper. Over dinner we talked about each other's day and she asked me the same question she had asked just an hour earlier. I gave her the same answer, figuring she wasn't paying attention the first time. After dinner we were sitting in the family room watching the television together when she asked the same question for the third time. I got frustrated and raised my voice, "My gosh, Laverne, that's the third time you've asked me that same question in the past hour. Haven't you been listening?" She had a hurt look in her eyes and that's when I realized we had a problem. I thought, *this can't possibly be happening. She's only sixty-seven.* Then I remembered that Laverne's mother had suffered from Alzheimer's disease for years before she died.

She saw a neurologist who confirmed the diagnosis. We were devastated, and Laverne was understandably frightened. She slowly deteriorated. She was still the sweet woman I had married, but over time, she no longer recognized me or the children. Doctors speculated that it might have been related to an inherited trait, but I always believed it was mostly the result of having taken the aggressive chemotherapy years previously. A physician friend once told me that almost any medication has the potential for toxic side effects. Chemotherapeutic agents are a prime example. "Chemo Brain" some doctors called it. While the medications kill cancer cells, they can also destroy normal ones at the same time. I believe that's what happened in Laverne's case. The chemotherapy damaged parts of her brain, and the effects didn't appear until years later.

It's easy to second-guess the decision, but at the time, we had no other choice. Without the treatments, she would have died at a young age from the metastatic disease. It was a horrible situation. She went through years of hardship and overcame what the doctors called an "incurable cancer" only to wind up with this. Regardless of the cause, it wasn't fair. I think I was probably frustrated and feeling sorry for myself. Then I felt guilty about feeling that way. Poor Laverne was the one with the problem. The emotional turmoil inside me was overwhelming. The love of my life was fading away and there was nothing I could do to fix things, other than to pray, which I did a lot. The family did the best we could, caring for her ourselves, but it was more than we could handle. The disease was taking its toll on all of us and we were in desperate need of help.

One afternoon my oldest daughter Susan, a registered nurse, spoke to me. She said, "Dad, I've scheduled a meeting for the entire family at the Cincinnati Alzheimer's Association. They help family members of those afflicted with this problem. We want you to join us." The following week we all went to the Association. They had a conference room where a counselor discussed the problem in great depth. I can't remember her name, but she was excellent and had a full understanding of what we were experiencing. Our situation wasn't at all unique. She reassured us that all the emotions our family was feeling were common. She explained that Laverne was completely incapable of overcoming her dementia difficulties. It's wasn't a matter of not trying or a failure to concentrate. The part of her brain that processed memory was failing just like any part of the body can. We just had to be patient and accept her as she was rather than trying to change her. Our feelings of frustration were normal, and we shouldn't allow ourselves to be plagued by guilt.

By the end of the meeting we were relieved and felt much better about the situation. We learned to accept the reality of the disease. The progression might be slowed with medication, but it couldn't be cured. Even though I was unable to fix the problem I vowed to do everything I could to keep my wife comfortable. I was a very fortunate man who had accumulated enough wealth to keep that promise. I had built a retirement center called Highland Crossing in Fort Wright years previously. That was one of the unexpected blessings I mentioned earlier. We owned it for about fifteen years before selling it. I called Betty Hanson who was the lady who used to manage the facility before she retired. I said, "Betty, would you and your husband be willing to join me for dinner some night next week?"

The following Monday, she and her husband met me. I asked, "Betty, have you heard anything about Laverne's problem?"

"Yes, I have, Matth. We're both so sorry."

"Well you've been in this kind of business for a long time, talking care of elderly people with special needs. I need some help. Laverne is getting worse and I'm afraid she's going to hurt herself. I need somebody to be with her at all times." I asked Betty if she had any ideas. She did.

"You remember that woman we had on the third floor managing the assisted living area?"

"Yes, Linda Jones as I recall."

"That's her. She's an excellent caregiver and has a great deal of experience dealing with dementia patients. We were talking a few days ago and Linda was complaining that the new owners of Highland Crossing were working her to death. She's been doing double shifts and would like to find something else to do. She might be exactly what you need."

"Oh my gosh, she sounds perfect. Would you call her for me?"

I hired Linda a week later and she has been a godsend. She and her husband lived in Villa Hills, less than five minutes away so she was readily available when needed. By the time she began working for us, Laverne was already having serious problems. Linda was a very patient, caring person who treated Laverne like a sister, maybe even better. She was always at Laverne's side, reassuring her and tending to her needs. We owned a home in Naples, Florida, and Laverne loved going there, even after her conditioned worsened. We would take Linda with us every year to help care for Laverne. The two of them would sit next to each other by the pool almost every day.

As Laverne continued to deteriorate, Linda remained at her side. We couldn't have gotten by without her. She was a saint.

Linda and Laverne

Laverne's disease had also taken its toll on me. The past several years had been overwhelmingly stressful. I had been burning the candle at both ends, caring for Laverne at night, supervising a multitude of construction projects during the day, and working behind the scenes on several major political campaigns. It was January 24, 2011. Ed Bessler and I were at the Greater Cincinnati/ Northern Kentucky Airport waiting for a flight to Washington, D.C. We had been invited to Rand Paul's Senate swearing-in ceremony. We were waiting at the Delta gate when I started feeling ill. There was no chest pain, but I began sweating profusely and thought I might pass out. It was similar to the way I had felt twenty years earlier when I thought I was having a heart attack. In retrospect, that's probably what had actually happened that day.

I looked so bad the Delta personnel became concerned and told me I couldn't board the plane. Someone must have called 911 because the next thing I knew I was in an ambulance on my way to the St. Elizabeth Hospital emergency room. My daughter Susan met me there and called Dr. Ray Will, a cardiac surgeon. He ordered an angiogram that showed multiple coronary blockages. Within hours he took me to surgery to perform quadruple bypass surgery. After several days they let me return home, but I was very weak. Fortunately, I had my family and Linda to take care of Laverne and me while I recovered. Once I was stable, I believed most of our troubles were behind us. As often happens, I was wrong.

Less than a month later, Laverne lost her long-standing battle with Alzheimer's. She died on February 16, 2011, at the age of seventy-nine. Though it was expected, the finality of it was rough on all of us. I was physically weakened and emotionally devastated. I felt that my own life had come to an end. Any measure of success I had enjoyed, any accumulation of wealth and material possessions became meaningless without Laverne to share them with me.

The visitation was held at the Middendorf Funeral Home. Hundreds of family and friends came to express their condolences. Lines of visitors extended all the way through the door and outside. It was a fitting testament to how many lives Laverne had impacted. The number of people attending was both heartwarming and exhausting. I can never thank them enough. I was still recovering from my heart surgery and after about an hour, I could no longer stand, so my family brought me a stool. I half-stood and half-sat for the remainder of the evening. A funeral service mass and burial were held the following morning. She was laid to rest at St. Mary's Cemetery in Fort Mitchell. Laverne and I had been together for over fifty-five years. A large part of me was buried along with her that day. I had my children and grandchildren to comfort me, but losing Laverne left a deep hole in my heart, one that could never be completely filled. The family made a sizable donation to the Cincinnati Alzheimer's Association in her memory to fund ongoing research and counseling to families impacted by the tragic disease.

About a month after Laverne passed away, Linda came to me and asked, "Matth, when would you like me to quit?"

"Linda," I said, "I would like it if you could remain here for as long as I live." She is still with me to this day, helping me with everything inside the house. Five days a week she comes in the morning and leaves after dinner, about seven o'clock. She organizes all my medicines, prepares meals, cleans, and makes sure all birthday cards for my children and grandchildren go out with checks on time every year. The entire family loves her and I will forever be in her debt.

POLITIC*S*

When I came to the United States in January of 1953, there was a requirement that I register every year on the anniversary of my entering the country. They wanted to know where I was living and whether or not I was supporting myself. The immigration rules then were much more stringent than they are today. I was always afraid I might be so busy I'd forget to register and that I might be subject to deportation back to Germany. I never missed the date, however.

After five years, I was permitted to apply for citizenship. I studied Civics and American History. Though I had learned the English language somewhat, reading was still a formidable challenge. Without Laverne's help I would have been lost. In the fall of 1958, I passed the written test and was thrilled. Several days later Laverne and I went to the Kenton County Courthouse where I and several other immigrants were sworn in. It was such a proud moment that it's hard to describe. I had the privilege of becoming a citizen of the United States, something that is too often taken for granted. The ceremonies were conducted by Judge Mac Swinford. He could have made it difficult by quizzing us on various aspects of the constitution, but he didn't. He simply admonished us that our new citizenship was an honor that came with the responsibility of following the traditions and principles of our great land.

I was now allowed to vote, a privilege not enjoyed by most people in the world. I had done some research on the two major political parties and I didn't like what the Democratic Party stood for, so I registered as a Republican. My initial sponsor George Kreutzjans congratulated me and asked if I had registered to vote yet. I replied that I had and would be voting as a Republican.

"Republican!" he laughed. "There aren't many of those in Kentucky. Why did you do that? You might as well not even bother to vote."

"I've seen the damage a powerful central government can inflict on its people. You don't know what it was like, George. You left Germany before it happened, before the Nazis took over and squeezed every ounce of liberty out of the citizens. The Democrats favor the same kind of powerful, centralized government and I'm concerned they could very well be headed down the same path. It might take a while but that seems to be the direction they're headed. I had enough living under a powerful socialist government. You must beware of those who promise everything. They treat their citizens like sheep. If sheep could vote, they'd probably select those persons who feed them even though those same people are the ones who would slaughter them later. I've seen enough of that approach under Hitler and I refuse to be a part of it."

After further discussion, George respected my decision and the courage to speak my mind. It was one of the many freedoms that the citizens enjoyed in this country. With that freedom comes a responsibility to treat others of differing opinions with respect. As a younger man, I'm afraid I might have been a little bull-headed, a trait I inherited from my father. When confronted with a dispute, I would stick out my chin, raise my voice, and draw a line in the sand. It was an approach that might have been necessary on occasion, but it eliminated any chance for resolution through discussion. Once drawn, you can't erase the line without being seen as weak or lacking resolve.

With Laverne's influence over the years I've learned a better way. She helped me soften some of those rough edges around my personality. I learned that in expressing your opinion, you shouldn't dig in your heels and bully others into agreeing with you. Rather you had to convince them with superior facts and logic. There is almost a duty to do so if it's in the interest of bettering the community. It's an obligation I have readily embraced. One example is the debate over whether Northern Kentucky should support the establishment of an eastern bypass or the more popular concept of building a new bridge between Kentucky and Ohio. I supported the bypass and chose to do so working in the background, out of the limelight.

To my way of thinking, the bridge made no sense. It wouldn't solve the problem of excessive traffic along the I-75/I-71 corridor. Studies had been commissioned and showed that an eastern bypass would cut traffic by over 30% if it was constructed properly. I had already studied the original plans for I-71 and it was never the intention of the engineers to have it merge with I-75. It was supposed to continue east as a separate interstate, passing through Boone, Kenton, and Campbell Counties prior to crossing the Ohio River and continuing to Northern Ohio. By constructing an eastern bypass instead of the bridge, both Kentucky and Ohio would greatly benefit while seeing a higher return on their tax dollars.

Many counties in Northern Kentucky and Ohio have already supported the idea. I've tried to convince any reluctant local officials that it was the best option for our community. Rather than trying to ramrod my position, I showed them the facts and studies. Their typical response was, "Matth, I understand and now I'm on your side." Most agreed to change their position as most great leaders are not afraid to do when presented with all the information. It's still a battle because many Cincinnati politicians and the local newspaper are enamored by the bridge concept. In reality, it would prove to be more expensive and a huge waste of taxpayer money with little economic benefit. I felt so strongly about the matter I wrote an op-ed piece for the *Enquirer*, included on the next page.

I wrote the following article for the *Cincinnati Enquirer* on August 6, 2015:

The proposed Northern Kentucky Interstate 71/75 Cincinnati Eastern Bypass consists of a 68-mile, four-lane highway that would begin in southern Boone County, and then cross into Campbell and Kenton counties before crossing the Ohio River and reconnecting with I-71 and I-75. The bypass is a significantly better alternative than the current plan to construct a new bridge next to the Brent Spence Bridge, and must be our region's highest priority.

While the Brent Spence Bridge plan would cost approximately $3.8 billion, the proposed 68-mile bypass through Kentucky and Ohio would cost approximately $1.1 billion.

In addition to the tremendous cost savings, the bypass would provide much more opportunity for growth in the region, as it would create thousands of permament jobs in Northern Kentucky and Ohio along the 68-mile stretch of highway that would have approximately 16 different interchanges. These jobs would benefit the region for generations to come. The current plan for the Brent Spence Bridge, on the other hand, provides little, if any, economic benefit to Northern Kentucky businesses or residents. And not only does the plan for the Brent Spence Bridge offer very little to the region in terms of economic benefits, but it also imposes costly tolls on commuters crossing the bridge, something the proposed bypass plan would not do.

Moreover, the bypass would markedly reduce traffic congestion on the Brent Spence and in the region's urban core, and these reductions in traffic would far surpass any reductions in traffic resulting from the Brent Spence Bridge plan. Specifically, approximately 25 percent of the daily traffic crossing the Brent Spence Bridge is regional through traffic, much of which is 18-wheeler trucks.

Diverting this traffic to the bypass would be the equivalent of adding an entire lane to each side of I-75 – both southbound and northbound.

Anyone who drives our local interstate system knows that the traffic exceeds the system's capacity. I-75 and I-71, both inside and outside the I-275 loop, are seriously congested, particularly during rush hours. I-275 is no different.

This congestion is costing commuters both time and money, increasing pollution and restricting job growth. Unlike the bypass, the plan for the Brent Spence Bridge offers no long-term relief for this congestion. The bypass would provide commuters with an alternate route during those frequent times that I-75 is congested due to repairs or accidents.

In short, the proposed bypass is a far superior alternative to the Brent Spence Bridge plan. It would cost less than half of what is being proposed for the Brent Spence Bridge plan, be much easier to finance, foster much more economic growth in the region, cut congestion in ways that the Brent Spence Bridge plan simply cannot and overall provide a positive impact on the Tristate region.

Why would one spend $3.8 billion of public money on a highway project when would could accomplish so much more by spending less than half that amount?

The answer seems simple, but it will take the efforts of individuals to persuade our leaders to do the right thing.

So let's build the bypass now – before it is too late and other development begins purchasing the available rights of way.

For more information on getting involved, visit www.nkyunited. com and www.cincyeasternbypass.com

THE ENQUIRER /// THURSDAY, AUGUST 6, 2015 7A

Scrap Brent Spence for new bypass

MATTH TOEBBEN

Matth Toebben is founder of Northern Kentucky-based Toebben Cos.

The proposed Northern Kentucky Interstate 71/75 Cincinnati Eastern Bypass consists of a 68-mile, four-lane highway that would begin in southern Boone County, and then cross into Campbell and Kenton counties before crossing the Ohio River and reconnecting with I-71 and I-75. The bypass is a significantly better alternative than the current plan to construct a new bridge next to the Brent Spence Bridge, and must be our region's highest priority.

While the Brent Spence Bridge plan would cost approximately $3.8 billion, the proposed 68-mile bypass through Kentucky and Ohio would cost approximately $1.1 billion.

In addition to the tremendous cost savings, the bypass would provide much more opportunity for growth in the region, as it would create thousands of permanent jobs in Northern Kentucky and Ohio along the 68-mile stretch of highway that would have approximately 16 different interchanges. These jobs would benefit the region for generations to come. The current plan for the Brent Spence Bridge, on the other hand, provides little, if any, economic benefit to Northern Kentucky businesses or residents. And not only does the plan for the Brent Spence Bridge offer very little to the region in terms of economic benefits, but it also imposes costly tolls on commuters crossing the bridge, something the proposed bypass plan would not do.

Moreover, the bypass would markedly reduce traffic congestion on the Brent Spence and in the region's urban core, and these reductions in traffic would far surpass any reductions in traffic resulting from the Brent Spence Bridge plan. Specifically, approximately 25 percent of the daily traffic crossing the Brent Spence Bridge is regional through traffic, much of which is 18-wheeler trucks.

ENQUIRER FILE

A new Brent Spence Bridge would cost more and do less than a new eastern bypass, a Northern Kentucky businessman writes.

Diverting this traffic to the bypass would be the equivalent of adding an entire lane to each side of I-75 – both southbound and northbound.

Anyone who drives our local interstate system knows that the traffic exceeds the system's capacity. I-75 and I-71, both inside and outside the I-275 loop, are seriously congested, particularly during rush hours. I-275 is no different.

This congestion is costing commuters both time and money, increasing pollution and restricting job growth. Unlike the bypass, the plan for the Brent Spence Bridge offers no long-term relief for this congestion. The bypass would provide commuters with an alternate route during those frequent times that I-75 is congested due to repairs or accidents.

In short, the proposed bypass is a far superior alternative to the Brent Spence Bridge plan. It would cost less than half of what is being proposed for the Brent Spence Bridge plan, be much easier to finance, foster much more economic growth in the region, cut congestion in ways that the Brent Spence Bridge plan simply cannot and overall provide a positive impact on the Tristate region.

Why would one spend $3.8 billion of public money on a highway project when one could accomplish so much more by spending less than half that amount?

The answer seems simple, but it will take the efforts of individuals to persuade our leaders to do the right thing.

So let's build the bypass now – before it is too late and other development begins purchasing the available rights of way.

For more information on getting involved, visit www.nkyunited.com and www.cincyeasternbypass.com

Build the Bypass Now!

I've always believed that it is incumbent on each of us to do all we can to improve the community. One of the best ways to accomplish this is by influencing the political discourse locally and nationally through support of honorable and honest candidates. The prevalence of professional lobbyists has made money far too available to politicians and that has resulted in widespread corruption. I made it my personal cause to help elect people who would shun the seduction of money and power while espousing my philosophy of smaller government.

US Congressman Gene Snyder was such a man. While I was president of the Home Builders Association, I had the opportunity to work with Gene on numerous issues affecting Northern Kentucky. I found him to be an honest person and a tireless worker for his constituents. For that reason, I did all that I could to ensure his political success. He served the people of Kentucky for twenty years. It was the personal contact with representatives like Gene that kept Congress honest. He was a good man who's vote could not be bought, a rarity in DC. I supported him in each of his campaigns and was honored to call him a friend.

Over the years I also felt privileged to support the campaigns of multiple presidential candidates including President George H. Bush, Senator Robert Dole, President George W. Bush, and President Donald Trump.

To Matth
Best Wishes

Laverne and I with presidential candidate
George W. Bush

To Matt & LaVerne,
With best wishes . . .

From left to right: Senator Mitch McConnell, Laverne, me and
presidential candidate, Senator Robert Dole

Left to right: Vice President Dick Cheney, me, Kentucky Governor Ernie
Fletcher

In August 2009, I received a call from Rand Paul. He was
the son of the well-known Libertarian congressman from Texas
and former presidential candidate, Ron Paul. Rand introduced
himself and said, "Matth, you don't know me but I'm running
for the Senate seat that has opened due to the retirement of Jim
Bunning."

I said, "Senate? Why are you just now entering the race?"

"I wanted to wait to see if Senator Bunning was going to
retire or run for a third term. If he did seek re-election, I wasn't
going to run against him in the primary. I didn't think it was the
right thing to do."

That level of respect for the incumbent senior senator impressed me. It showed me that he wasn't just another political opportunist. I saw that as a good sign. I said, "Well Rand, it's already getting late in the game. You don't have a lot of time." I knew who his opponent would be in the Republican primary. I knew the man's family well. They were friends of Laverne and me and were influential members of the Northern Kentucky region. I was aware that he had a great deal of support from the Republican leaders in the state and his winning the primary was almost a forgone conclusion. I had some misgivings about the frontrunner, though, and I was open to the possibility of another candidate. I asked Rand to tell me a little about himself and his vision for Kentucky and the country. I was impressed with his response but said, "Rand, I think you're a little too late. This primary has already been decided in Northern Kentucky."

"My team and I don't think so, Mr. Toebben. I wouldn't have entered this race if I didn't believe I had a chance to win."

The man was a fighter and had the necessary fire in his belly to pull things off. I liked that and wanted to give him a chance, but I didn't actually know him. No one else in Northern Kentucky did, so I said, "I need to know more about you. Why don't you send me some information? To be honest with you, I plan to make a few phone calls to check into your background." That's what I did and found out that he was involved in formulating some groundwork on conservative ideas coming out of the Bowling Green area. He was a true down-to-earth conservative. I called him back about a week later. "I've been thinking about your candidacy and I've decided to support you. If you work with me, maybe we can win this thing."

Rand Paul said, "I know you're expecting me to ask for a check but that's not the only reason why I called you. I've heard that if someone is going to run for any state political office, they must have you in their corner to help carry the Northern Kentucky region."

He wanted my open endorsement in the expectation that it would bring in more supporters from the area. "I tell you what, Rand. We need to talk in person. When can you visit? I would like you to meet some of my friends."

I called together a group of the most influential people in the area, ones who would be willing to open their checkbooks to support the right man. Twenty of us met with him in my offices on Buttermilk Pike. After I introduced Rand, he began speaking and continued uninterrupted for the next forty-five minutes. He had no notes. He spoke from the heart about what he thought was needed in our country. That indicated to me that he believed in what he said and wasn't simply throwing out talking points to pander to potential contributors. After he finished speaking, you could almost hear a pin drop. All were impressed by what he had to say. Rand fielded a dozen questions and handled them with the confidence of a seasoned politician, except he was like few politicians I had ever met. He was a man of deep principle and personal conviction, a man who could never be bought.

After he left, I asked everyone there what they thought. One man said, "My gosh, Matth, where has this guy been? This is the kind of man we need in Washington." Most of the others echoed his comments. Of the twenty there, most wrote checks and threw their support firmly behind this young man. Some had already contributed significant sums of cash to the opposing candidate but were willing to switch their allegiance and commit to Rand.

Within the week we opened a Northern Kentucky campaign office on Mall Road in Florence. It was a very visible spot and the battle for the hearts and minds of the voters began. Every Sunday, I, Bernie Kunkle, and about a dozen of Rand's supporters would meet to discuss strategy. Rand's opponent was well established in Northern Kentucky and that's where the fight would have to be won. Every week, Rand would talk to us on a conference call and discuss where we stood in the campaign and what needed to be done, what should be emphasized with the press and the voters.

When we started, Rand was sixteen points behind his opponent. After only six weeks the frontrunner's lead was cut in half to eight points but time was running out. We redoubled our efforts, seeking campaign contributions for television ads and increased our door-to-door canvassing of the neighborhoods. I told our staff, "I think that if we can get this thing within six points, we'll have it won." Newspaper polls in the state were notoriously unreliable. They had been backing the opposition and appeared to be willing to fudge their poll numbers accordingly to cast their candidate in a better light. Unfortunately, six points was as close as we could get, no matter how hard we worked.

I remember thinking, *This can't possibly be right. We're getting too much positive feedback from the community.* I called Rand and said, There's something screwy going on here. The poll numbers can't be right."

He told me, "We know, Matth. We don't want it to get out, but the true polling numbers show that we're only two points behind." I knew what that meant. Rand Paul was going to win the primary. Polls are inherently misleading because they don't factor in the number of people who will actually go out to the polls and vote.

Pat Runge, Senator Rand Paul, and me
in Naples, Florida

The mainstream press kept pecking away at him. They didn't want a true conservative to win. He wasn't part of the good-ol-boy establishment in Kentucky, the power brokers traditionally centered in Louisville, Lexington, and Frankfort. Regardless of the poll numbers, we knew we were winning the battle. The public loved an underdog, especially one that had a strong message. We kept pushing hard and it paid off. In May, Rand Paul won the primary by almost twenty-three percentage points. So much for the newspaper polls. Rand went on to win the general election by beating his Democrat opponent Jack Conway, 56% to 44%. Several months later he was sworn in as the new junior Senator from Kentucky.

◆◆●◆◆

Whenever I believe in a candidate, I will back them with my time and my checkbook. I always felt an obligation to do my small part in reshaping the political philosophy of our state. Another example was the campaign of Thomas Massie, a former judge executive from Lewis County. I found him to be a man of superior honesty who was a fiscal conservative and strong believer in personal rights. He also could not be bought by anyone, even his own party, no matter how much money or power was thrown in his direction. In an age when everything is influenced by the billions of dollars spread around by lobbyists, Massie has steadfastly refused their money, a rare character trait in Washington today. I have and will continue to support the congressman as long as he continues to serve our country.

Though I have traditionally supported Republican candidates for office, I was always open to consideration of ideas from members of the Democrat Party if they were consistent with my beliefs regarding government. Democrats campaigning for governor or other state offices would frequently call to solicit my support. Too often they espoused ideas I couldn't agree with. However, that didn't mean I wouldn't work with them for the benefit of the Northern Kentucky community. One such person was Democrat Governor John Y. Brown. During his tenure I was able to join forces with him on several occasions. Along with the help of many others, we were able to accomplish a great deal for Northern Kentucky. One example involved the extreme congestion of traffic during rush hour along Buttermilk Pike. In spite of all the development in Crescent Springs, it was still only a two-lane road. That presented a huge inconvenience for thousands of residents living there. Morning and evening commutes were almost impossible. Working with the Governor as well as many Democrats and Republicans in the State House, we were able to get the road widened to five lanes, a difficult project considering the fact that it entailed construction of a new bridge over I-75 and required partial funding approval from the United States Department of Transportation.

After construction on Buttermilk Pike was begun, Governor Brown called my office. He said, "Matth, I'm impressed by the work you did getting that Buttermilk Pike project organized. I would like you to spearhead a few more projects for the people of Northern Kentucky. Could you help me assemble a group of local leaders and give me a wish list of things that the community needs?"

"Governor, I'll do whatever I can to help." I recruited a group including: Dennis Griffin, Gordon Martin, Bill Butler, Wayne Carlisle, several others, and myself. We met with the governor on multiple occasions and a year later submitted a list of projects that would benefit the community. They included: the Mineola Pike interchange, Thomas More Parkway, and the exit for Northern Kentucky University. In addition, Governor Brown added some seed money for developments in downtown Covington.

I was very careful not to misuse my position on that committee. I knew in advance what was about to be developed and that presented a potentially profitable situation for me. However, acting upon that confidential information for my own benefit would be wrong. It was confidential information, not in the public sector like the Interstate plans from several decades earlier. I would not purchase a single foot of land where I might personally benefit from that inside knowledge. It would have been an abuse of the trust the governor had placed in me.

With success comes the accumulation of influence. It's a benefit that must be earned through honesty and respect. When you are able to exercise a level of influence, I believe you have a responsibility to use it to make a positive difference in your community. That's what the nation's forefathers did to create this great land. They were willing to sacrifice life and fortune for the benefit of the country. Now it's our turn and that of our children. We must lead in conjunction with many others to make good things happen. With influence comes the responsibility to use that influence for the benefit of the community and not for personal enrichment.

TRANSITION

L averne and I were blessed with five children: Susan, John, Diane, Bill, and Elizabeth. Each has their own unique personality and talents. I must give all credit to Laverne for raising them to be good adults who are givers rather than takers. She's the one who loved them, nurtured them, and molded them into what they are today. All have gone on to lead successful lives, each becoming a source of endless pride and comfort for Laverne and me.

Our children, from left to right:
My daugher Elizabeth Heist and her husband Tom; daughter Susan Ellison and her husband Glenn; John Toebben and his wife Dana; Bill Toebben and his wife Judith; my daughter Diane Marx and her husband Scott

As the we started to grow older, Laverne and I began thinking about the future and how the family business should transition to the next generation. It was a difficult task, so we hired Ellen

Frankenberg from the Gearding Institute, a company that specialized in family business planning. She and her staff did extensive interviews and testing on each member of the family to determine each individual's long-term expectations, their interests, strengths, and weaknesses. The process took almost three years and was very informative. A board of directors was formally established, and each child served as an equal voting member. It became apparent that the three girls weren't interested in the day-to-day management of the company. They each had their own lives and husbands with separate businesses that needed their attention. That left operations up to my two sons, John and Bill, both of whom had worked in some capacity for the company since they were fourteen years old.

After graduating from Covington Catholic high school, John attended Trinity University in San Antonio where he majored in construction management. His career was derailed for several years due to his tragic boating accident. After overcoming those injuries, John worked for Toebben construction, gradually working his way into a position of supervisor. When he was twenty-six, I felt he was ready to take on more responsibilities. I called him into my office and said, "John, I'd like you to assume the job of running our entire residential division."

He was a little surprised. "I don't know if I'm ready for that yet, Dad. I'm pretty happy where I am right now."

It was a Friday evening, so I said, "I'll tell you what, John. You know the business well and I know you're ready. I have complete confidence in you. Why don't you think about things over the weekend and we can talk about it more on Monday morning?"

That Monday we met again, and John said, "Dad, I'm going to give it a try, but I'll need you to help me for a while until I'm more comfortable."

"You'll not regret this, John. I know you're going to do a great job."

For the following six months I would go with him once a week to see how things were progressing on various projects and offer advice when needed. Finally, I was satisfied and said, "John, as of today, the residential division is all yours." I never looked back. He has served as president of Toebben Builders and Developers ever since.

He has remained very successful in that position because he prides himself on insisting upon the same quality of work that I had provided to customers. Recently John began construction on the final home at Country Squire Estates. It marked the end of a forty-year project and was celebrated with a ribbon-cutting ceremony. John is now focusing his efforts on our new Rivers Pointe Estates in Hebron. It's a one-billion-dollar development of a 450-acre site with over a mile of frontage overlooking the Ohio River. In addition to many estate homes it will include a large section for midrange homes. The community will feature hiking trails, equestrian facilities, and its own village with a grocery and other retail stores. John and his wife Dana have already built their own home there. It has a horse stable and an indoor training track available to interested residents.

Newest Toebben development: Rivers Pointe Estates
in Hebron, Kentucky

My youngest son, Bill, attended Bradley University in Illinois where he also studied construction engineering. He ultimately returned to work for the Toebben Company and when ready he was promoted to the position of director of the industrial division. In that capacity, he spearheaded the continued development of the Florence Industrial Park, a four-hundred-acre industrial development site along Mt. Zion Road in Boone County. He has also managed the construction of a multitude of shopping centers in Kentucky, Ohio, and Indiana. Fifteen years ago, Bill took over as president of Matth Toebben Construction and Toebben Limited, a holding company that manages all our various divisions including residential construction, commercial construction, property management, Interstate leasing, and Stand Energy.

Two generations of the Toebben Companies

John's oldest son Jake has been interested in the construction business since his late teens. He majored in construction management at the University of Colorado. We now ask that any family members joining the company spend five years working elsewhere in the construction field in order to learn ideas from other developers in different regions of the country. As a result, Jake has been working for a company based in Denver. He was just starting work on a $40 million project when we talked to him about returning to Toebben Construction. He joined us in 2017. The plan is to rotate him through the various company departments in an effort to groom him to eventually take over the business when his time comes.

Jake's younger brother Zachary has also graduated from the University of Colorado with a degree in construction management. He is presently working for a company in the Colorado area but we are looking forward to the day when he can also return to join Toebben Construction.

I'm proud of the success all my sons and grandson have enjoyed. I feel comfortable that our company will be in good hands for generations to come. I'm equally proud of the rest of my children and grandchildren for the careers they've each established in their own fields of interest.

A NEW COMPANION

Not a day goes by that I don't miss my sweet Laverne, her smile, her laugh, the gentleness of her touch. I occasionally think I can hear her voice calling me from another room, but reality quickly dictates otherwise. I love my family dearly but losing her left an emptiness in my heart. Loneliness became my companion as I simply existed from day to day, trying to distract myself with work.

Sometimes life can change when you least expect it. About a year after Laverne passed, I was eating by myself at John Phillip's Restaurant in Crestview Hills. Sitting at the table next to me was an elegantly attractive woman. She was tall and had short white hair. I noticed her blue eyes seemed to sparkle when she smiled. After a while I introduced myself and was surprised to hear her response. "Oh Matth, I know who you are. I'm Pat Runge. You built a house for me just down the street from yours."

We struck up a conversation and found that we had much in common. I explained that my wife had passed away about a year ago. She mentioned that her husband had died of lung cancer six years prior. We talked about how hard losing a spouse and being alone can be with nothing but our own thoughts to keep us company. I discovered that Pat was retired but used to work for the *Cincinnati Enquirer*. She was the director in charge of procurement and facilities, a position in which she managed a budget in excess of several million dollars. We spoke for quite a while and I found her to be as caring and intelligent on the inside as she was lovely on the outside. Before we knew it, over an hour had passed by. It was an enjoyable evening for both of us, so we decided to get together for dinner the following week.

We went to Dee Felice Cafe in the Mainstrasse region of Covington. It featured New Orleans cuisine accompanied by live jazz music. We ran into mutual friends of ours, Frank Henn and Alice Sparks, both of whom had previously lost spouses. It was comforting to be with others who had experienced the same loss we had. The four of us had a delightful evening together, sharing stories and listening to the music. Being with others and laughing together was a pleasant relief from the hours spent alone in my house. It was the first time I had had that much fun in years.

Pat and I began to see each other on a more regular basis. In time our friendship blossomed into a wonderful relationship based upon love and mutual respect. Since both of us are independent people, we each continue to maintain our own homes and live separate lives. Still, we have dinner together most evenings and have attended multiple social gatherings and fundraisers as a couple. We have also spent a great deal of time traveling with many of our good friends. Every winter we escape the cold winter weather up north by traveling to Naples, Florida, for several months.

Pat and I on the beach

A few years ago, I took Pat and some friends to see where I grew up in Germany and to meet my family in Lorup.

With friends in Lorup. Left to right: Bill Bray, Pat, me and Chris Bray

Pat has also been at my side during some difficult times. My home in Country Squire has a large tile patio. I was rushing across it one afternoon, trying to get out of a heavy rain, when I fell and fractured four of my ribs near the spine. It was the worst physical pain I had ever experienced, even worse than my kidney stones or heart attack. I was completely incapacitated, and breathing was so difficult I was unable to take care of myself. Fortunately, I had Linda to attend to me during the day while Pat stayed with me every night, remaining at my side until I recovered. She did the same thing when I needed surgery for acute appendicitis several years ago. She was always there, always giving, always caring for me, and I love her dearly.

Many men go through life without having a single loving woman at their side. I was blessed enough to have had two. I know Laverne would have approved and she would be thrilled to know I was no longer alone. I look forward to enjoying many more years together with Pat.

Family Reunion

SUNSET THOUGHTS

Over sixty years ago, I was fortunate enough to be welcomed into this great country with open arms. All that was asked of me was that I abide by the laws and principles laid out by the forefathers in the Constitution. That's what I have always tried to do while continuing to strive for success and provide for the future of my family. I no longer run the Toebben Companies, but I still go into the office every day to be available just in case there are questions. I attend meetings but seldom say much unless someone asks for my opinion or advice, which has become less and less frequent over the years. It gives me great joy knowing that the business is in such good hands and that all my children have become successful. It would have been easy for them to fall back on the Toebben name and allow that to carry them along. They realized that any favorable benefits derived from the family history would soon dissipate as time moves forward. Instead, each of them has decided to forge on, creating their own legacy to pass on to their own children. That's how it's supposed to be and I'm extremely proud of each of them.

Though I have pretty much bowed out of the corporation, I remain involved in regional and national politics. I'm afraid our country has been headed in the wrong direction for too long and I try to do whatever I can to turn that around by supporting the right people for the right job. I have lived under the oppression of a powerful central government and will continue to struggle to keep that from happening in this great land.

━━━━━━━━━━◆•◆━━━━━━

As I get older, I tend to become more philosophical about life. The same is probably true for most people. I now reflect upon the many things I was too busy to consider in my younger years. Life is a strange journey that ultimately leads us all toward the same destination. There are simply many ways in which we get there. It's the unpredictable and capricious ways in which life evolves that continues to amaze me. I often think about all the random twists and turns my own story has taken. A tailor dies of a sudden heart attack in Lorup and my apprenticeship ends before it started. As a result, I go on to become a cabinet maker which lays the foundation for my future career as a home builder. Without those series of events I would very likely still be living in Germany. I decided to attend a dance in Cincinnati where I first met Laverne. Without that chance meeting, my children and grandchildren would have never been born and our business wouldn't have prospered. A man on a horse happens to ride along and sell me a piece of land on Amsterdam Road. The seed that would eventually grow into The Toebben Companies was planted. Life has been such an incredible journey, a blessing I'm not sure I deserve. So much seems to happen by chance. Maybe it's guided by Divine will. I don't know for sure, but I like to think so. I thank God every day for all He has given me.

———————————◆•◦•◆———————————

I came to this great country as an immigrant with only ten dollars in my pocket. I couldn't speak a word of English, but with the help of friends and the support of my family I was able to build a successful business and accumulate some degree of wealth. However, that was never my ultimate goal. It was simply a by-product of what I did to make things happen the best way I knew how. I was fortunate in that my career was also my passion. I took great pride in constructing something out of nothing. It was always the challenge rather than the paycheck that motivated me. Whether it be building a family's dream home or orchestrating improvements for the community, the desire to make a difference was always there, in the back of my mind. One must be careful to avoid making the attainment of wealth your primary focus. It's an obsession that can quickly turn its head around and devour your life. In the end, the pursuit of wealth and the accumulation of material possessions is transient and meaningless. Things are just stuff, items that are sold at auction or garage sales after you are gone. What is enduring is one's good name and the legacy one leaves behind.

Even more important is one's family. Mine will never fully understand how much I cherish them and the moments I get to spend with my children and grandchildren. They have their own lives now, so I don't get to see them as often as I might like. On weekends I occasionally head down to the family farm in Carrolton. I have many fond memories of the times Laverne and I enjoyed with family and friends, the cookouts, hunting with my sons, and fishing with my grandchildren. I wish I could relive those moments, but moments are just that, little snippets of time that are gone too soon, leaving just the memories. I've learned the painful lesson that anything or anyone important can be taken from you at any time so you must seek out and cherish the good moments whenever you can because you might not get the opportunity again in the future.

Our grandchildren: Christmas 2015

One of my grandchildren was involved in the development of a computer programming business that he sold after several years for a sizable profit. He called and asked me my advice on what I thought he should do now.

"You have the benefit of enjoying good success fairly early in life, but you must keep everything in perspective. Nothing is permanent. Success can beget subsequent failure so save as much as you can for the future. Bad times arise when you least expect them, so you must be prepared. The best advice I can give you is the same thing my father told me when I was just a boy in Germany. If darkness comes into your life, and it will, remember to just keep pushing forward until you see a light at the end of the tunnel. Never give up. Do that and you'll be fine."

Before we hung up, I said, "There's one other thing."

"Yes Grandpa."

"Send your wife a dozen roses and tell her you love her. Do it first thing after you hang up. Be sure you tell her that every day. Remember, your family should always come first."

"I will. And Grandpa..."

"Yes."

"Thanks for everything you have done. I love you."

"I love you too, buddy." There can be no more cherished words for a grandparent to hear than those. They brought a smile that remained on my face for weeks.

———————————◆◆●◆◆———————————

One of my grandsons has his own steel manufacturing company in Newport, Kentucky. On Christmas several years ago, he gave me a beautiful elevated deer stand that we put together on the farm in Carrolton. He made extra-wide steps so his old Grandpa could make the climb inside. It has windows on all sides and two comfortable swivel chairs so you can easily see in all directions. I enjoy sitting there in the evenings from time to time, just before the sun sets, listening to the singing of the birds along with the other peaceful sounds of the woods.

In those private times I wish Laverne could be there sitting next to me. I think of her and all the friends I was fortunate enough to know over the years and the wonderful times we enjoyed together. Many of them are no longer here and I miss them all.

Left to right: Me, Laverne, Ed Bessler, Maureen Bessler, Irma Drees, Ralph Drees

At Pebble Beach; left to right: Ray Erpenbeck, Jim Berling, Ralph Drees, Jim Huff, Mark Arnzen, Bill Robinson, Ed Bessler, and Me

Left to right: Me, Fran Carlisle, Sue Butler, Bill Butler, Pat Runge, Wayne Carlisle

Friends posing with me next to my old plywood suitcase. Left to right: Rudy Pohlabeln, Marie Kreutzjans, Me and Bill Gerdes

Those things that seemed important in my younger years are no longer so important now. I guess as you get older, you have a deeper appreciation of the simple beauty of life. I feel content and it gives me the chance to reflect upon my years, to recall the many warm memories. It has been a life full of unimaginable happiness. Laverne and I have been able to raise a wonderful family and enjoy the company of good friends along the way. I thank God and this magnificent country for the opportunities given to me. I have been greatly blessed and now more fully appreciate what my mother meant when she said, "Every day has been a blessing. I hope to enjoy another day of blessings tomorrow."

Looking out the windows of the stand I gaze at the variety of wildlife. I marvel at God's workmanship, the magnificence of His universe, and His elegant design of life. I am humbled. When the animals wander close enough, I shoot them...but I now use my camera instead of a rifle.

No matter how much you try to do, it never seems to be enough. One looks back on life and often decides he could have done more. I'm no exception, but I learned long ago to avoid second-guessing my own actions. All you can do is to live life the best way you know how, and to use the gifts God has given you as fully as you can. I have fought my share of battles, both corporate and personal. I've lost a few but won most by always keeping in the back of my mind the words of my father, "Keep pushing through, Matth. Keep pushing through until you see the light at the end of the tunnel." That's what I have always done and will continue to do, just keep pushing forward toward the light of another day.

·

T. MILTON
MAYER

He is a graduate of the University of Cincinnati College of Medicine. He's a former Major in the United States Air Force and a retired Otolaryngology surgeon. After leaving a thirty-year career in medicine, he embarked on a new career in writing. His previous works include political action thriller, *Scorpion Intrusion*. His next novel, *Quantum*, is a techno-thriller. It's projected for release in the summer of 2020.

CPSIA information can be obtained
at www.ICGtesting.com
Printed in the USA
JSHW012142081122
32875JS00001B/1